Death's Futurity

THE VISUAL ARTS OF AFRICA AND ITS DIASPORAS

A Series Edited by Kellie Jones and Steven Nelson

The Visual Life
of Black Power

Death's Futurity

Sampada Aranke

Duke University Press

Durham and London

2023

Designed by Dan Ruccia
Project Editor: Ihsan Taylor
Typeset in Futura and Portrait by Westchester Publishing Services, Inc.

Library of Congress Cataloging-in-Publication Data
Names: Aranke, Sampada, author.
Title: Death's futurity : the visual life of black power / Sampada Aranke.
Other titles: Visual arts of Africa and its diasporas.
Description: Durham : Duke University Press, 2023. | Series: The visual arts
of Africa and its diasporas | Includes bibliographical references and index.
Identifiers: LCCN 2022028095 (print)
LCCN 2022028096 (ebook)
ISBN 9781478019305 (paperback)
ISBN 9781478016663 (hardcover)
ISBN 9781478023937 (ebook)
Subjects: LCSH: Black Panther Party. | Black power—United States—
History—20th century. | Black Arts movement—United States—History—
20th century. | Political art—United States—History—20th century. |
African Americans in art. | African American art—History—20th century. |
Politics in art. | Social problems in art. | BISAC: SOCIAL SCIENCE / Ethnic
Studies / American / African American & Black Studies | ART / History /
Contemporary (1945–)
Classification: LCC E185.615 .A736 2023 (print) | LCC E185.615 (ebook) |
DDC 322.4/20973—dc23/eng/20220815
LC record available at https://lccn.loc.gov/2022028095
LC ebook record available at https://lccn.loc.gov/2022028096

Cover art: Detail of *Attica Book,* edited by Benny Andrews and Rudolf Baranik.
Illustrations; 11 in. × 14 3/16 in., 1972. Courtesy of Thom Pegg, Black Art
Auction.

Duke University Press gratefully acknowledges the Dean of Faculty and
the Department of Art History, Theory and Criticism at the School of the
Art Institute of Chicago, which provided funds toward the publication of
this book.

Publication of this book has been aided by a grant from the Millard Meiss
Publication Fund of CAA.

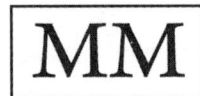 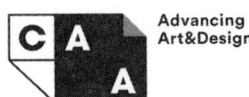

Contents

Acknowledgments

That books often open with thanks has always felt right. These intellectual endeavors are never really singular and as such are collective forms of study, dissonance, thoughtfulness, and care. In that spirit, I start this one with endless gratitude for all those who fought and continue to fight for Black liberation, and especially to Bobby Hutton, Fred Hampton, and George Jackson. I hope this book embodies some of the energy you gave as a testament to how your murders have never left us and remain within the revolutionary aims of today. Thank you to the artists and visionaries whose works grace these pages, who remind us that politics means little without art, and crucial to any idea of revolution is an idea of seeing and living anew.

The enormity of this undertaking would have been impossible without the endless support of my intellectual and personal community. First thanks goes to Benjamin Jones, my thought partner and lifelong collaborator. Thank you for always lending mind, eyes, heart. This project lives today because of the endless support of Kemi Adeyemi, Nicole Archer, Megan Bayles, Delinda Collier, Huey Copeland, Nijah Cunningham, Andrea Dooley, duskin drum, Armin Fardis, Hannah Feldman, Jeremy M. Glick, Keith Hennessy, Benjamin Jones, Nick Mitchell, Amy Mooney, Jed Murr, Magalí Rabasa, Leigh Raiford, Nikolas Oscar Sparks, Omar Ricks, Blake Stimson, Krista Thompson, Julia Bryan-Wilson, and Frank B. Wilderson III, who engaged so many early conversations and iterations of this project and who always came back with rigor, enthusiasm, and some of the most insightful engagements with this project. Thank you.

Death's Futurity would not have made it without the ongoing, refined, and incredibly careful attention of Huey Copeland, Hannah Feldman, Amy Mooney, and Krista Thompson—a writing group of my actual dreams. I'm so humbled to be in a thought-experiment with you four. I am indebted to Penelope Deutscher's generous support of this book through multiple invitations. I especially want to highlight the workshop "Decolonizing Critical Theory: Decolonial Aesthetics and Epistemic Violence" and thank Mlondi Zondi and Le'ah Kaplan for their fine-tuned engagement and the book workshop "Appropriation and Its Discontents" Penny cohosted with Huey Copeland, and am so incredibly grateful to æryka hollis o'neil, Jordan Mulkey, Harrison Graves, and Alex Weheliye for their incredibly thoughtful responses to the book. I am especially grateful to the dean's office at the School of the Art Institute for providing generous support for this project. There are so many colleagues that have invited me to share versions of this research along the way. Thank you to Andrew Aisenberg, Kirk Ambrose, Katie Anania, Janet Dees, Joan Giroux, Mark Godfrey, Carlos Jackson, Tirza Latimer, Richard Martin, Deborah Obalil, Rachel Schreiber, Krista Thompson, and Zoé Whitley for the invitations.

Teaching at the San Francisco Art Institute was undoubtedly transformational, as my students and colleagues taught me about how artistic practices are crucial to any and all conceptions of research. My colleagues at the School of the Art Institute of Chicago make teaching, publishing, and partying look easy. Your ongoing support, incredible dedication to the lives of art and artists, and your ability to make the university fun is seriously unparalleled. I am so grateful to everyone who has made and supported me along this journey.

Thank you to Ken Wissoker who guided this project into publication and has believed in it since day one. Thank you to Ryan Kendall for so kindly shepherding me through the project.

My parents, Aai and Baba, who have encouraged me to take on my passions, regardless of how idealist or unknown they seem, and my brother

Sarang, who taught me how to study and party, are woven into this book. This book is dedicated to my family, Benjamin, Nina, and Lorenzo, who make home a place and a feeling. Finally, thank *you* for reading this book. I hope that what comes next generates the radical spirit, dedication, and energy that comes with radical critique, unwavering movement building, and revolutionary art.

The Visual Life of Black Power

The Black Panther Party for Self-Defense (BPP) was founded as a response to the sustained and ongoing murders of Black people at the hands of the police. Along with murder were other forms of state and police violence, ranging from racial profiling, economic disenfranchisement, political suppression, lack of access to basic human resources, including funded schools and health care, to name but a few. In fact, the BPP's first public appearance was in Richmond, California, after the April 1, 1967, murder of Denzil Dowell at the hands of the Richmond Police Department. As a follow-up to that rally, the BPP made its first issue of the *Black Panther*, dated April 25, 1967 (plate 1).[1]

This first issue was a four-page broadsheet that included the first appearance of the Black Panther logo, which was an explicit citation of the original 1965 Lowndes County Freedom Organization drawing. The issue also included sections on the BPP's philosophy and proposals, a detailed account of police inconsistencies and explicit lies surrounding Dowell's murder, and a call for an organizing meeting. This issue would come to embody the future of the *Black Panther* newspaper, which would keep these foundational principles: a commitment to political praxis, exposing and educating the masses on state violence, and engaging in political direct action. The fourth principle is of central concern for this study: the production of radical Black visual culture aimed toward revolution and liberation. From its inception, the BPP was well aware of the political power of visual culture, making room for illustrations, photography, and graphic typesetting in their inaugural publication. This attention to the visual qualities of print media would only expand as the party grew, and, arguably, the development of an iconic aesthetic aided in the growth of the BPP. Indeed, these aesthetics would last, sedimenting the party's legacy as a cultural, as well as a political, icon.[2]

Death's Futurity analyzes how Black radical death was rhetorically and visually imagined as a generative means toward political liberation in ways that responded to state-sanctioned violence during the Black Power era. Mobilizing archival findings that have never been published, I critically analyze the ephemera surrounding the murders of three Black Panther Party members—Lil' Bobby Hutton (1968), Fred Hampton (1969), and George Jackson (1971). I argue that these spectacularized murders mark a transition from Black Power to prison abolition. In order to track this historical and theoretical shift, I focus on how Black radicals transformed these state-sanctioned murders into opportunities to engage political action, primarily through the use of innovative compositional techniques that draw on a broader Black art-historical canon.

Photography, documentary films, journalistic print media, and political posters take center stage during these brief years as a means to produce and catalogue the generative potential death held for Black radicals in anticapitalist and antiracist revolutionary struggle. The proximity between Black life and Black death is of central concern in this book. The cultural productions organized in this book give us images of the dead Black body—photographed, collaged, filmed, and drawn—as a means of contextualizing a long history of anti-Black violence. These images reveal how the role of corporeality—and corpses in particular—played out in efforts to shape visions of a Black future free from white supremacy and capitalism by recomposing Black death as a means for liberation.

This monograph thereby curates a counter-history to understandings of state repression and death as solely destructive in the making of 1960s and 1970s Black radical politics. Instead, my extensive archival research documents how Black radicals' uses and manipulation of figuration, composition, perspective, and narrative took shape around photographic reproduction, visual composition, color saturation, juxtaposition, sequencing, and camera focus—all of which aimed to reimagine death as generative for visions of Black liberation grounded in futurity. This study examines artistic productions from within and outside the party in an attempt to demonstrate broader approaches to a Black radical imaginary, particularly in and through print- and lens-based media. For the purposes of introduction, I want to return to the *Black Panther* as a foundational object of print and alternative media for the BPP and for Black radicals across the country.

By 1969, the *Black Panther* circulated over one hundred thousand copies weekly and by 1970, that number quadrupled to over four hundred thousand.[3] While these numbers might seem astounding, they reflect a popular investment in the newspaper as a leftist resource for critique, coverage, analysis, and visual propaganda. The *Black Panther* was one of many forms of alternative media that emerged out of the 1960s as documents of the social, political, and cultural upheavals of the time. As artist and print media historian Geoff Kaplan insists, "In the 1960s, a media revolution was afoot as explosive as the revolutions taking place in the streets of Chicago and Paris, Prague and Mexico City."[4] Indeed, in the case of the BPP, this media revolution was crucial to the call for Black autonomy and self-determination. A Black radical aesthetic was a foundational element in reflecting and imagining Black life outside of the constraints of mainstream media plagued by white supremacist ideations of Black people, whether covert, mild, or outright in their racist beliefs. In what follows, I focus on lens-based and print media that enacted a Black radical aesthetic prompted by the *Black Panther*.

Emory Douglas took over the design and vision of the *Black Panther* in 1967 and became the minister of culture for the BPP. Douglas insisted that propaganda, or "revolutionary art," was an essential element in building radical culture because it "enlightens the party to continue its vigorous attack against the enemy, as well as educate the masses of black people" by "showing them through pictures—The Correct Handling of the Revolution."[5] Douglas's artistic vision formed the party's identifiable Black radical aesthetic as he appropriated and reinvented forms of illustration, collage, photomontage, and graphic design. Douglas created an aesthetic that could be immediately understood by Black people as undeniably revolutionary, therefore enacting methods of political education at the level of the image aimed to prepare Black people for revolution.[6] Strikingly, death was central to this mode of instruction for Douglas. Douglas did not emphasize images of Black revolutionary death, however, and instead focused on drawing "deadly pictures of the enemy—pictures that show him at his death door or dead—his bridges are blown up in our pictures—his institutions destroyed—and in the end he is lifeless."[7] The emphasis on depicting Black revolutionaries successfully overthrowing white supremacist and state powers activated Frantz Fanon's notion of anticolonial revolution and visually argued that Black liberation was dependent upon the oppressor's death.[8] These depictions flooded the pages of the *Black Panther* and eventually was oft-cited as fodder for the state to wage its repressive campaign against the party. Along with these depictions, I would argue, images of Black radical death emerged as invocations toward a politics that would also enable Black liberation struggles.

Indeed, a key intervention that this book offers is that the visual life of Black power is activated through Black radical death. In order to undergo such a provocative project, I have turned to formative interventions in Black studies around reconceptualizing how the Black radical body throws into crisis theories of object/subject relations, histories and afterlives of slavery, and revolutionary approaches to reshaping the world. Concurrently, I offer an emergent and provisional set of provocations that I hope will contribute to and challenge performance theories of embodiment. The visual ecologies presented in this manuscript offer alternative forms and compositions of Black corporeality vis-à-vis the corpse. The corpse might best be understood as a political, relational, and aesthetic form in the book and one that might give us tools to understand how Black radical life and Black radical death are lived, activated, and regenerated as vibrant and ongoing mobilizations toward Black liberation.

Anti-Black Violence and Its Visual Reproduction

The images in this book oscillate between degrees of graphic intensity. That this project centralizes images of Black radical death requires an acute attention to the nuances of display, as both an element of documentation and a possible source of reproducing the initial violence in question. While there are glimpses of state violence shown as is, in its barest form, I focus on how these objects deploy creative modes of rendering, photographic manipulation, and narrative sequencing in order to make meaning of that violence and turn it toward revolutionary ends. When this project started, I knew that these works were not only compelling in their direct, unassailable force but they urgently needed to live in a more public form in order to account for their historical power. However, I was also skeptical of such an impulse in light of the ways in which anti-Black violence often requires an audience, one that delights in the libidinal, social, and political pleasures of partaking in consuming such degradation.[9] As a scholar, I have been concerned with the politics of visual reproductions, taking on how artists and cultural producers directly address the dangers of proliferating scenes of such violence while also making space for the necessary visual confrontations of these realities across audiences. While this political line is delicate, its shape is dynamic. In the same spirit as at the BPP, this project aims to stage encounters with these images that make room for the spectrum of rage to grief, horror to analysis, disaffection to reflection that are required of such violent deaths.

Ever since Fred Moten staged a debate surrounding the reproduction of scenes of anti-Black violence in *In the Break: The Aesthetics of the Black Radical Tradition*, this question has taken center stage as a revisited element of scholarship about the Black body.[10] While Moten was not first in raising these urgent questions, his presentation of a narrative engagement through visual terms has proven to be a significant touchstone for projects like *Death's Futurity*. In the opening pages of the book, Moten invokes and engages Saidiya Hartman's uptake of Frederick Douglass's narrative, specifically surrounding the question of his witnessing Aunt Hester's brutal beating in *Scenes of Subjection*. In a 1999 review of Hartman's seminal text, Moten provides a lucid glimpse at what would become a lasting argument in his book some four years later. Speaking to the "intense dialogue with Douglass that structures *Scenes of Subjection*," Moten notes how the "dialogue is opened by a refusal of recitation that reproduces what it refuses."[11] "The question here," Moten poignantly asserts, "concerns the inevitability of inescapability of such reproduction even in the denial of it."[12] While reproduction ensures a kind of repetition of the initial condition of harm, even if refusing to restage it requires a kind of supplemental form of that initial violence. The relationship here between reproduction and refusal depends upon the responsibilities of the writer and of writing as a practice. Taken as a priority, the outgrowth of these concerns leads to calculations about how and when such violence must be attended to and how and when it must be directly engaged, dissected, overwrought, and obsessed over and therefore taken as a given in order to engage what comes out of that violence or another kind entirely.

How this violence appears—in what context, shape, degree of intensity, and to what extent this violence reenergizes white supremacist power and retriggers its effects—speaks to the prescient state of violation that accompanies seeing the pained Black body. When it comes to if or how to write about the political repercussions of such violences in the context of the production of aesthetic objects, whether or not those images should be seen, raises the stakes of these debates. The visual consumption of Black pain structures and shadows all images of Black life, as has been extensively noted across eras and lines of study. Looking at these images, coupled with the question of whether or not to write about them, exhausts an already fatigued image-cast that centers anti-Black violence as an everyday visual practice. In his writing for the book that emerged out of the controversial exhibition *Without Sanctuary: Lynching Photography in America*, Hilton Als lyricizes the complex relationship between looking and feeling that emerges out of a visual encounter with images of anti-Black violence: "I didn't like looking at these pictures, but once I looked, the events documented in them occurred in my mind over and over again. . . . And it is as one that I felt my neck snap and my heart break, while looking at these pictures."[13] For Als, looking simultaneously invokes a recurrent meditation on the historical specificity of these events while also initiating an embodied, felt transmission that registered such violences at the level of sensation. This kind of looking practice is of key concern for this book as the images in question aim to reconsider the radical Black body as a locus of collective sensation through which revolutionary action may be transmitted.

This book heavily involves an engagement with theories of the Black body as a historical, sensorial, and aesthetic force. While the field's influence might often be concealed from chapter to chapter, performance studies has undoubtedly shaped this book's approach. I have turned to those studies that centralize Black studies approaches to questions of corporeality, sensorial matter, and the historical and contemporary reconceptualizations of the Black body. Two such theories of the Black embodiment prove to be particularly generative for this book: Joseph Roach's account of "surrogation" as a constitute practice of Black aesthetic presence and

Harvey Young's insistence that histories of anti-Black violence are always active within forms of Black embodiment.

Joseph Roach's study *Cities of the Dead: Circum-Atlantic Performance* of histories of performance grounded in memory and forgetting offers up a compelling set of corporeal possibilities. Roach foregrounds those various anti-Black historical events and practices that give rise to a limited range of possibility for Black people to access and enact those narratives so necessary for self-definition and self-determination. Describing those practices that attempt to retain, enact, and share those histories, Roach offers a theory of "kinesthetic imagination," where a performing body might activate a kind of "displaced transmission" in order to recount a past (in all its incompleteness) for a desired future.[14] Roach goes on to describe these practices of displaced transmission as "surrogation," a dynamic process of substitution where "culture reproduces and re-creates itself" as an act of survival or defiant attempts to fill the "cavities created by loss through deaths or other forms of departure."[15] Roach offers us a process that is incomplete and fails by virtue of its pursuit; who or what is lost can never be fully replaced, and therefore we are left with the kinds of gaps, limitations, or excesses made visible through this failed act of an attempted substitution. For this project, surrogation is another way to account for how Black bodies and objects interplay in moments of flashing juxtaposition or uncanny harmony. Because the process leads us to the incompleteness of substitution as an act and therefore calls attention to the incompatibility and similitude marked by one in relation to the other, Roach's approach to theories of embodiment provides a rich and dynamic language to register the long and violent history of Black bodily objectification while also opening up a space where the object might prove a generative means to account for the Black body's potentials for refusal and resistance.

Harvey Young's study explores the disquieting proximity between Black embodiment and objecthood and opens up a dynamic conversation with Roach's concept of surrogation. His book *Embodying Black Experience: Stillness, Critical Memory, and the Black Body* explores how acts of anti-Black violence appear as constitutive elements in modes of Black embodiment, making the object status of Black life of central sensorial concern. Young's book charts the ways that Black life has been constituted within and against normative access to sensorial and bodily coherence, requiring new methods to think about the Black body as a whole. This corporeal exceptionality mostly takes shape around forms of white supremacist violence that have adhered understandings of Blackness and therefore constitute modes of looking, embodiment, and cohabitation that fall outside of a reliance upon "the body" as a uniformly assumed and understood category.

Lynching is the most poignant example of a performance of anti-Black violence where white spectators' impulses to gather flesh as souvenirs was fueled by a desire to somehow commemorate their participation in these acts. These collecting practices are, borrowing from scholar Rebecca Schneider's theory, kinds of "performance remains," a noun and a verb that indicates a "temporally ambiguous object that existed in the past (and was saved), exists in the present, and will continue to exist in the future."[16] In the case of lynching, where Black victims' fingers and toes (among other body parts) were often dismembered and pocketed by enthusiastic onlookers as souvenirs, these remains compel a looking practice that can "imagine the hand, and by extension, the body from which it was taken" and "restage (in our minds) the process of its removal"—similar to Roach's notion of kinesthetic imagination.[17] Young offers a visceral description of how the dismembered Black body's remains signal the active presence of anti-Black violence as ongoing and constitutive of how the Blackness is made legible.

Both of these scholars are concerned with how Blackness is formed both via the constitutive logic of violence coupled with the generative uptakes of that violence toward another kind of presence. Their historical studies prove to be crucial in this study, as the events, practices, and cases they examine are also foundational reference points for the murders that take central stage here. This project works with theories of both performance and embodiment in the spirit of these scholars. Performances speak to both state actions of durational violence as well as instances of radical refusal. Embodiment is a category not assumed for the Black radicals here. The weight of picturing the Black body is radically reconstituted to account for modes of corporeality marked by anti-Black violence, and thus fragmentation, abstraction, and surrogation act as indicators of forms of Black corporeality. These approaches to thinking about Blackness in its corporeal form are indeed multivalent and considered. Putting Young and Roach together, my approach to Black corporeality here turns to how Black radicals motivated a way of reading and looking that at once aimed to account for an understanding of the Black body as a site of immense anti-Blackness and of radical possibility.

Camera and Gun: Bullet Hole as Aperture

The camera is key to the material, political, and rhetorical registers of *Death's Futurity*. This book focuses on the photographic image, documentary film, and political posters as its main objects of analysis. The camera operates as a central apparatus in chapters 1 and 2, and even while it does not take center stage in chapter 3, the artworks in question have to deal with its nonpresence as an indication of the state's desire to withhold the conditions behind Jackson's murder.

The camera, as an apparatus that captures both the still and moving image, contributed to the production of radical cultural and aesthetic forms at a rapid speed in the 1960s. Social movements wrenched the gun away from the state's stronghold in order to radically resignify the gun as a tool for revolution. Similarly, the camera's ability to "shoot" made the device an ideological weapon for social movements around the world. Étienne Jules-Marey's 1882 chronophotographic gun is oft-cited as a clear foundational alliance between both the camera and the gun. Inspired by the gun's physical structure, Marey mimicked the rifle's design as a "point-and-shoot" device in order to capture images for scientific animal-motion studies through a mechanism whose line of sight was much stronger than the human eye's.[18] The relationship between hunting and shooting, in Marey's creation, is seamless, as the camera is modeled after the very weapon intended to kill, whose power lies in the ability to capture an image more precisely than can be achieved through the human eye. Critics and theorists of the still photograph have also reflected upon the material and representational relationship between the camera and the gun. Indeed, Susan Sontag's 1977 polemic that the "old-fashioned camera was clumsier and harder to reload than a brown Bess musket. The modern camera is trying to be a ray gun" hardly seems provocative now.[19] Frederich Kittler's insistence that the "history of the movie camera thus coincides with the history of automatic weapons. The transport of pictures only repeats the transport of bullets" offers a concise illustration of the intimacy between both apparatuses as varying mechanisms of capture, violation, and force.[20] Tracking this history's impact on nineteenth-century formations of the Western liberal subject, Jason Puskar has insightfully detailed how the camera gun supplemented the rifle for "camera hunting" and activated "aggressive fantasies of violent capture," which "configures the subject of the photograph as a fugitive that the photographer must seize suddenly and violently."[21] While the objects of study in Puskar's essay are made circa 1880, their relationship to the sustained modes of capture and captivity for Black people in the wake of slavery's formal end seems particularly relevant. As has been noted, the various afterlives of slavery that continued to index anti-Black violence often oscillated between the physical/psychological and the representational, between criminality and capture, between lynching and the minstrel show.[22] Characterizing the photographic subject as fugitive here bears a particular kind of historical resonance when we think about the eponymous status of Black Americans in the nineteenth century under the 1850 Fugitive Slave Act. The fugitive status of Black Americans legally emerged at the very same moment that Louis Agassiz and J. T. Zealy's experiments in daguerreotype relied upon enslaved peoples, thus making any history of photography inextricable from the ongoing production of capture mobilized by the camera in the nineteenth century and beyond.[23]

The disquieting relationship between photography and anti-Blackness converges most clearly around the lynching photograph, a topic that has been covered extensively.[24] Jacqueline Goldsby's *A Spectacular Secret: Lynching in American Life and Literature* provides a dense and attuned study of how photography's open promise depended upon anti-Blackness, as the populist drives in the technological form (i.e., that the realm of representation was suddenly open to the masses and not solely the property of the elite and wealthy) were quite often weaponized against Black Americans. Key to this book is Goldsby's insistence that lynching "helped shape the experience and meaning of American 'seeing' at the start of the twentieth century, just as those new modes of sight helped make lynching the distinctly visual phenomenon it was," and the images produced out of these acts "inscribe how practices of racial violence were used to cultivate the experience and meaning of sight itself."[25] Goldsby insists on this triad among the production, circulation, and reception of the lynching photograph as a popular and populist form of cultural education that informed questions of citizenship and nation building. Building from this nineteenth- and early twentieth-century tradition, the visual objects produced in the wake of Black radical death in this study also serve as instructive forms of cultural education.

While the lynching photograph is indeed one example of the ways that the photograph circulated as a form of visual culture intended to restrain, discipline, and fundamentally threaten Black life, it is also the case that these photographs were also used as galvanizing objects that could also open up the possibility of activism, accountability, and alternative modes of sight. Take, for example, Goldsby's uptake of the notion of "what we would call the 'frame narrative'—printing images that depict the mob's victims before and after their deaths; paying empathetic visual care to the victims' bodies—appears to have been a distinctly black tradition in lynching photography. Inviting viewer to imagine the life histories of black lynch victims as they look at the pictures, this aesthetic challenges the popular ideology of the spectacle."[26] Indeed, as Goldsby highlights, Black spectatorial practices were "varied and unpredictable" in ways that encouraged "resistant or oppositional looking" as well as practices of outright refusal to look as a way to protest the repressive force of these images.[27] What is clear nonetheless is that whether explicitly resistant or organized around a refusal to look, the lynching photograph's circulation and reception encouraged a mode of seeing that accounted for the camera's power as a historical agent. In both Goldsby's work and *Death's Futurity*, the camera (and by extension the photograph as the technology's record) is presented as a weapon whose effects were repurposed and reconceptualized to encourage new ways of seeing the violence presented in the photographic capture of the lynching act. This notion of the violence of the camera would never leave the technology's function and would be similarly repurposed by movements for Black liberation.

While rooted in and often commenting upon a history of the development of white supremacy and state power, the camera as gun was reconceptualized in the mid-twentieth century as a revolutionary device that contributed to the cultural development of a global left. With the rise of viable anticapitalist alternatives to the state formation as best represented by successful anticolonial movements globally, such as the former USSR or the People's Republic of China, the camera and the gun were two sides of the same project: the ushering in of a new world that required revolutionary violence *and* revolutionary ways of seeing. In the opening words to her groundbreaking 1978 essay on the documentary form in Latin American leftist movements, Julianne Burton penned,

> The metaphor of the movie camera as gun is as old as the apparatus itself. Étienne Jules Marey, credited with inventing the first motion picture camera in France in 1882, described the instrument he sought to invent before the fact as "une sorte de fusil *photographique*." What he designed was in fact the size and shape of a rifle. The metaphor

acquired renewed currency in the Latin American context. There is a marvelous photograph of Sergei Eisenstein on location for the ill-fated *Que Viva Mexico!* Eisenstein is posed behind a camera on a tripod; draped over him and the camera are the cordage belts made famous by the soldiers of the Mexican revolution. In the sixties, Argentine documentarist Fernando Solanas and Spanish-born Octavio Getino reappropriated the metaphor, sparking a kind of guerrilla cinema movement and declaring, "The camera is a gun which shoots twenty-four frames a second."[28]

The phrase of central concern, "une sorte de fusil *photographique*" translates into "a kind of photographic rifle," thereby seamlessly marking a continuum that positions the movie camera as an apparatus linked to the gun—physically, metaphorically, and ideologically. In this spirit, there is a shared revolutionary spirit between the camera in 1960s Latin America and the United States as a tool for building political consciousness and as an aesthetic device aimed to build radical culture. Black photographers and filmmakers also took up this notion of the camera as an ideological tool. Gordon Parks famously titled his 1967 autobiography *A Choice of Weapons*, chronicling his fight against racism and poverty through his documentary photographs, and Haile Gerima notably reflected on being "happy [he] grabbed the camera as a weapon" in his uptake of the device in filmmaking.[29] This emphasis on the camera as a tool for ideological warfare was compatible with the ongoing call for armed self-defense by Black radicals in the United States. The gun and the camera were both considered revolutionary weapons, and in the hands of Black Americans, these devices would be aimed toward the abolition of racism and capitalism and the creation of a new world composed of Black freedom.

Since its inception, the BPP featured armed self-defense as a centerpiece to their ten-point platform. Coupled with nuanced consideration, control, and engagement with their signature aesthetic, the BPP had a deliberate calculation of the power of images over local and national media coverage of the movement. Kara Keeling's stunning book *The Witch's Flight: The Cinematic, Black Femme, and the Image of Common Sense* accounts for how the armed Black radical image ruptured national consciousness around anti-Black violence and the possibility of Black revolution in the United States. "The appearance of American blacks with guns," writes Keeling, "revealed that those commonly shared memory-images which previously supported perceptions of a black were inadequate to a present perception of blacks with guns because American blacks with guns was not a component of the common sense through which the black appeared."[30] Working backward from Keeling's insights, images of common sense that shaped how Black Americans were seen did not include self-determined, armed Black revolutionaries committed to the Black freedom struggle. Coming off the heels of the civil rights movement, more common were images of nonviolent activists who endured white supremacist violence and did not fight back. In stark contrast, the images of radical resistance embodied by the BPP cast an image that refused to comply to any notion of nonviolence, thus destabilizing assumptions regarding what forms of anti-Black violence Black Americans would continue to endure. The answer, quite simply, was none. Black Americans would no longer endure sustained white supremacist violence and were broadcasting an aesthetic and material message that linked militancy to armed resistance. Crumbling the previous images of Black Americans that shaped national consciousness, the BPP provided a confrontation at the level of sight, a warning shot that should Black Americans need to defend themselves against white supremacist violence, they will be armed and prepared.

This image of "Blacks with guns" undoubtedly heightened the state's repressive apparatus against the BPP specifically and Black radicals broadly. Abolitionist scholar and radical activist Angela Y. Davis's 1994 essay "Afro Images" suggests the urgency of both the historical conditions that gave rise to such images as well as their impact on contemporary culture. As Davis so poignantly notes in her reflection on the ways her image from the 1960s, as circulated through photographs of the activist, continued to follow her, she said:

> But it is not merely the reduction of historical politics to contemporary fashion that infuriates me. The distinction of being known as "the Afro" is largely a result of a particular economy of journalistic images in which mine is one of the relatively few that has survived the last two decades. Or perhaps the very segregation of those photographic images caused mine to enter into the then-dominant journalistic culture precisely by virtue of my presumed criminality.[31]

Photography, in her analysis, is up for political grabs. We can extend Davis's analysis out to account for productions of images writ large, as they shaped the ways that Black radicals could be seen. While Davis was never formally a part of the BPP, the organization's visual efficacy undoubtedly impacted her. Davis's image became conflated with her being. The circulation of her photographic image contributed to a groundswell of global solidarity while simultaneously contributing to the policing and surveillance of Black women who wore their hair natural or were self-styled in any manner readily seen to resemble Black militancy. Davis insists that the photographs shaped a public image of her: the "most obvious evidence of their power was the part they played in structuring people's opinions about me as a 'fugitive' and a political prisoner."[32] As in Davis's recollection, the image opened up real consequences in which guns, whether radical or reactionary, would indelibly shape the future of Black radical resistance.

Bullet holes appear throughout this book as shared and consistent causes of death for each slain Panther presented across all three chapters. Reports indicate that Bobby Hutton was shot over twelve times,[33] two deliberate gunshots killed Hampton though police fired between ninety and ninety-nine into his bedroom,[34] and two fatal gunshot wounds are responsible for George Jackson's death, though there are contested accounts of the incident.[35] While the bullet is responsible for the violent tearing through of flesh, muscles, bone, artery, and organ, the gunshot is what activates the deterioration of corporeal integrity. The gunshot exposes the vulnerable elements of the body, now torn apart, to the external environment, forcing the body's protected internal apparatus to release into the outside world through rapid blood loss and other possible escapes through the gunshot's entry and/or exit hole. This vulnerability accumulates with each and every gunshot endured by the victim, thus creating a series of exposures that scenes the brutality of anti-Black violence as well as the spectacular and quotidian nature through which that violence gets articulated at the level of the body. This kind of corporeal exposure is marked by and through the bullet hole. The bullet hole operates in this study as the site where the question of Black corporeal integrity meets the production of a way of looking.

Upon closer examination of the details of each murder, coupled with the insistence in each object to focus upon the bullet holes themselves, I have come to theorize the bullet hole as an aperture and as a way of looking. To understand the bullet hole has an aperture is to suggest that the bullet's violent rupture, which takes the form of the hole itself, does not only point to the devastating emptiness it leaves behind. As aperture, this hole filters light and composes the interplay of positive and negative space from which an image emerges, whether in focused clarity or as a blur that passes the viewer's eye. This attention to the contours that the aperture helps to expose requires an attention to the body itself as well as the figurations of the body that enable a mode of looking that both contextualizes and politicizes the scene. Bullet holes, particularly their appearance and reappearance, illustrate an attention to one particular photographic portrait of Bobby Hutton as it develops across mediums and media immediately after his death. In chapter 2, I refer to this kind of contextualization as *politicized looking*, in an effort to discuss how the camera lens in *The Murder of Fred Hampton* instructs the viewer to look *for* Hampton's slain body vis-à-vis its absence and through the objects left in his wake. In chapter 3, I suggest a version of this mode of looking as a kind of *fugitive imaginary*, where artists composed visual records of the conditions of Jackson's murder with little or no evidentiary proof and instead turned to Black visual histories in order to picture the scene. These approaches share an assumptive claim around the centrality of the bullet hole as a shared exposure that enables a mode of looking that engages the afterlife of Black radical death as it is pictured in and through mediation.

Looking for and Enacting a Black Future

Key to this development of modes of looking is attention to the relationship between the evidentiary and the imaginative elements of each object of inquiry. Expressing his skepticism of the seeming acceptance and embrace of the medium as evidence, Webster Melcher, in a 1922 think piece for *The Central Law Journal*, questioned the alleged neutrality of the camera, insisting rather that "any photograph is a correct representation of *that which the camera sees, and as the camera sees some*; but this by no means settles it that the camera actually sees *all* that is before it, or sees in a *truthful form* that which is there."[36] This skepticism is central to this study, even while the documentary and photographic uses aim to reconceptualize the evidentiary away from the state and into the people's hands.

This particular utilization of the evidentiary claim does not solely rely upon truth-claims in the legalistic sense but rather these objects centralize the aesthetic as an imaginative device that allows artists and activists to turn to common-sense knowledges that would otherwise be denied, refuted, or ignored by the state. Take, for example, the development of speculative claims in lieu of governmental transparency regarding the specific conditions of George Jackson's murder. These artists mobilized a visual language that offered suggestive illustrations of the placement of Jackson's fatal wounds and in so doing encouraged a way of seeing that pushed viewers to the limits of evidentiary mandates into a beyond in which Jackson's death required a generative political engagement. These modes of looking encouraged an activation of context, a refusal to accept state narratives, and an active engagement with Black visual histories that cite and sight a long history of the Black freedom struggle. Crucial to this approach was that the viewer not only take stock of the murders presented but invoke the transformative capacities of the image before them toward political regeneration. Recently, Deborah Thomas's *Political Life in the Wake of the Plantation: Sovereignty, Witnessing, Repair* brings together the ethnographic with the visual in order to open onto various sets of embodied knowledge that emerge as a response to systemic violence in Jamaica. The question of reception is crucial to her project. Thomas has provided a useful framework for this kind of viewing practice, which she calls "Witnessing 2.0."[37] An "embodied practice," this form of witnessing "makes visible the ways affects operate in multiple temporalities and across levels of consciousness" and "involves assuming responsibility for contemporary events."[38] While I find Thomas's uptake of embodied practices and divergent forms of affect across temporalities to be a helpful resource, the kind of looking I turn to is not about morality but about a political generativity that recomposes one's subjectivity toward a notion of a future already in motion rather than in relation to moral responsibility. This future takes death as a necessary facet of a radical life and requires a looking practice that strives toward action and activity, an active destruction of all inheritances of white supremacy (from the camera to the gun), and a Black freedom so vibrant and all-encompassing that liberation might mean a collective one after all.

Historians suggest that at its peak in 1969, the BPP had five thousand members.[39] In their comprehensive study on the BPP's internationalist and antiimperialist practices, Joshua Bloom and Waldo E. Martin have noted that despite police violence and state repression, "young black people embraced the revolutionary vision of the Party," which resulted in "many thousands" joining the BPP.[40] So much so that the FBI, CIA, Defense Intelligence Committee, and National Security Agency noted that "43 percent of blacks under 21 years of age" expressed "great respect for the [Black Panther Party]."[41] What this information suggests is an overwhelming support for and participation in the party by Black youth. Indeed, the BPP's founders themselves were much older than their first recruit, Bobby Hutton, who was sixteen when he joined the party and would soon be one of many others his age. To call the BPP a youth organization is not an exaggeration. While much of the most visible leadership was older, members drew from a demographic between sixteen and twenty-four years old, making the political base of the party radically different from the kinds of movements that preceded Black Power. This links directly to a key concern in this book regarding an orientation toward futurity. As Huey Newton noted in a 1968 interview with members of the Students for a Democratic Society, "The revolution has always been in the hands of the young. The young always inherit the revolution."[42] Newton gives us a nonnormative notion of inheritance here, where one's relationship to politics is what determines what one receives and gives for the future. Guided by youth, those less associated with a reproductive and financial normativity, the kind of futurity at play, prioritized revolution toward the promise of a more egalitarian order of society writ large.

In this direction, Keeling's contributions on the topic of futurity in her second book, *Queer Times, Black Futures*, act as a useful roadmap for *Death's Futurity*. In Keeling's analysis, one of the many ways anti-Black racism operates is through an attempt to forcefully align particular approaches to time:

> Persistent anti-Black racism continues to delimit otherwise visionary movements and possibilities, shaping existing geopolitics and other present realities. In this context, the long arc of Black existence contains vital elements that might be recombined to call forth new relations for all. Black existence has called modernity-as-progress narratives into question since the dawn of modernity during the transatlantic slave trade and the European colonization of African, Asian, Aboriginal and other Indigenous peoples' lands. It carries within it alternative organizations of time in which the future, if there is such a thing, has not been promised; it has had to be created by reaching through and beyond what exists.[43]

Keeling's emphasis on alternative organizations of time in which a future is dependent upon creation resonates with how the BPP engaged a practice toward Black liberation. To create a future, in this vision, depended upon a notion of moving *past* the existing construction of everyday Black life and toward *enacting* the kinds of future-oriented practices otherwise seemingly impossible under white supremacy and capitalism. In other words, the BPP, as but one of many examples, worked toward living a Black future in their present while also working toward a more comprehensive futurity through revolutionary praxis. My implementation of the term *futurity* is akin to Keeling's seminal engagement. Black futurity is a "political imagination that posits radical socioeconomic and geopolitical transformations."[44] These transformations, as facilitated through revolutionary action, required a commitment to aesthetic forms of creation. Imagination, according to Keeling, "participates in the construction of the present through a combination of past and present elements that are not necessarily attached to a presently perceptible reality."[45] This radical aesthetic practice necessitated a responsiveness to the present while also keeping a robust eye on the future. In sum, death's futurity could be simply identified as revolution itself.

Some of the objects of interest for this study were meant to die, so to speak. Newspapers and political posters especially were meant to be used despite their fleeting status: cheaply produced on nonarchival paper; wheatpasted and posted in public areas; pinned, stapled, glued. Others, like the books and documentary film, were meant to survive. These objects were to be used because of their enduring status: to be read and circulated; screened across the world; shelved, preserved, reproduced. Across their specific forms of media and mediation, all the objects in this study were created with an aim toward Black futurity, toward political regeneration through the deaths they focus on and image. Political regeneration works toward a notion of Black futurity that is facilitated in part through forms of politicized looking, a way of looking at and through the aesthetic object for clues of a future "to be created through and beyond what exists."[46]

Notes on Structure

From wake work to waywardness, my research has been indelibly touched by the stunning and recent contributions of theorists and historians like Christina Sharpe and Saidiya Hartman who have offered innovative and cutting insights into the contours, dangers, and possibilities of Black radical politics in and through the archive.[47] While this project does not explicitly engage these and other more recent vital works, I can say without hesitation that my reading and writing practice has been shaped and reshaped by these and other scholars whose writings approaching the question of Black radicality will undoubtedly inspire an entire generation of thinkers whose projects more thoughtfully engage the complexities of these scholars' works. Instead, in what follows, I trace the choices I made regarding the inclusions, exclusions, and methodological approaches that characterize *Death's Futurity*.

This book is far from a comprehensive study of the BPP. As such, I take as a formative premise the understanding that "incomplete history remains a worthy pursuit" and as such have compiled a study that will undoubtedly continue to be regenerated and renewed.[48] Instead, it is my hope that this book is offered as a compendium to many of the works cited as predominant scholarship on the party. This is a study of a brief moment in the BPP's history, from 1969 to 1971, roughly marking a transition from Black Power to prison abolition. I offer this project as a way of thinking through a sliver of the BPP's political theory with the aim of expanding our notion of how Black radical deaths have been engaged to insist on and shape the futurity of Black radical life. I have attempted to let particular objects lead this approach in order to keep each chapter focused in its provocation and minor history. This is aimed toward an attempt to retune my approach to Black studies through levels of description, questions of appearance and reappearance, and aesthetic praxis.

Each chapter in this book is self-sustaining—meaning that the theory and history are specific to both the historical conditions of the murder detailed and the aesthetic objects that emerged as responses to those murders. In this way, I have tried to respect the specificity of each case while also opening up broader conceptual and historical avenues so that we can track how each case is related. Secondary texts that appear from outside of the historical moment at hand are included as forays into historical accuracy, key theoretical interventions, and moments of analytic exposition in relation to each case. Central to this approach is an involved attempt to balance storytelling with first-person narratives, archival coverage, and political theory from the era. In an attempt to attend to the specific artistic interventions in each case, each chapter pairs one kind of object with each murder. Chapter 1 focuses on journalistic print media as it created a framework for understanding the political conditions of Bobby Hutton's 1968 death. Chapter 2 considers the documentary film *The Murder of Fred Hampton* and its role as a tool of political education and regeneration in the immediate aftermath of Hampton's 1969 murder. Finally, chapter 3 examines political posters as they reimagine George Jackson's slain body in relation to the political prisoner's writings and an alternative canon of the Black body as posed by artists. The book's epilogue considers how artists and activists turned to the 1971 Attica state prison rebellion as a way to radically centralize prison abolition as an act of Black revolutionary imagination. Ultimately, each chapter shares in its drive toward repositioning the generative capacity of death in Black radical life as a way of working toward the egalitarian promise of Black liberation.

1

"1,000 Bobby Huttons"

Robert James Hutton, affectionately known as Lil' Bobby, never made it past seventeen. Just a few weeks out from his eighteenth birthday, on April 6, 1968, he was murdered by the Oakland Police Department. His image, however, would circulate long after his life was taken and would serve as a revolutionary call to arms and action by the Black Panther Party for Self-Defense (BPP). Disseminated in flyers, newspaper articles, and other journalistic publications, Hutton's image was reproduced widely as a way to call attention to both the political conditions and the political uses of his death. Various iterations of the same photographic image considered in this chapter appeared in the wake of his death yet each served a distinct purpose. In this portrait, Bobby Hutton, with a black leather jacket adorned with political buttons draped over his shoulders, looks knowingly at the camera. He offers up direct eye contact with the camera's lens, and the twilight of a smile is gestured in passing. There is no surrounding context, and no one else appears in the photograph with him; just Hutton, alone, wearing a collared shirt, sweater, leather jacket, and cap. Three buttons are pinned to his jacket, one centered decisively on a discernible iconic photograph of Huey P. Newton, cofounder of the BPP. The photograph is cropped from the waist up. No clear clues appear about the environment, place, or circumstances of the photograph. Seeing that this is not a formal political portrait per se, Hutton's political agency or relationship to the photographer is clued for the viewer at the level of accoutrement. This photograph, the original and origin of which is uncertain, appears at least three distinct times in the cultural productions made in the immediate aftermath of Hutton's April 1968 murder. Some speculate the image was a family photograph or a candid photograph taken by a party member or a movement photographer close to the Panthers.[1] Others suggest that that the source image is unattainable, and the copy is all that matters (plate 2).[2]

This photographic image of Hutton lasts, but with each iteration, we're presented with an adjustment, a reorganized detail, an added layer, a clipping. Each uptake of Hutton's photograph differs, most notably through the presence and absence of a superimposed layer of bullet holes: the placement of bullet holes, the juxtaposition of his body within the frame, what does and does not surround the image, and how clear or impeded the image is within the clutter of the page correlate to how the image functions in each of its afterlives. These details matter in light of the fact that the original source photograph is a reminder of Hutton's youth and his short-lived status as a member of the BPP. The photograph acts as an object that registers an evidentiary claim to Hutton's life even while that claim is formally shattered, cracked, isolated, and rendered still, thus ontologically questioned if not unsettled. In the photographic iterations discussed here, reworkings of an image of Black death is signified and mobilized through varied transfigurations of an image of Black life.

There are a few other photographs of Hutton that circulate with frequency. In one, he is standing armed, with a gun pointing down, dressed casually in non-Panther uniform and a fedora in front of the Oakland Police Department jail building. In another, fedora-clad Hutton walks ahead of Bobby Seale, gun tucked under his right arm, followed by suited reporters armed with cameras and boom mics at the famed California state capitol demonstration. Often, Hutton is caught looking out of the corner of his eye at something or someone, an ocular turn away from the photographer that embodies what Krista Thompson has theorized as a "sidelong glance," a cool, perhaps detached look that accompanies a Black aesthetic.[3]

This cool sensibility is captured in many images of Hutton, suggesting that being young, armed, and militant came with ease and was both a common and everyday mode of Black living. Hutton's youthful cool is made apparent in these images, as he's often surrounded by suit-clad middle-aged men or next to his mentors Bobby Seale (b. 1936) and Huey Newton (b. 1942) who were almost twice his age. This emphasis on the teenager as a locus for revolutionary activism would be emblematic of the Black Panther Party's eventual rise and, most importantly, to the way they shaped an orientation toward Black revolutionary futurity. But Hutton's own life would be quickly stolen, thus marking a shift in the ways the BPP would speak of and aim to mobilize a revolutionary future, primarily through the visual culture of Hutton's image itself (plates 3–6).

In what follows, I track the varying iterations of the uptake of this photograph as it appears on the covers of the *Berkeley Barb* and the *Black Panther*, a flyer, and a political poster. What all of these mobilizations share is an invocation of the photographic image as reproduced through offset printing as an attempt to make sense of Hutton's murder in lasting terms. As a medium organized around an evidentiary claim, Hutton's photograph works to call attention to a deep concern within the BPP to reckon with the conditions of his death while also entering his revolutionary life in the historical archive as a future-oriented practice. What motivates this concern with the afterlife of Hutton's death is a commitment to a post-revolutionary future in which Hutton's murder would not be delimited to the monotony and mundane quality of anti-Black violence in the United States.

Flash Points and Other Notes on Structure

In what follows, I present a speculative and incomplete set of suggestions on the objects presented in this chapter. This mode of presentation is not unique to my research but is in fact indicative of what it means to conduct research in Black studies more broadly. As a clear example of systemic racism, many of the institutional archives about the BPP and surrounding radical organizations are incomplete or poorly maintained, as indicated by the broken chains of continuity that accompany searching for objects, correspondences, or other materials crucial to this chapter. Many institutions or organizations that have worked to chase down, preserve, and house many of these ephemeral objects are underfunded and overtaxed.

Not surprisingly, these organizations tend to be primarily staffed by Black Americans or political activists who work tirelessly to keep this history alive with limited preservation budgets, little to no resources for facilities maintenance, and an overabundance of materials to maintain. These institutional practices have significance when it comes to this chapter, as many of the materials collected here have required footwork on my part in order to secure information regarding artistic authorship, networks of relation and circulation, and crafty yet informed speculation based on glimpses and fragments of select works in documentary photography and footage. This mode is continuous with those working in Black studies who have worked against the grain of proper archives that tend to erase, abandon, or outright ignore Black presence.

I have chosen, however, to take these institutional gaps and elisions as indications of how to work with the objects selected here. In other words, I have taken the lack of archival consistency as an indication of Hutton's photographic fugitivity. What makes this study unique is how Hutton's image subtends structures of appearance as the image—through repetition, re-presentation, and reconsideration—enables an approach to archival practices that mirror the processes of fugitivity that the object itself activates. The visual, in this register, flees the stillness of an archive and pops up in use—as its appearance conditions the very ephemerality of its original circulation. This is why I have chosen to "follow the object's lead" as a methodological project that slips away from institutional capture.

The original production and chains of circulation of these objects have at least two probable circuits. In what I have decided is the most likely chain of events, the original photograph (which I have not been able to track in terms of both provenance and patterns of emergence and adoption) is utilized in a flyer that mobilized for a memorial march and rally. This flyer, a graphically punctuated and clearly formatted offset multiple, was made in the immediate aftermath of Hutton's murder and passed through the hands of hundreds of activists, sympathetic and nonsympathetic community members, and strangers within the Bay Area. Which is to say, Hutton's photographic image in question for this chapter circulated through the hands, homes, shops, and public spaces frequented by hundreds if not thousands. This detail would make it highly likely that the photographic image was then repurposed to grace the April 12, 1968, cover of the *Berkeley Barb*, which I believe utilized a process of double exposure to overlay the source image onto a glass surface and wall that was punctured by bullet holes. A highly refined symbolic gesture, this process is compatible with scant access to forensic evidence surrounding Hutton's murder and instead aims to image the narrative details that accompany stories of his death. Seeing both that the Black Panther Party made alliances with radical and hippie organizations and publications like the *Berkeley Barb* and that the entire issue of the publication included "exclusive" interviews with BPP leadership, it is highly probable that the minister of culture Emory Douglas was aware of the issue's cover. In the final objects analyzed in this chapter, I argue that Douglas cites the April 12, 1968, *Barb* cover and repurposes elements for a subsequent issue of the *Black Panther* in two subsequent graphic images for the weekly newspaper: a 1970 front-page image and a 1971 political poster. Considerably, visual attention to the images points to the fact that Douglas creates a photomontage that sites and sights the forensic in order to locate Hutton's murder as central to a Black revolutionary future (plates 7 and 8).

I include these details in order to at once set the stage of the course of this chapter while also offering up the speculative nature of some of the "hard" evidence that has emerged in my research. Much of this chapter relies upon research conducted through first-person narrative, politically left propagandist coverage, personal correspondence with living artist-activists from the era, imprecise knowledge of the technologies that were available in the production of these objects, and a broken sense of the networks in which these objects circulated. These structural conditions of intellectual production press upon the very nature of the sociality activated through the political use of these objects: they point to the highly urgent, presentist needs of the BPP to respond to state violence in such a way that elevated a sense of political belonging and activism. Leaning on the visual as a mechanism for mobilizing and gathering, these improper, everyday paper objects provide a striking visuality that resist a sense of stability in terms of archival access and historical knowledge.

Instead of attempting to establish (or better yet force) a normative chronological narrative about the relationship between these objects, I flesh out the ways that each object was used—individually and in tandem—toward the revolutionary aims of the BPP, including rhetorically and materially establishing the grounds of the Black freedom struggle. These processes were not only concurrent but often overlapping, thus making possible a historiographical approach structured around simultaneity as a flash point where objects emerge, collide, coincide, and move together.

I have chosen to structure each subsection with the aims of coupling an object of inquiry with particular historical details of and around Hutton's murder in order to create space for a consideration of the entanglement of aesthetics and politics. Part of a subplot in this venture is to contend with how the photographic image flees from one form to the other, even while the photographic portrait at hand remains identifiable. A type of photographic fugitivity, this relationship between the identifiable image and its movement transforms the photograph into an aesthetic object whose afterlife generates a political sensibility that is future-oriented, and revolutionarily so.[4]

The Social Life and Afterlife of the Photographic Object

This approach to chasing the life of the object is in harmony with Huey Copeland and Krista Thompson's invocation of the "Afrotrope" as a "shorthand way of referring to the recurrent visual forms that have emerged within and become central to the formation of African-diasporic culture and identity."[5] In their lucid development of this conceptual apparatus, Copeland and Thompson introduce the Afrotrope as an analytic mode of engagement[6] and vital heuristic that poses a "challenge to Western theories of the object, the self, authorship, and chronological narration" and instead highlights "the mercurial flow of the black image across the globe."[7] These recurrent visual forms emerge and circulate at uneven speeds and levels of density but nonetheless signpost how Black cultural production leans on the possibilities within transient networks, accrual and dispersion, and matters of time. Like Copeland and Thompson, I too am concerned in this chapter with how visual forms "materially manifest affective investments and historical necessities not only at their moments of appearance but also through their circulation and appearance."[8] Hutton's image could comfortably fit as an Afrotrope precisely because of the ways his image is "transformed and deformed in response to the specific social, political, and institutional conditions that inform the experiences of black people as well as the changing historical perceptions of blackness" of the time.[9] To borrow and repurpose a phrase from Copeland's book, it was as if Hutton's photograph was bound to appear if "given the right set of conditions, experiences, and technologies."[10] Hutton's photographic portrait takes on a life of its own as a feature across various print media in the aftermath of his death.

Taking the Afrotrope as a key framing device, this chapter is also guided by a theoretical concern with the overlaps and differences between photographic forms in both the quotidian and spectacular forms of anti-Black violence.

Historians of photography have charted how the photographic object is ontologically oriented toward a future. This temporal orientation functions as a device of particular significance for my study, primarily because of the medium's compatibility with the BPP's revolutionary aims. It is simultaneously produced as both the social life and afterlife of the object whose making is organized toward capturing a moment in order to preserve it for a future unknown. Embedded within the logics of this future-orientation is also a given sociality of the photograph. At its base, the image produced assumes a relationship between photographer, photographed, and a possible subject who views the photograph. Ariella Azoulay has notably described these temporal and social functions of the photograph as "the civil contract of photography" where users of photography are enabled "to produce images that go beyond the simple technical actions required to produce them, attaining something that transcends the here and now."[11] The medium's technical apparatus—the mechanics that are necessary to apprehend in order to take, process, and produce a photographic object— are only one part of what it takes to "produce" an image. The production of a photographic image is also inextricable from the function of the object to move beyond the presentism of its taking in order to circulate in a future immanent to the photograph's initial origin. The key, in Azoulay's formulation, is that the photograph *requires* a spectator in order for it to act: "Even when a spectator merely glances at a photograph without paying special attention to what appears in it, the photo rarely appears to the gaze as a mere object. The photo acts, thus making others act."[12] Thus, a key social function of the photograph is to act and to make others act; the photograph spurs action/activity beyond the boundaries of its frame yet contained within its social apparatus. Azoulay's attention to action is central to the arguments presented in this chapter, where the appearance and reappearance of Hutton's photographic image serves to mobilize the revolutionary political aims of the BPP. Thus the temporal and social functions of Hutton's photographic image collide to *enact* a revolutionary future.

This concern about the social function of the photograph is enlivened in Leigh Raiford's illustrative engagement with the BPP's visual cultural productions. Taking the BPP's visual cultural productions seriously, Raiford charts a deeply rigorous engagement with the role of the photograph in the cultural and aesthetic apparatus of the organization. Raiford's account is what she calls a "dialectics of seeing," which "describes the process by which one can better understand history through its condensation and assemblage in the material, visual object."[13] Just as Azoulay, Raiford's theory of the photographic object is dependent upon the viewer who, in this formulation, engages with not only the photograph but with "another visual or viewing subject."[14] Whereas for Azoulay the photograph acts and, by extension, makes others act, for Raiford, the photograph provides an occasion for both a better understanding of history and a sociality between viewing subjects. The visual object, then, acts as mediator but not necessarily as actor. Therefore, the appearance and circulation of the photograph reflects the historical and social circumstances in which the BPP used the object. Raiford charts how many of the photographs used by the BPP were taken by photographers who worked for both mainstream publications (waged work) and for social movements (unwaged work), and that by extension these photographs tended to appear in both venues at the same time.[15] This striking historical fact opens up how the "fluidity of photographic circulation at the same time" marks "how mainstream media and the Panthers shared a visual repertoire of the party that at some moments they created simultaneously."[16] While Hutton's portrait does not appear in mainstream media publications, Raiford's insights on the fluidity of circulation and simultaneity of appearance also apply to the alternative press publications covered in this chapter. Key to this chapter, however, is that the photographic portrait in question has no definitive photographer. Captured by an anonymous source, the portrait appears and reappears in different yet related contexts in such a way that the *movement* of the image itself signposts a life and afterlife of the photographic object.

The relationship between photographic appearance and circulation is taken up dynamically by Hito Steyerl in her 2009 essay "In Defense of the Poor Image." While this essay takes on the role of the ubiquitous digital photograph in an increasingly globalized market of exchange, her essay strikes a chord with the low-quality, cheaply xeroxed, quotidian objects that feature Hutton's portrait. "The poor image," writes Steyerl, "is a copy in motion. Its quality is bad, its resolution substandard. As it accelerates, it deteriorates."[17] Steyerl's uptake of both the material qualities of technological reproduction and the conceptual assessments that fall out of such qualities are of particular relevance to Hutton's portrait's reproduction and circulation. For Steyerl, the poor image is worth defending not only because it describes the ubiquity of photographic production in the contemporary but also because the poor image is a *popular* image, it can be made and seen by many. The poor image is, in so many words, the people's image—"not assigned any value within the class society of images," "resistant and non-conformist," and "resolutely compromised: blurred, amateurish, and full of artifacts."[18] These photographic images access and are accessed by the everyday, quotidian subject whose antiprofessional knowledges produce an object that can live poorly but fully among the masses of other objects (and subjects) among which it circulates. Having "disappeared from the surface into an underground of alternative archives and collections," the poor image produces to an alternative system of value organized around "the permanence of the 'original,' but on the transience of the copy."[19] Hutton's photographic portrait, which appears in this chapter as always a copy, accrues political value through its poor quality as a xeroxed object to be circulated, posted, and used by the masses. Hutton's reproduced portrait comfortably embodies Steyerl's theorization of the social life of the poor image: both work to create visual bonds that link the masses with each other.[20] This life, in all its political weight, is mobilized toward the revolutionary aims of the party and in so doing secures Hutton's place in history as a primary force of radical social change.

"The First One Out Was Bobby Hutton"

The *Berkeley Barb*, an infamous, countercultural weekly underground newspaper, dedicated its April 12, 1968, issue to Bobby Hutton. This was strange content material for the *Barb*, considering that most publications addressed the then-ongoing Vietnam War or campus-driven Free Speech Movement at the University of California, Berkeley. The *Barb* was a 1960s countercultural weekly magazine known for its coverage of popular hippie youth cultural and social events. It is estimated that the magazine's circulation grew in the mid-1960s between twelve hundred to eighty-five thousand copies.[21] The magazine was known for its vocal support of the use of illicit drugs, equal access to pornographic films and film clubs within the gay and lesbian community, and the ability to connect people for sex trades. The combination of an emphasis on illicit underground cultures coupled with coverage of the antiwar (particularly antidraft) and free speech movements, was popular among the *Barb*'s mostly white hippie base.[22] To have an entire publication dedicated to the BPP was an unusual editorial decision (plate 8).

A bullet-riddled image of a young Hutton graces the cover of the April 12, 1968, edition of the *Barb* (plate 9). Strikingly, the issue date is the same date as Hutton's funeral, which also took place in Berkeley. Pictured next to prominent BPP member Kathleen Cleaver, Hutton's image is demonstrably reflective of his particular relationship to violence. On the cover, under the banner "IN COLD BLOOD HOW THEY KILLED HIM," a caption reads, "BOBBY HUTTON 1950–1968." Below the caption sits the photograph in question.

Hutton's gaze is disorienting, as the look he gives the camera is strikingly intimate. Four bullet holes are concentrated to the right of his photographed body. These bullet holes geometrically highlight circular shapes, which otherwise appear in the form of the buttons on Hutton's shirt and political buttons on his lapel. Proportionately, the size of the bullet holes distort the scale of Hutton's face, amplifying optic attention to both the cracks that shatter across his neck, chin, cheekbones, and upper right edge of his forehead. Cracks disperse from the bullets' impact, destroying the integrity of the photograph. The bullet holes destroy the photograph's integrity because although Hutton's body is unmarked by bullet holes, the impact of the bullets disassemble the photo into what look like jagged puzzle pieces.

The photograph in this image seems to be superimposed onto an image of a reflective surface affixed to a wall.[23] This is of particular importance because the photograph is punctured by three visible bullet holes, as evidenced by the clear signs of entry of each into the wall, as well as the shattered glass that surrounds one bullet hole. Strikingly, these bullet holes do not directly hit Hutton's image but instead shatter the structural integrity of the photograph itself. The image is fractured by the impact, impeding the viewer's line of sight and thus dramatizing Hutton's murder in sharply aesthetic ways.

There is a productive conceptual tension within this image. Hutton is representationally shattered by the bullet holes while his bodily coherence remains intact. Despite the bullets' intended symbolic and material consequence, Hutton's body does not register the material and fleshly damage that would otherwise appear after a bullet's impact. The bullets fall short of representationally killing Hutton even though Hutton's murder was a real consequence of gun violence. This representational preservation of Hutton's image makes its placement in the *Barb* particularly ripe with argumentative force. The decision to print this as the cover image, as opposed to one of several images of Hutton participating at political rallies or Black Panther Party events, suggests a desire to portray his life as not only political but sentimental in value; his death as not solely destructive but perhaps generative for any potential Black revolution. The first sentence underneath the photograph reads, "The first one out was Bobby Hutton." Hutton appears in a kind of political family portrait.

The grief of his premature death is marked by the tension between signifiers of personhood and signifiers of violence, all discursively framed via press coverage and the journalistic imperatives placed upon the photograph within the print media covered in this chapter. The *Berkeley Barb*'s cover embodies the journalistic and evidentiary associations wedded to the photograph as an object organized around seemingly certain "truth claims" and a weighted sense of "proof." The photograph as an evidentiary device is ripe with potential in the wake of a murder that required the emergence, circulation, and reaestheticization of Hutton's photographic portrait as a means to take stock of the revolutionary politics at stake.

In what follows, I offer an account of the April 6 events as culled from primary and secondary sources, which point to the narrative events of the police encounter, subsequent shootout, and murder with declarative certainty. While I too present the details of the event as certain, there is still relative speculation given the fact that besides Cleaver's recollection and the police record, there are no other eyewitness accounts recorded. Needless to say, the broader implications of such nontransparency in the records show the ease with which state findings take shape and remain uncontested or unchanged as normative police and state practices. This phenomena will reappear in chapter 3, as George Jackson's murder illustrates a more extreme version of such nontransparency. As in the case of Hutton, state procedures and protocols kept Jackson's murder hidden, making it near impossible to get a clear sense of the events leading to these deaths and making any substantial political response to these murders challenging, thus preventing effective and substantive structural change at the level of police violence. Focusing back on Hutton, even if we had a robust archive of eyewitness accounts, police documentation, and other historical evidence, this data would only partially reconstruct the escalation that eventually led to a wounded Cleaver and Hutton's death. With this in mind, I present the details in a narrative voice in an attempt to set the scene for the subsequent uptake of Hutton's photographic image as a tool for imaginative evidence for the Panthers.

First-person narrative accounts of Hutton's death all confirm relatively minimal facts surrounding his murder. In a posthumous collection of his writing edited by Kathleen Cleaver, Eldridge Cleaver discusses the events that eventually led to Hutton's murder and its significance for organizational leadership.[24] Bobby Seale, in his book *Seize the Time*, also discusses Hutton's murder as a formative moment in his own personal history as well as that of the BPP. According to first-person narrative accounts, on April 6, just two days after Martin Luther King Jr.'s assassination, Bobby Hutton and Eldridge Cleaver took shelter in a Panther safe house on 28th and Union Streets in Oakland, California. Moments earlier, Oakland police had harassed several Panthers, including Cleaver and Hutton. Parked adjacent to a local school basketball court, Cleaver and Hutton sprinted into the house when police officers called for reinforcement. Both assumed the Oakland Police Department were simply interested in harassing the BPP and would quickly continue their patrol. Unfortunately, the evening intensified as the Oakland Police Department shot into the building for several hours and eventually tear-gassed Hutton and Cleaver out of the West Oakland holdout. Cleaver, Hutton, and the other Panthers were immediately placed into police custody. Hutton stood in silence while commanded to strip to his underwear with his arms raised to prove that he was unarmed. Several police officers immediately fired dozens of shots into Hutton, who was killed on the scene, just outside of the house.[25] Cleaver and several other Panthers were also wounded by police fire that day. Murdered in front of his revolutionary comrades, Hutton's death was the state's first terminal warning to the BPP. Hutton was not only the first killed in the state's war against the BPP, he was also the first official member of the BPP, thus making his murder particularly formative for the organization.

To date, journalists and historians have no clear sense of the conditions that led up to Hutton's murder, but they all agree on an excessive use of force by the Oakland Police Department in his murder.[26] Additionally, as historians Waldo E. Martin and Joshua Bloom have extensively accounted for, two police officers involved in the shoot-out disavowed the murder, even while one wished for not the death of the young Panther but for his incarceration, arguably a death by other means. In his 1998 interview with African American studies scholar Henry Louis "Skip" Gates for PBS, Cleaver recalls a visit by Oakland Police Department lieutenant Hilliard before he gave his testimony against Cleaver.[27] In the transcript, he remembers their interaction steadily and with certainty: "He said, 'the reason that they have not been rushing you to court is because of my testimony and the testimony of 13 other police officers who were that night who do not agree with what the police did in the way they killed Bobby Hutton.' He said, 'They murdered Bobby. They murdered my prisoner.' That's what he said."[28] The ease with which Hilliard, according to Cleaver, declares Hutton's death as "murder" exposes the ease through which police killings of Black people are a part of an everyday life so quotidian that the aftermath affords no record beyond that of a single memory of testimony.

It is important to note, however, that in Cleaver's account, Hilliard divests himself from the murder scene. "*They* murdered Bobby," he declares, "*They* murdered my prisoner."[29] I believe Hilliard's refusal to place himself as an active participant in Hutton's murder, and his investment in state systems of incarceration ("they murdered my *prisoner*" [emphasis added]), reveal the complex network of desires anti-Black violence creates.[30] In other words, in my reading of his testimony, Hilliard recognizes Hutton's murder as an act of violence by "other" cops while also revealing his own desires to see Hutton incarcerated—a version of "life" sustained in permanent carceral death.[31] To corroborate Hilliard's assertion that Hutton was murdered by the Oakland Police Department, Bloom and Martin provide additional journalistic evidence:

> Eight Panthers were arrested, and six Panthers and two policemen were wounded, none critically. Accounts differ about how the shoot-out began and what the BPP were doing there. There is also conflicting evidence about the conditions under which Hutton was killed. Two Black Oakland police offers involved in the conflict, Gwynne Peirson and Eugene Jennings, testified that Hutton was outright murdered by white police officers after surrendering to them. This testimony was repressed, and the grand jury found the killing of Hutton justified. Gwynne Peirson left the police force and completed a PhD at Berkeley. His 1977 doctoral dissertation, "An Introductory Study of Institutional Racism in Police Law Enforcement," discusses the incident. . . . Officer Jennings's April 10, 1968 testimony, also describing Hutton's death as a murder by white police, was secret until thirty-seven years later when he released a copy of the original testimony transcript."[32]

As detailed in this footnote, Bloom and Martin's archival discovery of Peirson and Jennings's lost testimony (which attested to how officers killed

Hutton) recontextualizes the historical conditions in which Hutton was murdered. Both Peirson and Jennings offered testimony that reflect how white police officers murdered Hutton. This information, along with its eventual exclusion from the grand jury hearing, counters state narratives that referred to Hutton's murder as a justified response by officers under duress. What strikes me in this discussion is also the ongoing censorship of Jennings's testimony, which was kept secret until he himself released the original testimony transcript more than thirty-five years later. Both the initial exclusion of the original testimony, coupled with the more extended thirty-seven year censorship, attends to how Hutton's murder was an exercise in and extension of the state's investment in the violent repression of Black radicalism. Rather than securing state narratives that the police responded appropriately, this testimony corroborates Panther narratives that the police violently and intentionally murdered Hutton.

However, none of this institutional data, nor any historical retrospection, was available to the BPP at the time of Hutton's murder, which is why the turn to the visual as a means to make an evidentiary claim about anti-Black violence is particularly generative as a way to insist on the political nature of Hutton's murder. While the public nature of his murder indeed created a scene for passersby and community members to witness parts of the scene, there is counterintuitively a dearth of visual evidence that would have supported Panther insistence of the brute force of the Oakland Police Department's raid. This lack of accessible visual evidence from the scene is also another aspect shared between Hutton and George Jackson's murders, the difference being the extreme sealing off of the prison from any public access at all, making this lack of visual evidence even more extreme. That is, in a seemingly paradoxical turn, in light of the dearth of photographic evidence surrounding this murder by both state and grassroots sources, the photograph becomes the primary medium through which radicals claim the "truth" behind the conditions of Hutton's death.

The framing, here, is crucial. Unlike the immediate registration of evidence forensic or crime scene photography might wield, the BPP's lack of photographic evidence surrounding Hutton's murder made for a unique conundrum in terms of representation. Rather than strive to stage or even imagine the conditions of his death (as would later happen in the case of Jackson as explored in chapter 3), the photograph of choice was that of a living Hutton, and the imaginative force laid upon that image would gesture toward the violences of his murder without attempting to re-create the scene. This choice would at once destabilize the assumed corollary between the photograph and evidence as a state technology while it also points to alternative modes of visually composing and signposting violence as a condition of everyday Black life.

Photography's peculiar relationship as an evidentiary device is inextricably linked to an assumed realism within the medium's captured subject. While the moving image, particularly via the documentary film, would serve as a kind of evidentiary method in the case of Fred Hampton's murder covered in chapter 2, the photograph's ability to "freeze" time and present itself as unedited made for its unique application as objectively revealing the truth about its given subject. While this history has been tediously accounted for and disputed,[33] with the absence of photographic proof of the conditions of Hutton's murder, the task of proving the spectacular violence of his death had to be uncoupled from an evidentiary approach to the photographic object. Evidence, a case of legal jurisprudence, is often determined by the whims of state technologies that decipher, collect, and assess given materials of "proof" within a court of law. Often undertheorized, however, is the role of trying a case informally in the court of public opinion—where the instability of evidence and its alleged decipherability is up for public debate and disagreement. Legal historian Katherine Biber has called for a "jurisprudence of the visual" in order to reveal the "fantasy that permits law to imagine that decades of criminological, historical and cultural inquiries into race and representation, dispossession and deviance had not intercepted its capacity for vision."[34] A social force, the photograph, as John Berger once claimed, "has no language of its own. One learns to read photographs as one learns to read footprints or cardiograms. The language in which photography deals is the language of events. All its references are external to itself."[35] If we understand the law to be both a material and discursive apparatus, the notion that the photograph requires a language to translate its alleged truth always already destabilizes its ontological security as a realist object. The racial language spoken through a photograph is plentiful precisely because of reliance upon both the legal and extra fantasies that form its status as an object of proof.

These issues are both redeployed and accelerate in the case of Hutton's bullet-ridden *Barb* cover. Here, the bullet holes signify the brutality of Hutton's murder and by extension viewers are compelled to think about the force of anti-Black violence that structure such institutions like the police that protect and promote such violence. The evidentiary case made here is not reliant upon the state's demand for reading an image as unmediated and realist but instead call attention precisely to the *manufactured status* of such violence. These apparatuses are man-made and perpetuated at the hands of those who act as guardians for white supremacy and state violence. By manufacturing an image that literally produces the applications and implementation of violence (as signified by the bullet holes) against the Black body (as embodied by Hutton's portrait), this constructed image provides a set of visual and linguistic cues that frame Hutton's murder as first and foremost political. The creative act—superimposing bullet holes upon a portrait of a living Hutton—articulates a direct claim in the court of public opinion, attempting to foreclose the alleged criminality, deviance, and delinquency that traffic out of legal and social associations with an image of Black youth among a general public. With this photographic portrait, we are given a politics of militancy that preempt and usurp the state of its process of criminalization in order to picture Hutton as but one of many victims of state violence. This visual strategy adopted by the BPP and those they worked in solidarity with was strong enough, in fact, to be taken on by the state via the Oakland Police Department.

In a press conference held shortly after the fatal shoot-out, Oakland chief of police Charles Gain vehemently defended police actions on April 6.[36] Gain predictably justified the Oakland Police Department's actions, notably citing that Hutton posed a viable threat given the fact that he allegedly attempted to run away from officers who thought he was armed at the time of the shooting. Based on KTVU footage of the press conference, the opening thirty seconds included Gain charting police findings that ultimately conclude that the police department's conduct was lawful. He then goes off script to declare that the BPP "poses a real threat to the peace and tranquility of the city of Oakland"—five months before J. Edgar Hoover would go on to make the same claim about the BPP on a national stage.[37]

While his claims that the BPP are irrational and unlawful are hardly shocking, Gain does make a peculiar move in this conference. In order to substantiate his position, he turns to various examples of print media utilized by the BPP and other community organizations to rally around Hutton's death. Repeating the phrase "take a look," Gain holds up ink-on-paper drawings, two separate editions of the *Black Panther*, and a community flyer featuring the same exact Hutton portrait in question in this chapter in an attempt to delegitimize the local power of the BPP. In the process, Gain unwittingly reinforces the power of the images produced in the service of the BPP's revolutionary aims. The restaging of these images in light of Hutton's murder highlights their worth and power more generally. These cultural productions demonstrate influence and impact: at the very least, they represent the circuits of visibility of these objects; they were beginning to be synonymous with the aims of the BPP. At best, these objects come to mark the BPP's threat at the local and state levels. Coming off the heels of the May 1967 state capitol armed protest, Gains argues that the BPP's visual objects serve as examples of the need for state violence against the BPP while also pointing to the state's burgeoning fear of the party's efficacy.

In Gain's hands, these visual cultural productions become evidence of the BPP's criminality—incitements of violence against the police, dangerous ideologies that target the state and capitalism, and "proof" that the BPP are threats to society. Gain attempts to transform these objects that utilize the photograph as central in their making into prosecutorial forms and thus returning to versions of photographic documentation that have formed the historical processes of criminalization and surveillance that structure Black life.[38] There is striking similarity here in how the mugshot has historically been used for similar outcomes against Black people.

Here, it is useful to point to the ways that Gains leans on articulating a dominant narrative in order to build a case in public opinion and in order to do so, he turns to the visual as an evidentiary means. While he aims to defame the images, Gain instead marks their significance in not only the narrative surrounding Hutton's murder but also in the broader project to repurpose that death for political means. What Gain's demonstration portrays is the complexity of the visual as a terrain for politics. The revolutionary images produced by the BPP posed a cultural threat that was coeval with the political critiques and organizing leveraged against the state. A flyer for Hutton's march is presented between that of BPP images that depict the police as pigs and call for armed self-defense. That Hutton's flyer appears in this context is an example of how the production of his image is assumed to encourage the political aims of the BPP.

The political power of the photograph accrues as the original source image is manipulated in various media publications. The *Berkeley Barb* cover speaks primarily to the ways that the details surrounding Hutton's death required a visual response that could account for the exaggerated scale of police violence. Subsequent findings confirm that Hutton was shot at least ten times by the Oakland Police Department.[39] While the details of those findings were yet unavailable to the BPP and surrounding activists, the public and graphic nature of Hutton's murder communicated the ways that the BPP would be targeted by local police departments and state agencies. Hutton's death symbolized the murder of Black people at the hands of the Oakland Police Department, and activists and community members believed that the death was violently public in order to teach a lesson for anyone who would be a part of the BPP and engage in revolutionary activism.[40] By 1968, the BPP had built a reputation as a militant vanguard organization that aimed to organize Black people to build a revolution to overthrow the state and capitalism in the United States. Only two years out from its founding, the BPP had come to symbolize the force of Black Power and struggles for self-determination by Black people globally. This accelerated rise was in large part due to early events that catalyzed the BPP as a force to be reckoned with, including Hutton's status as the first recruit and the first murder within the Black Panther Party.

Recruited in 1966 at the age of sixteen (the summer before the BPP was formally founded), Bobby Hutton ("Lil' Bobby" as he was affectionately referred to) was the first official member.[41] Born Robert James Hutton in 1950, Hutton and his family relocated from Jefferson County, Arkansas, in 1953 following a racist confrontation by the Nightriders, a white supremacist group of vigilantes known to terrorize Black people in the state.[42] Hutton's Panther recruitment came out of his friendship with Bobby Seale during the summer of 1966. Hutton participated in a summer program facilitated by the North Oakland Neighborhood Anti-Poverty Center for which Seale was hired as a lead foreman.[43] This program employed one hundred Black youth who were paid in exchange for doing basic manual labor.[44] Seale took the job in an attempt to "teach Black American History" between work projects as well as "teach them responsibility" in relation to "their own people living in the community."[45] Seale's occupation is a reflection of both a historically and politically specific moment in which one's work was ripe with revolutionary potential and one's revolutionary commitment was a facet of their work. Coupled with the long labor history of organizing within one's workplace, Seale's decision to take the job in order to facilitate the politicization of Black youth reflects a non-romanticized everyday notion of how politics saturated one's everyday life.[46] This kind of approach to politics signals a deep investment in consciousness-raising within everyday contexts, like the workplace and classroom and during leisurely activities. By using his waged work to facilitate his political work,

Seale politicized his wage by engaging young Black men in questions of their political, economic, and historical genealogies. Within this everyday act of subversion, Seale leveraged his workplace as one where a different kind of subject position could emerge.

Seale and Newton met Hutton while doing this work. This also was the time that Hutton began his own process of politicization. A few months after their initial meeting, Hutton was the first to join the Black Panther Party. In the first two months of the nascent organization's development, Hutton took to the streets, circulating thousands of copies of the "10-Point Program" in an attempt to build a broader mass movement across Black communities in Oakland.[47] Seale noted how Hutton developed astute political responses to questions and concerns from tentative and wary community members.[48] Family members reflect on his intellectual rigor at such a young age, noting that Hutton was reading Richard Wright's *White Man Listen* and W. E. B. Du Bois's *Black Reconstruction*—a 750-page volume—around the time of his murder.[49] Often characterized by his adept rhetorical skills and ability to articulate the severity of systemic poverty and violence, Hutton's early politicization demonstrated leadership promise within the organization.

All these historical and biographical details add texture to the *Barb*'s cover photograph. The shattered photograph is but one object of many devastated by bullet holes during the April 6 shoot-out. Reporter Stu Glauberman noted that a sited memorial emerged on the sidewalk where Hutton's blood had pooled and where he fell to the ground. That memorial included white lilies, red roses, a shattered framed print of James Earle Fraser's *End of the Trail*, and, eventually, the broken face of a television set.[50] The *Barb*'s photograph of the memorial is cropped to focus on these lilies and Fraser's print, which is punctured by a bullet hole in the bottom left corner that fracture the image to create faultiness on its surface. An emphasis on this popular print's wound uncannily emphasizes the wound of the subject depicted, both person and historical content, and illuminates the overlaps between both Native genocide and localized anti-Black violence as concurrent processes in US nation making.[51] The makeshift memorial grounds the gunshot as a wound with continuity and one that surfaces on the visual plane as one of many locations of violence. This image, therefore, is compatible with the cover image presented. The bullet hole serves as a representational device that could be repurposed to point to the political nature and potential of his murder. By choosing a source image that was, at the time of its circulation, already associated with a rally, march, and political aims of the BPP, and pictured Hutton clad in then already-recognizable BPP garb, the *Barb* chose an image of Hutton already imbued with revolutionary potential. The combination of the portrait image and the bullet-shattered glass compositionally adhered to form a visual production that could hold the revolutionary promise of Hutton's life with the political conditions of his death—an aesthetic argument coupled with a political imperative (plate 8).

"1,000 Bobby Huttons"

A flyer deploys the same photograph of Hutton—in this instance calling for a memorial procession rather than reconstructing the conditions of his murder. Here, the photograph appears for us in an organizing context, made for a different kind of circulation and remembrance than that of the *Barb* cover. Hutton's photograph is cropped so that Hutton's body seemingly floats on the white page. In this iteration, Hutton's photographic bodily integrity is also not compromised. While his portrait is indeed cropped and isolated to float against the white paper's background, Hutton's photograph is seemingly untouched by creative flourishes, compositional impositions, or other forms of embellishment. Because of this lack of compositional elements, this might be the closest to the original source photograph at hand. Similarly, this might be what made the photographic object readily available for uptake by others; it was a relatively clean copy that could be creatively adjusted and compositionally extended. Simple, black, bold, and large text accompanies the photograph, "Bobby Hutton MURDERED By Oakland Pigs," along with the date, time, and location information for the scheduled march. A text box appears in the bottom third of the page; in it, the text reads, "Procession to jail for Eldridge Cleaver Following Memorial." There are twinned aims with this flyer: to both offer memorial to Hutton and to transform that legacy into action for a comrade who survived the violence that Hutton himself did not. The political use of this object, like others, was intended to mobilize (plate 7).

Buried on April 12, 1968, two thousand people attended Bobby Hutton's funeral service at Ephesians Church of God in Berkeley, California. At the family's behest, the service itself was a closed ceremony. Regardless, the church became a central location for radical cadres from throughout the Bay Area to give their condolences and organize around Hutton's murder. Recorded footage from outside the funeral shows attendance by Huey P. Newton, Kathleen Cleaver, Bobby Seale, Eldridge Cleaver, and even actor Marlon Brando (who became radicalized by the Black Power and American Indian movements).[52] Panther rank-and-file members provided security for the funeral. In a uniformed effort, these members lined up in front of the church to deter police and white supremacist organizations from disturbing the funerary proceedings.

Hutton's mother decided on an open casket for her son.[53] She also asked the BPP to serve as pallbearers and carry the casket into the hearse and ultimately to the grave. One cannot think of this maternal decision without thinking of the influence and legacy of Mamie Till's decision to have an open casket for her son Emmett's 1955 funeral. Mamie Till, in an act of unthinkable force, urged the public to view her son's brutalized face such that they would never be able to a forget the violences of white supremacy that led to his death. Till's 1955 decision left an indelible mark on many within Black communities in the United States and is often referenced as an unforgettable turn for many youth who would go on to be key figures in subsequent Black Power movements.[54] It would be sensible to assume that in addition to adherence to religious traditions that encourage a final viewing for the deceased, Dollie Hutton wanted her son to be viewed as a political gesture. Several reports and a first-person account by Bobby's surviving brother Jay Hutton Sr. recall how the Hutton family was in support of Bobby's activism, therefore making the decision to view his body in final rest a likely means of solidarity with the Till family and others who lost their children to acts of police violence.

Dollie Hutton's decision to have a final viewing of her son Bobby opens up the maternal apparatuses of witnessing within a Black radical tradition. Fred Moten has poetically described Mamie Till's (then Mamie Till Bradley) decision as Black performance:

> Ms. Bradley opens, leaves open, reopens, the violent, ritual, sexual cutting of his death by the leaving open of the casket, by the unretouching of the body, by the body's photograph, by the photograph's transformation in memory and nightmare of which many speak (for instance Roland Barthes, about whom more later). That leaving open is a performance. It is the disappearance of the disappearance of Emmett Till that emerges by way of exhibiting kinship's wounds (themselves always refigured and refinished in and as and by

exogamous collision). It is the ongoing destruction of the ongoing production of (a) (black) performance, which is what I am, which is what you are or could be if you can listen while you look. If he seems to keep disappearing as you look at him it's because you look away, which is what makes possible and impossible representation, reproduction, dream.[55]

Moten insists that by charging and demanding an active practice of *looking at* her son's face whether in situ or through photographic reproduction, Till activates a Black performance that relies on the looking at/looking away, production/reproduction, appearance/disappearance—all of which converge to inform an image and afterimage of Emmett that undeniably mark the looker's memory. What makes this act one of maternal force is not only Mamie's status as Emmett's mother but, most significantly, the elements of her decision that enact a radical insistence on exposure and encounter between those looking. To engage in this particular Black performance, which is to say to engage in the dynamics of looking and being unable to sustain that look, is an activity central to Black performance. In this modality of looking, Till opens a pathway to consider how her son's murder lays bare the political force of anti-Black violence.

Dollie Hutton's inheritance and reproduction of this staging too considers a lineage of a Black maternal performance. Unlike Emmett Till's open casket, Hutton's visage was not reproduced via the photographic image. Rather, there is but one photograph from Hutton's funeral that circulates, and it was taken by Stephen Shames who was covering the funeral with permission from Hutton's family. In this photograph, Hutton's open casket is visible, and the silhouette of his body is discernible from afar. The photograph overwhelmingly frames the many attendees of the funeral who fill the pews at the funerary service. Open for the duration of the funeral, Hutton's casket is front and center, right beneath the pulpit. Reserved and somber, the photograph is quiet and attentive, unlike the photographic portrait of Hutton circulating among those outside the church walls. This photograph asks for a kind of looking that exposes the looker to the physical contours of Hutton's murder and stages an encounter with the act of looking embedded within these traditions of Black performance. The emphasis here on the crowd of attendees—all those present to look and look away—is doubled when we consider those who circulated a radically different photograph of Hutton that day (plate 10).

Hundreds who were unable to attend the funeral sent letters, including Betty Shabazz (the late Malcolm X's wife), as well as the executive secretary of the Organization of Solidarity of the People of Asia, Africa, and Latin America (OSPAAAL). Some of them subsequently published tributes in the May 4, 1968, edition of the *Black Panther*, commemorating Hutton. Among these letters was one by Stokely Carmichael whose prose details the significance of Hutton's death:

> Little Bobby was in the vanguard of revolutionary brothers who clearly understood that power comes from a gun. His death proves that if we are to survive America we must follow by these examples and pick up the guns. . . . In his death thousands of other Bobby Huttons will rise from our communities to carry on where he left off.[56]

We can see how Carmichael refuses the potentially isolating rhetoric of Hutton's murder. Carmichael does not understand Hutton's murder as an exceptional case of police misconduct but rather contextualizes Hutton within systemic violence against Black people. By suggesting that Black survival in the United States requires revolutionary violence, Carmichael adheres to the BPP's declarations of war. Carmichael's call for "thousands of other Bobby Huttons" collectivizes and pluralizes Hutton's murder toward a call for continued revolutionary violence. Black survival requires power, and "power comes from a gun."[57]

This understanding of survival addresses the coconstitutive deployment of revolutionary violence alongside the "survival programs" that were so crucial in the early years of the BPP. In Carmichael's model of survival, anti-Black police violence can only be combated through Black revolutionary violence. Survival *requires* revolutionary violence. If we take Carmichael's commemoration letter as an indication of the potential of revolutionary violence, then we can better understand the radical use of Hutton's murder toward revolutionary action. This connection sheds light on Carmichael's call for a thousand Bobby Huttons. Journalist Charles Howe discusses how the state's repressive apparatus affected Panther membership:

> Each time a Panther is beaten or jailed or shot or killed—the score is now one dead, three wounded, at least a dozen in jail and scores "rousted"—their membership grows. Starting with one 14 year-old boy in 1966 the Party—members and non-member sympathizers—now may number 1000, State-wide.[58]

Accounts like these substantiate that BPP's membership in 1968 expanded rather than contracted under the state's repressive regime. This surge in organizational membership and capacity suggests that the generative power of Black radical death was, in fact, wedded to notions of Black futurity. This shift puts Bobby Hutton's murder within another insightful political context. Rather than stymie the organizational growth and mass participation toward death, Hutton's murder catalyzed, renewed, and fortified investment in the Black freedom struggle. Rather than make claims to Black life in the utopic sense, the BPP's early invocation of warfare, and Hutton's subsequent first fatality within that guerilla warfare, contributed toward a vision of a Black future for which Black radical death was a certainty.

Immediately following Hutton's funeral, the BPP held a rally at Lake Merritt in Oakland as an attempt to situate Hutton's murder within a broader framework of ongoing state repression against Black revolutionaries. Following speeches by Brando and Seale, Kathleen Cleaver read a short letter written in response to Hutton's murder. In it, she continues Carmichael's refusal of nonviolent strategies by inverting the rhetoric toward self-defense. "It is not a question of nonviolence versus violence," Cleaver declares, but one of "self-defense." In her formulation, self-defense combats state narratives that depicted the BPP as revolutionary agitators aimed at instigating unrest. In a world where Hutton was "shot down like a common animal," self-defense against state violence requires militant Black revolutionary violence. Hutton's murder immortalized him as a "warrior for Black liberation," which sparked the call for thousands of Bobby Huttons to rise in his wake.[59]

The rhetoric of self-defense, as deployed by the BPP, is a lucid systemic analysis of the foundations of anti-Black violence in the United States. By honing in on the particularities of state violence, the BPP were effectively able to frame taking up arms as an act of self-defense against police and other white supremacist violence.[60] In doing so, they radically repositioned the right-wing assertion of the constitutional Second Amendment and recaptured it in the service of leftist revolutionary violence. The BPP extended their declarations of war, as embodied within the 10-Point Program, toward revolutionary praxis. This extension dismantled state narratives that Black men and women somehow deserved the onslaught of state-initiated violence and replaced these narratives with the embodied threat of armed Black people killing police in an act of self-defense. This productive inversion radically redetermines the conditions of possibility for revolutionary violence. If we understand, like the BPP did, that anti-Black violence is the permanent and intensified offensive force in the durational management of Black bodies, then any form of revolutionary violence to annihilate state terror is always and already an act of self-defense.

Mumia Abu-Jamal, in his memoir *We Want Freedom: A Life in the Black Panther Party* written from the Pennsylvania State Correctional Institution at Mahanoy, notes that between 1966 and 1968, "the Revolution seemed as inevitable as tomorrow's newspaper."[61] The comfort of knowing with certainty that tomorrow's newspaper will come is mirrored with the certainty of knowing that revolution too is inevitable. We can assume that much of this certainty was established in the Black Panther Party's weekly newspaper publication the *Black Panther Community News Service*, which often published articles and political posters that reflected the "here-and-now" qualities of revolutionary action. The first edition of the *Black Panther* called for people in the Black community to "arm themselves to put an end to exploitation and oppression" in order to pursue "self-defense, serving the people, national liberation, and revolution" and ended with the phrase, "THIS IS OUR DAY!"[62] Indeed, it is the final phrase of the paper that reflects the viable promise of revolution. By claiming, with the utmost certainty, that revolution was present, the *Black Panther* aimed to performatively call revolution into being among its popular base as the only solution to ongoing state violence.

Against the backdrop of global insurrections, and in reaction to political assassinations like that of Dr. Martin Luther King, the formation of COINTELPRO (the Counter Intelligence Program) in response to radical organizations like the BPP, and subsequent murder of revolutionaries like Bobby Hutton, all make explicit the threat Black radical politics presented to the state and capitalism. In a May 1968 letter to the editorial staff of the *New York Review of Books*, just one month after Hutton's funeral, an unlikely grouping of authors and activists, including John Gunther, Charles V. Hamilton, and LeRoi Jones, articulated their condemnation of state responses to the BPP.[63] Written on behalf of several signatories, the letter indicted the Oakland police force for being "determined to exterminate" the Black Panther Party's leadership.[64] In addition, the letter condemns the "murder of Bobby James Hutton and the wounding of Eldridge Cleaver as acts of violent white racism" that reflect the ongoing persecution of Black men and women "for their militant position on Black liberation."[65] Because of its publication source, the letter reflects a mainstream understanding of the state's early attempts to repress the Black Panther Party's active pursuit of revolution. The BPP threatened the sanctity of white supremacy as protected by the police and capitalism precisely because they dared to shoot back. In this way, FBI director J. Edgar Hoover's September 1966 proclamation that the BPP were the "greatest threat to the internal security of the country" evidenced the influence of the BPP on other mobilized radical organizations.[66] Being a threat, in other words, means waging a war against the state and capitalism and therefore the attendant strategies, tactics, and rhetorics that reinforce such systems. Bobby Hutton's murder, as evidenced by the circulation of his photographic image, demonstrates the intensification of that status as a threat by the BPP. Hutton's murder, and the cultural productions attached to that event, were utilized as a means to further motivate revolutionary activity.

Hutton's death—as the *first* recruit and member of the BPP as well as the *first* Panther to be murdered by the state—intensified the BPP's antistate and anticapitalist warfare. Within this intensification is the BPP's understanding of historical continuity (linking police violence to histories of lynching acts as but one example of this phrase), as well as an account of the shifting political and economic conditions of the 1960s (the particularity of global resistance movements within which the BPP situated itself). When taken together, the BPP made use of both of these structural operatives in their narrative application of Hutton's murder ultimately toward revolutionary ends. In doing so, these aims became most impactful as an articulation of war against the state and capitalism—an articulation that secures the BPP's influence on histories of radical resistance.

In Huey Newton's 1968 letter written from jail, his first public response to Hutton's murder, he writes of Hutton's place within the Black Panther Party's history. Newton calls Hutton "the beginning" who "gave himself" and "asked neither for security nor high office."[67] He goes on to describe Hutton's legacy in the "struggle for life, dignity, and freedom." As though disaffected, Newton writes, "We salute Lil Bobby and his family for what they have given us. He was the beginning of the Party. Let us make his thinking, his desires for his people become a way of life." Here, Newton distances himself from the emotional response commonly afforded to this kind of egregious murder in order to pragmatically approach Hutton's murder as a necessary sacrifice in the plight of revolutionary violence. While he acknowledges Hutton's exceptional position as the "beginning of the party," Newton repetitively uses "given" and "gave" as verbal cues to the nature of Hutton's death. Note how Newton does not engage in rhetorical fervor, nor does he present the language of victimhood. With calculated and delicate diction, Newton articulates Hutton's murder as a timely event in the service of revolution. Hutton's murder coincided with a "struggle for life." Hutton's death marked a conjunction—between the "beginning" of the BPP and the first death—presenting a new political terrain in which the BPP strengthened their commitment to revolutionary violence rather than abandoning the call for arms. Through this letter, Newton *uses* Hutton's murder as a way to build mass-organizational participation. Instead of responding to Hutton's murder with a call for political retraction, Newton intensifies efforts in an attempt to further polarize Black radicals from the police by calling for directed revolutionary commitment.

Bobby Seale corroborates Newton's calculated response to Hutton's death. In a message sent through his lawyer, Newton charts how Seale should publicly respond: "Huey sent a tape back, and told me to remember to tell the people not to spontaneously riot, but to tell them to organize themselves. . . . Huey told me to tell the people to arm themselves and put arms in their homes, and to say that if they see racist cops brutalizing and murdering our people, that we have but one alternative—to go forth as an organized force."[68] Newton instructs Seale to put Hutton's murder to revolutionary work in order to build a collective and organized response by—and for—the masses against state violence. In line with the BPP's overall organizational politics, Newton calls on Seale to build around potential revolutionary violence by advocating the collective pursuit of arms. What is significant in his instruction is Newton's insistence to control any potential spontaneous riot—which in many ways was an effort to control mass emotional response. Seale reflects on Newton's instructions when he notes, "I knew Huey was right, and I made it a point not to function off of emotions because emotions won't guide a correct revolutionary struggle."[69] For the first time in Panther history, they needed to account for the tension between "emotional" versus pragmatic political responses to Hutton's highly charged murder.

This differentiation between emotional and pragmatic responses to Hutton's murder is echoed on page five of that same May 4, 1968, edition of the *Black Panther* that includes Newton's aforementioned note: a drawing by Joan Tarika Lewis, the first woman to join the BPP in 1967. Lewis was a frequent contributing artist to the newspaper under the pen name Matilaba. Lewis, then a high school student herself and who, according to several sources, was a good friend of Bobby Hutton's, depicts a familiar scene of police harassment on a nameless city street corner. Tucked behind a wall away from police sight lines are three Panthers, armed and witnessing an act of police violence against a young Black kid. Posted on the wall that safeguards them from police vision hangs a drawn rendition of the same portrait of Hutton in question in this chapter with the phrase "Bobby Hutton Murdered by Oakland Pigs." This drawing is captioned with the declaration "NO MORE RIOTS" in bold, black ink. The reconstruction of Hutton's photograph in drawing form appears as a wheat-pasted poster and is paired with a prowling black panther, readily signposting the party and its public visibility for the viewer. Well aware of the mass circulation of this particular issue of the newspaper among communities directly affected by Hutton's murder, Lewis's image marks a clear message intended for those who want to rage against the Oakland Police Department and their violent practices (plate 11).

At least three political messages become particularly clear through this drawing. Firstly, Hutton's memory is called upon as a lasting presence in the streets, as his image is invoked in the pursuit of Black radical activity. Secondly, there is a bold call against rioting, which echoes Seale's account of what Newton felt was the correct course of action for community responses to Hutton's death. Finally, while both these political stances require disciplined militancy, they also require a tactical call to arms; the revolutionaries wait patiently around the corner, armed and ready for the revolutionary call.

As a self-defined revolutionary vanguard cadre, Newton, Seale, and Cleaver decided to discourage spontaneous rebellion in the service of organizing an armed (and eventually trained) organized militia. Crucial to this task was the abandonment of emotional responses that might cloud strategic revolutionary vision.[70] As an outcome of this party line, the BPP encouraged Black nonmembers to transform their emotional rage around Hutton's murder into Panther membership and armed self-defense. Hutton's murder, the first murder (of many), required Panther leadership attend to Black radical murder's generative potential for revolutionary warfare against the state. What is clear is that this kind of measured response to violence was best embodied in some of the most notable BPP actions, including the April 1967 rally to protest the police killing of Denzil Dowell in Richmond, California, and the May 1967 armed march on the state capitol in Sacramento, California.

The rally to protest the Richmond police was the BPP's first public appearance as an organization. Hutton was present at the rally, equipped with a recording device and camera to document any police harassment. Making their inaugural public appearance at an antipolice violence rally is significant in that it marks just how the lived reality of violence within Black communities was a priority in early BPP organizing, as this violence comes to mark the very conditions of the revolutionary guerrilla warfare they strived toward.

In a speech delivered at the rally, Huey Newton characterized the place of war within the Panther's revolutionary framework. Being such a noteworthy organizational event, this speech's provocation toward revolutionary violence was especially telling: "The masses of the people want peace. The masses of the people do not want war. The Black Panther Party advocates the abolition of war. But at the same time, we realize that the only way you can get rid of war, many times, is through a process of war."[71] The realization that the "only way you can get rid of war" is "through a process of war" speaks to how cognizant the BPP were of the potential of revolutionary violence. This declaration also reinterprets and redeploys Frantz Fanon's assertion that "the colonized man liberates himself in and through violence," a praxis that "enlightens the militant because it shows him the means and the end."[72] Adopting Fanon's justification of the means and the end, Newton similarly showcases the theory that the pursuit of war ensures the abolition of war. Fanon's framework allows the BPP, in these early formative years of organizational life, to justify the use of revolutionary violence for radical ends. In a way, the BPP adopt Fanon's theoretical work for its radical use and deploy his oeuvre for implementation. The use of revolutionary violence by colonized peoples allows the BPP to imagine the use of revolutionary violence within the United States. Fanon allows the BPP to access the anticolonial imaginary he details, from which the BPP declare their own antistate and anticapitalist uses of revolutionary violence. In this way, the declarations of war posited by the BPP show the conditions of white supremacy that structure Black life in the United States in order to approximate the limits of thinking about Black freedom without revolutionary violence.

"He Was the Beginning"

To conclude this chapter, I want to focus on two final appearances made by Hutton's portrait in the *Black Panther*. The first is for the April 6, 1970, cover, which memorializes Hutton's death two years to the day. On this cover, Hutton's portrait is cropped and scaled to fit the broadsheet. Unlike the rally poster, here he rests against a stark black frame. The black background is delimited by ten white silhouettes of assault rifles, which strike contrast to the black box that they frame. Text to the right of Hutton's photograph includes his years of life, and to the left reads, "HE WAS THE BEGINNING LIL BOBBY JAMES HUTTON." At the bottom, in italicized font, sits a quote by Huey Newton. This cover serves to function as a journalistic memorial, one that rehearses a commitment to memorializing Hutton as in the first iteration of his portrait. The gun here gestures toward the gunshot, but through the mechanism that produces such violence, not the material registration the gunshot leaves behind. The repetition of the gun here is compatible with the measured, organized call to arms made by the party in the wake of Hutton's murder. To call revolution into being, the gun must be repurposed as not only a technology of state anti-Black violence but also of revolutionary potential (plate 12).

Dynamically, only one year later, in the April 3, 1971, issue of the *Black Panther*, Emory Douglas includes a poster that directly visualizes a revolutionary afterlife of Hutton's death. Douglas, who adamantly opposed picturing images of dead Black people and asserted that revolutionary Black art should only show Black people resisting or thriving, includes the source photograph as a wheat-pasted poster in one of his now iconic graphics.[73] In this poster, a child who shares a resemblance with Hutton himself stands atop a garbage dumpster holding a newspaper that reads, "COMMUNITY CONTROL OF POLICE." Another figure is included in the image, though facing away from our view. Behind this Hutton-like figure is a brick wall, and to the left is the very same photograph of Hutton, shaped and presented like a poster wheat-pasted to the wall. Recall Tameka Lewis's drawing that takes Hutton's photograph, renders it into a political poster, and displays it as fixed onto a brick wall. It seems that Douglas, in his occupation as both mentor and the art director of the *Black Panther*, readily cited Lewis's drawing here. Instead of turning to his iconic illustrative style, he chose rather to reproduce Hutton's photographic portrait and, à la *Berkeley Barb*, include his own documentary superimposition (plate 13).

This poster is seemingly out of step with Douglas's aesthetic political line, but just like the *Berkeley Barb* version of this same photograph, Douglas's photographic reproduction features Hutton alive, though his image is also riddled with bullet holes. However, unlike the *Barb* image, Douglas's reproduction features bullet holes that strike Hutton's torso and neck. What is significant about Douglas's composition is that he sources the bullet holes from the same May 4, 1968, edition of the newspaper that included Lewis's drawing. The photograph homes in on five bullet holes, and the caption reads, "Police murdered a man, imprisoned a man, jailed seven others, ruined this house at 1218—28th St, Oakland, and showed the country and the world the exact nature of the racist oppression in the U.S." Douglas rotates that 1968 photograph by ninety degrees and overlaps it onto the photographic portrait of Hutton (plates 14 and 15).

Taken at precisely the location of Hutton's murder, Douglas's use of the bullet holes works as almost forensic image.[74] Taking on yet another iteration of the conditions of his death, the doubling of one photograph onto another, of one reproduction onto another, gestures toward the entry and exit points of bullets strewn across Hutton's body. Here, the poster, positioned in the background of the scene in front of it, is a part of the structure (the brick wall) that stages the political activity at hand. The photomontage is in aesthetic conversation with the illustration that surrounds it. Leigh Raiford has noted how Douglas pursued a strategy of "combination," where he would add other creative elements to enhance the meaning of the photograph and in so doing created a composition that was compatible with the aims of the political message strived for in each work.[75] The relationship between the forensic invocation of the photograph as it is produced to lay claim as evidence and the rest of the poster as illustration opens up a striking visual argument around the afterlife of Hutton's murder and its direct political actions in the present (plate 16).

As such, through this material application, there is a more direct referent to the political conditions of Hutton's murder. The image is set against a quotidian scene of engagement, as the young Panther pictured surrounds himself with political signifiers. Like Hutton, this figure emerges out of, and in relation to, the aims of the BPP. The appearance of this Panther, recruiting in front of a photograph of the party's *first* recruit, makes it easy for the viewer to build a bridge between the bullet-ridden young boy presented in the poster and the one who stands in front of us. Famously, Douglas insisted that "the ghetto is itself a gallery," and in this image, he indeed suggests that the transformation of Hutton's bullet-riddled image into a wheat-pasted poster is a form of "Revolutionary Art."[76] The poster in this formulation structures the scene in front of it, suggesting Hutton's murder is a constant reminder of both the stakes and promises of the BPP's everyday modes of revolutionary organizing. In other words, the work before us offers a scene where we might see the makings of one thousand Bobby Huttons.

Indeed, Hutton's murder may have been the first, but it would not be the last. In the chapters that follow, I conduct a close examination of two of many deaths of Panthers at the hands of the state. Fred Hampton's and George Jackson's fates were a part of the future orientation marked by Hutton's murder. In both cases, the BPP responded in similar rhetorical and visual ways, which gestures toward how the response to Hutton's death set a precedent for the urgency and relevance of the aesthetic in serving the political goals of the party. By galvanizing the movement for Black liberation around these murders, the BPP worked toward that initial call for one thousand Bobby Huttons and by result created a visual language around Black radical death that lived on well into the future. By offering these various iterations of Hutton's portrait made anew, I believe the BPP aimed to mark such a future orientation. This future, which is present as a revolutionary instantiation, is mobilized through the appearance and reappearance of Hutton's image. While this portrait flees from one form of print media to another, its Afrotropic qualities become more and more dependent upon Hutton's presence as both Black radical, first recruit, and first death in the party. The image's return, its repetition, accrues in revolutionary value as a poor and popular image, an emergent and coincidental one that marks revolutionary potential and power. Making one thousand Bobby Huttons is inseparable from seeing Hutton's image again and again, as a reminder of the future that is present in the aftermath of his death. That futurity, that horizon line, is a Black radical aesthetic imagining as seen and activated through Hutton's ever-present image.

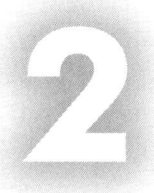

Fred Hampton and
the Political Life of Objects

I don't believe I'm going to die slipping on a piece of ice . . .
I believe that I will be able to die as a revolutionary in the
international revolutionary proletarian struggle.
—Fred Hampton, 1969

I came into this world anxious to uncover the meaning of
things, my soul desirous to be at the origin of the world,
and here I am an object among other objects
—Frantz Fanon, *Black Skin, White Masks*, 1952

This chapter is about radical Black life. It is about a Black life articulated, imagined, and visualized through death. It is about how revolutionary Black life and death can be narrated in filmic footage. It is about the life that takes shape and transmutes into a group of revolutionary objects. This chapter is not about an active flattening or reduction of Black life to the status of nonsentient object. It is not about simply equating Black life to Black death, as much as it is not about suggesting that objects are equal to Black people. Rather, this chapter is about Fred Hampton's life via his death and his anticipation of his death. It is about how documentary form works to visualize his life and death. This chapter is about how looking for Hampton's life and afterlife means looking for all those objects that composed his Black radicalism. This chapter is, ultimately, about how Hampton's Black life can be seen through death and through the objects that he left behind.

Some of these objects are presented to us in the form of black and white footage. Guided by the lens of a shaky, handheld camera, the viewer has landed in a small room in disarray. Newspapers, records, and clothing litter the floor. Natural light seeps in, illuminating pockets of space in some areas while creating stark shadows in the corners of the room. The well-lit parts guide our sight. Tucked underneath a stack of pamphlets hides *The Wretched of the Earth*. Exposed and positioned in clear view on a bloodied mattress rests *The Autobiography of Malcolm X*. Other clues offer insight into the scene. Rumpled papers pile on the floor. A battered poster is pulled from the pile and the blurry profile of a figure mid-speech is featured prominently. Rounded and fractured records are strewn on the ground; they still sit, gently touching as if once stacked. Unsheathed, their dark black forms are a stark contrast to the white papers they touch delicately. These objects accompany each other in the chaos of the scene. We jump from the room to a camera zoomed in on a figure speaking, someone who looks uncannily like the one depicted in the poster from a few frames ago: "I'm the deputy Chairman of the State of Illinois Black Panther Party, Fred Hampton." The frame holds still, and bold, white typeface is overlaid above Hampton's head, tilted downward. The text reads declaratively, "The murder of Fred Hampton" (plates 17 and 18).

In the twilight hours of December 4, 1969, the FBI and Chicago Police Department raided Fred Hampton's West Monroe home, where several members of the Black Panther Party for Self-Defense (BPP) were staying, including Hampton's pregnant partner, Deborah Johnson (age twenty). Hampton (age twenty-one) and Mark Clark (age twenty-two) were gunned down as part of a police raid later attributed to the FBI's COINTELPRO (Counter Intelligence Program).[1] Informant William O'Neal, Hampton's bodyguard and head of security for the Chicago chapter, had infiltrated the BPP and provided the FBI and Chicago Police Department with the floor plan of the apartment.[2] Court filings estimate that between eighty-two and ninety-nine shots were fired within the apartment.[3] The spectacular and excessive scene of the violence perpetrated by the Chicago Police Department was unsurprising to many in the BPP, even while it shook radicals locally and nationally. As a response to Hampton's murder, the BPP opened up the slain Panther's home in an attempt to prove, through invitation, engagement, and site-specific forms of looking, that the FBI summarily executed Hampton. Thousands visited the apartment as tours were available all day until around 8:00 p.m. Most of the visitors were Black, though *New York Times* coverage of the open house includes descriptions of working people from all corners of industry, including painters, office workers, and postal workers in addition to middle-aged women and the elderly.[4] The *New York Times* reported that "the areas of in the apartment where the police were are clear of bullet holes. The areas where the Panthers were are riddled."[5] The police sealed off the apartment and refused entry for tours on December 17, 1969.[6] In *New York Times* reporter John Kifner's coverage of the weeks following Hampton's murder, and specifically of the open house exhibition strategy mobilized by the BPP, he notes the political function of the open house. Kifner opines that the five-bedroom apartment had "become a combination shrine and political indoctrination center as the Panthers led tours of hundreds of people through it each day since the killings."[7] Kifner's coverage offers insights on both the number of visitors to Hampton's house as well as a sense of the kind of political interventions the exhibition practice motivated among working people, distinguished politicians, journalists, and the like who visited the site. By pointing to specific details of the crime scene and how they evidenced the fictive details manufactured by the Chicago Police Department—the bullet holes that only marked entry into Hampton's room and no evidence of bullets leaving Hampton's room toward the police, for example—the BPP had effectively used the brutality of the crime scene against the state's case. This strategy depended upon cultivating a kind of looking practice that I will go on to describe as *politicized looking*. This exhibition practice operationalized the state's case as false while it simultaneously worked to make meaning of Hampton's murder.

Given both his untimely death and uncanny way he anticipated his murder, the 1971 documentary *The Murder of Fred Hampton* acts as a central object of inquiry for this chapter and one that opens up modes of presentation and mediation in order to engage politicized looking among its audience. Howard Alk and Mike Gray, two members of the progressive filmmaking collective the Film Group, initially intended to make a film about Fred

Hampton's political leadership in the Chicago BPP. The original 1968 film project about Hampton became quite a different project after his murder in 1969. To capture this intensity, the filmmakers deployed experimental techniques in filming, editing, and sequencing the documentary. I focus on the documentary because of how the film's formal strategies emphasize scenes from Hampton's life and death and by doing so suggest a series of conceptual and temporal lapses. The film spends about equal time on footage of Hampton from rallies and meetings and footage in the wake of and discussing the factual debates resulting from his murder. These scenes, combined with various conceptual and temporal lapses, encourage a complex mode of looking that showcases an anticipatory relationship to radical death. The documentary's sequencing helps clarify Hampton's own salient anticipation of his murder, with a focus on the objects that form the ground of a particular Black radical political consciousness. In this way, the film makes space for a consideration of Hampton's afterlife through intense visual meditations on the matter of his murder—blood, propaganda, books—that open up the possibility of a politics that live on.

Mike Gray, Howard Alk, and the rest of the film's production crew declined formal credits on the film in its original circulation, likely as an act of solidarity that resisted the spotlight and market authority given to filmmakers in an attempt to keep Hampton's story at the center of discussion.[8] By October 1971, the film had only been screened domestically in New York, Chicago, and Washington. The documentary hit the international festival circuit with screenings in Stratford, Ontario; Berlin, Leipzig, and Mannhein, Germany; Pessaro, Italy; and Cannes, France.[9] The most high profile of these screenings was at the Museum of Modern Art (MoMA) in New York City and at the Cannes Film Festival in France.[10] In a press release to publicize the screening, MoMA noted the film's small but mighty force, which is likely why the museum chose to host the national release of the documentary.[11] In that release, MoMA referenced reviews by two high-profile publications, *Variety* and *Newsweek*, both of which highlight the film's social efficacy as a document that presses urgent questions about governmental overreach and police violence.[12] The *New York Times* reviewer A. H. Weiler began the film's review boldly: "History is, or should be, recorded after exhaustive contemplation, but 'The Murder of Fred Hampton,' the documentary about the slain Chicago Black Panther leader that was shown yesterday and is being screened again today at the Museum of Modern Art, makes immediacy an attribute of history."[13] Even those who believed documentary should be relegated to events and circumstances with historical distance from our present could not deny the urgent force of the documentary's commentary on a history of the present.

Prior to the film's national release in September 1971, Gray hosted a limited screening of the film in Chicago's Three Penny Cinema.[14] Gray reflected on the lukewarm response to the film, noting how "even with the good reviews we got, Chicagoans were reluctant to take a chance."[15] He points out the film's quality or "murky rhetoric" as possible causes for a reluctant Chicago audience.[16] Alk, however, interpreted the film's reception as yet another collective avoidance to take responsibility for Hampton's murder:

> People like to feel righteous. But they like to feel righteous about other people. They don't like to bring it home. It is possible to draw the conclusion that Fred Hampton's death was a case of state murder. Some people in Chicago don't want to draw the conclusion that Fred Hampton's death was a case of state murder. Some people in Chicago don't want to draw that conclusion because then they'd have to share responsibility for doing something about it.[17]

Knowing the members shared political investments, it might be assumed that Alk's use of the phrase "some people" refers implicitly to liberal or even left-leaning white audiences, whose combined outrage for atrocities elsewhere and tacit compliance with anti-Black state practices in their locales is taken to task by Alk. What is particularly striking here is how both Gray and Alk reflect upon aesthetic judgement of the film and the politics of it. An audience who judged the film based on aesthetic terms (poorly made, amateur quality) likely, even if unconsciously, did so as an extension of a general political divestment based on the content of the film itself. The Chicago premiere, as the story goes, was cold, and local audiences needed national embrace of the film to account for its worth and significance.

The MoMA screening, for Gray, was an opportunity to demonstrate the film's national appeal. The film was selected by Adrienne Mancia, associate curator of the Department of Film, as a part of the museum's Cineprobe Series launched in 1968 to showcase and "provide exposure for independent and experimental filmmakers."[18] In this context, the film was celebrated for its technical and formal development of sociopolitical content. The press release notes how "a hand-held camera was used in many scenes which could not have been filmed otherwise," demonstrating an interest in the experimental qualities of the film's undertaking as a practical outgrowth of its recording device. Ultimately, the film was chosen because Mancia believed it was "representative of contemporary filmmaking," a bold and declarative statement in an era booming with both palatable and contentious presentations of Black life.[19]

This embrace of the cinematic and political qualities of the film was, I contend, demonstrated in a notable 1970 screening of the film in Chicago. However, strikingly, no reviews of the film refer to this smaller screening in February 1970, which predated the aforementioned May 1971 premiere in Chicago at Three Penny Cinema. The Black Student Union at Loop College (renamed Harold Washington College in 1987) screened the film on February 27, 1970. There are two noteworthy details about this screening, as described in a seventy-six-word announcement that appeared in the *Chicago Daily Defender*: (1) the film is described as "The Life of Fred Hampton," and (2) it was screened as a double feature with Gillo Pontecorvo's 1967 explosive film *The Battle of Algiers*.

While it could be assumed that the misnaming of the film was accidental, I find the substitution of "Murder" for "Life" to be richly telling. One premise of this chapter relies on the suggestion that Black life and death share temporal intimacy for Black radicals like Fred Hampton, for whom death was not only immanent but palpable. The slippage in this announcement between life and death reflects the tension that naming motivates when addressing anti-Black violence.

While I find the slip here instructive, I also hold it as a reminder for the premise of this chapter (and book): that the narratives of Black life and death that take shape in the 1960s and 1970s are not only controversial but are deeply personal, thus making the stakes high both at the time of Hampton's murder and also now. What this misnaming validates is a notion that has remained central to me since I began writing about Hampton's murder. So much about Hampton's death is actually about Black life: the pains and possibilities of taking a radical position, working in community and against those whose policies and practices perpetuate anti-Black violence, moving toward a utopic revolutionary ideal in which the world can be reordered to be more egalitarian and more free.

This project is not about reducing Black life to death but rather about the generative potentials of death as mobilized by Black radicals and catalyzed through cultural and aesthetic forms. The stakes of this project dovetail with Hampton's own presentation of life and death, such that the misnaming of the film might be better understood as an invocation on the disquieting proximity between life and death for Black people. The fact that the film was presented alongside *The Battle of Algiers* might also suggest that life and death's proximity for Black radicals might be mobilized toward revolutionary action.

The 1966 film, directed by Gillo Pontecorvo and starring Jean Martin and Saadi Yacef, is an iconic revolutionary film that depicts the harrowing struggle for Algerian independence from France. The film was banned in France until 1971 because of its acute attention to the violence of colonization and the redistributed violence of anticolonial resistance. The film pulled no punches in its depiction of the horrors of colonial violence and gestured toward cinema verité in Pontecorvo's use of a handheld camera that "wobbled, zoomed, and reframed as though excitedly clawing at the action."[20] This technique, which I will elaborate upon later, was also utilized by the Film Group during their filming of *The Murder of Fred Hampton*. At the time of its release, *The Battle of Algiers* was adopted by radicals around the world, many of whom, like the BPP, adapted the film into training manuals.[21]

As noted in the previous chapter, Frantz Fanon's theorizations of the liberatory potential of anticolonial violence was crucial for the BPP's call for self-determination and self-defense. In fact, Fanon appears across all three chapters, as his writings were crucial in Black radical imaginaries. Many of these theorizations enabled Black Americans to articulate the need for revolution in solidarity with peoples of the Black diaspora across the world. The Chicago chapter of the BPP included an "internal education cadre" consisting of fifteen members and facilitated by Billy Brooks.[22] Each member was required to read a dozen radical books, including one by Fanon, and engage in a dialogue toward collective understanding of these foundational political texts.[23] Fanon's uptake in Black Power movements was generally part of a culture of Black resistance. As Martin Luther King Jr. described months before his assassination in his 1968 reflections on the rise of Black Power in America,[24] Fanon was embedded in the heart of a Black radical politic:

> Over cups of coffee in my home in Atlanta and my apartment in Chicago, I have often talked late at night and over into the small hours of the morning with proponents of Black Power who argued passionately about the validity of violence and riots. They don't quote

Gandhi or Tolstoy. Their Bible is Frantz Fanon's *The Wretched of the Earth*. This black psychiatrist from Martinique, who went to Algeria to work with the National Liberation Front in its fight against the French, argues in his book—a well-written book, incidentally, with many penetrating insights—that violence is a psychologically healthy and tactically sound method for the oppressed. And so, realizing that they are a part of that vast company of the "wretched of the earth," these young American Negroes, who are predominantly involved in the Black Power movement, often quote Fanon's belief that violence is the only thing that will bring about liberation.[25]

King goes on, later in this chapter, to do a close reading of Fanon's writing in an attempt to provide context for the rise of Black Power in the United States as the movement stood in contradistinction to King's own nonviolent commitments. What presses in this excerpt is the force through which even King himself acknowledges Fanon's insights as both "well-written" and "penetrating," thus articulating the relevance his theories of liberatory violence have in Black Power politics. Fanon, according to the famed leader, names the international community of which Black American youth are a part—these "wretched of the earth" righteously turn to the anticolonial framework for violence as a means to achieve Black liberation at home.

Fanon was crucial to not only to the BPP's notion of self-determination and self-defense but also in the film *The Battle of Algiers*. The anticolonial thinker's work can quite directly be seen to influence the 1966 motion picture. Fanon, whose studies of colonialism's impact on the colonized subject's mind, body, and realm of political possibilities, theorized revolutionary violence as a necessary road to freedom. *The Battle of Algiers* visualizes this "Fanonian spirit," sequencing one young man's politicization and declarative use of anticolonial violence as a psychologically liberating force.[26] In fact, many scenes in the film visually manifest phenomena, observations, and theorizations from Fanon's experience in Algeria during the long war for independence.

The BSU's joint screening of *The Battle of Algiers* alongside *The Murder of Fred Hampton* demonstrates the impact of the question of violence—both by those in power and those who fight for freedom within that racialized structure—on Black people. Most of Fanon's experiences with violence as oppressive and as a liberating force are catalogued across writings but most significantly in *A Dying Colonialism* and *The Wretched of the Earth*—the same work tucked away in Hampton's room. What seems like a strange coincidence might actually be best understood as a reflection of heightened popular interest in revolutionary resistance. In this instance, Fanon acts as a bridge between an anticolonial struggle for freedom in Algeria and a domestic revolutionary struggle for US Black Americans. Fanon's *Wretched of the Earth* is a common guide between both examples, and in Hampton's case, the book itself is an object that facilitates a kind of life after death. This object, and many others in Hampton's life, appear throughout *The Murder of Fred Hampton* as signals for another revolutionary promise.

Through the documentary form, other objects make themselves known. With focused attention on Fanon, whose volume and theories were central for the BPP, I will turn to how the objects left behind at the murder scene act as surrogates for Hampton's radical Black body.[27] What these objects promise is an unequivocal commitment to Black liberation for all—a course that Hampton would never see come to fruition, but his surrogate objects would work to enact in his afterlife.

"You Can Murder a Liberator, but You Can't Murder Liberation": *Predicting Death, Sequencing Life*

In 1969, the Chicago chapter of the BPP was one of the most radical community organizations in the country. A glimpse into Hampton's biography reflects the extraordinary social conditions that gave rise to the young leader. Born in Summit Argo in 1948, a southwestern suburb of Chicago, the Hamptons were neighbors of Mamie Till and her son Emmett. Iberia, Fred's mother, would occasionally watch Emmett, who was affectionately called "Bobo" until the Hamptons moved to Blue Island in 1951.[28] Four years later, fourteen-year-old Emmett Till's gruesome murder would reshape national consciousness around the brutal and persistent qualities of white supremacy, all of which would be initiated and mediated by Mamie's decision to have an open casket at her son's funeral. Fourteen years after Till's murder, Fred and Emmett's stories would converge once again: Iberia decided on an open casket for her son whose service, like Till's, took place in the Rayner Funeral Home.[29]

Hampton was politicized at a young age, as family members, peers, and others often recalled him reading Malcolm X and W. E. B. Du Bois.[30] Unlike many teens his age, Hampton "was always talking about 'the movement'" and was Maywood's National Association for the Advancement of Colored People's president of the youth council.[31] A skilled and talented orator as a child, Hampton's politicization included recording and memorizing speeches by Martin Luther King Jr. and Malcolm X, developing his own style for delivery and charisma by being a student of these radical thinkers.[32] An unnamed childhood friend of Hampton recalls his consistent attention to reading: "I never saw him when he didn't have a book in his hand."[33] Shortly after a July 10, 1968, arrest for an alleged ice cream truck robbery, Hampton joined the Chicago chapter of the BPP, an organization he had long admired for their commitment to self-defense coupled with their direct support of community and mutual aid programs.[34] These qualities help to contextualize Hampton's speedy rise as chairman of the Chicago BPP.

Hampton offered militant leadership in a city that was devastated by unbearable systemic poverty that disproportionately impacted Blacks. Under Hampton's leadership, the Chicago BPP implemented five different free breakfast programs, a free medical clinic, and an emergency heat program during the winter season, which pressured landlords to repair the heaters of their poor Black tenants.[35] Hampton was also responsible for brokering a working relationship with local gangs across racial lines as a way to try to halt violence within Chicago's mostly Black and Latinx communities and turn that energy against white supremacist policies and practices in the city.[36] The Chicago BPP thrived under Hampton's leadership and gained national recognition from radical Black organizers primarily because of their success building autonomous structures in a city notorious for its corruption and police brutality.

Hampton's work in Chicago was part of a broader radical political analysis that was invested in the complete overhaul of US capitalism, imperialism, and racism, often signposted by a frequent call for revolution. By 1968, the year often romanticized as the year of insurrection for Western and European countries, forty-one formerly colonized African countries fought and won independence.[37] By 1970, ninety-two formerly colonized nations became member states of the United Nations.[38] This historical data sheds light on the urgency with which the BPP and other social movements called for revolution. In many ways, they followed the leadership of third-world countries and wanted to ensure that history did not leave them behind.[39] Hampton's militancy was fueled by the seemingly global consensus that revolution was the logical end of the ongoing radicalization of a people.[40] The question for Hampton, and other militants, was not *if* revolution would happen but *when*. The certainty with which radicals engaged in revolutionary praxis is crucial to understanding state repression. Because of organizing practices like those of the BPP—which sought to realize self-determination and autonomy by creating transitional parallel institutions that undermined the dependency on, and therefore the legitimacy of, the state—the US government responded to this revolutionary promise with unprecedented institutionalized and militarized force.[41] The state identified radical organizations like the BPP as a serious indictment of both the US and capitalism.

In response to the active counter-state community organizing methods these radical social movements practiced, the US government implemented a severe campaign to restore "law and order" by further enhancing repression tactics against radicals.[42] However, barring the obvious police violence, surveillance, and harassment that took place every day, radicals and radical organizations in the 1960s had little documented proof at the time that the state was invested in the short-term repression and long-term eradication of these political movements. Radicals expected to be consistently policed, surveilled, incarcerated, or killed as the state executed its counterrevolutionary goals. Although several movements across racial, gendered, and class differences were impacted by state repression, the BPP, and other Black radical organizations, were disproportionately impacted by these repressive government programs.[43]

Hampton, like most Black radicals at the time, understood and publicly articulated the inevitability of his death at the hands of the state. In a speech at an August 1969 rally after his release from jail for an alleged seventy-one dollar ice cream robbery, Fred Hampton extensively elaborated upon a prediction of his own murder by state officials.[44] Presented at the end of the documentary, Hampton's voice is dubbed over a transcription of a speech given after a stint in jail. Hampton speaks with certainty about how he will die and for what reasons:

> Let me say in the spirit of liberation. . . . I've been gone for a little while. At least my body's been gone for a little while. But I'm back now. And I believe that I'm back to stay.
>
> I believe that I'm going to do my job. And I believe that I was born, not to die in a car wreck. I don't believe that I'm going to die in a car wreck. I don't believe I'm going to die slipping on a piece of

ice. I don't believe I'm going to die because I got a bad heart. I don't believe I'm going to die because of lung cancer.

I believe that I'm going to be able to die doing the things I was born for. I believe that I'm going to be able to die high off the people. I believe that I will be able to die as a revolutionary in the international revolutionary proletarian struggle.[45]

With certainty and ease, Hampton declares the inevitability of the political conditions of his death. Wrapped up in the word "believe" is a repeated sense of a truth that is assured, though not yet proven. Belief here signals a kind of pessimistic faith in the state's violent apparatus, a trust in the repressive modes of state power that have Hampton, like other Black radicals, in its crosshairs. This belief, articulated through the future simple tense of "will be able to" reflects Hampton's understanding of his service to the people as one of active meaning and value grounded in a future worth his death. To be able to die as a revolutionary is to be able to die for a more egalitarian future, a future that surpasses the repressive conditions of Hampton's present.

He insinuates the way he will die by offering coincidental examples of how he will *not* die. In other words, by affirming his death will not be because of happenstance (because he slipped on ice or died in a car wreck), Hampton speaks to the political nature of his future assassination while also warning his community to be skeptical of state narratives that might attribute his death to an accidental cause. In this way, Hampton predicts his own murder through a performative practice of insinuation and negation and moves toward one of affiliation and certainty. He begins by declaring all the ways he will *not* die and then moves into how he will die. His affiliation with the international revolutionary proletarian struggle provides certainty for the mechanism of his future murder. It is this affiliation, what Hampton calls "his job," his lifetime labor, that leads him to a declaration of his death. Hampton finishes his speech with a series of affirmative requests expressed through the negative: "Why don't you live for the people. Why don't you struggle for the people. Why don't you die for the people." For Hampton, life and death are bookended with struggle—which itself is "for the people." Here, one's revolutionary commitment will always and inevitably lead to death. Within this articulation of certainty, Hampton attempted to offer affirmative and declarative predictions to his fellow Panthers.

However, on December 4, those predictions provided little solace to Hampton's comrades. They knew before it was made official that the FBI, in conjunction with the Chicago Police Department, killed Fred Hampton. In fact, his predictions of his own death marked the shocking and spectacular nature of his murder as an unwelcome but all-too-real condition of a Black radical in relation to the state. Hampton's predictions clearly articulate a version of what Abdul JanMohamed deems "the death-bound-subject": a deeply vexed recombination of life and death where the Black subject embraces death as a means of rethinking the politics of bondage and freedom.[46] JanMohamed locates this subject-position within the theoretical and historical contours of philosophies of slave life in order to make space for the ways these realities touch the lives of Black Americans postemancipation. In his philosophical contribution to theories of the master-slave dialectic, JanMohamed notes that "for the slave, death is not an eventuality that somehow 'comes' or 'arrives' in the natural course of events (which are privileged terms within existential analysis), but, rather, something deliberately brought and imposed on him by another, by the master"; therefore, the "fact that, on the political register, death is brought by another allows us to open up the entire issue of the 'ownership' of death."[47] In this light, "the slave's ability to appropriate the death that is brought by the master and to embrace his death as property of his own subjectivity radically transforms the political economy that the master had constituted around the threat of death."[48] Hampton, like George Jackson, often referenced the long afterlife of slavery in the making of his contemporary Black life. Therefore, the turn here to JanMohammed's theorization of the slave is fitting in relation to the ways that dialectic continued to structure the political and rhetorical language used by Black radicals to describe the structural conditions of Black life. The question of ownership over one's death, while additionally vexed in light of the uncanny proximity between subjecthood and objecthood in Black life (which I will discuss in further detail later in this chapter), helps us rethink Hampton's predictions of his murder. What is striking in the context of Hampton, however, is how the reclamation of ownership over one's death is anticipatory insofar as Hampton predicts the political nature of his assassination well before it is made official that the state targeted Hampton. As opposed to a retroactive claim, Hampton's prediction and articulation frames his death and allows for a nuanced understanding of anti-Black state violence writ large. Death-bound and unabashedly so, Hampton's political life is thrown into stark relief precisely because of his own anticipatory reclamation of his murder. His prediction makes clear that his death would be one of many examples and his murder one of many ways to do the crime.

The documentary makes visible the horrors of Hampton's untimely and predictable death. One of the many features of the documentary form that separates it from other cinematic genres is an acute attention to the drama of nonfiction as presented by the filmmakers. After Hampton's 1969 murder, the Film Group sought out another kind of filmic political education: they created a film that sequenced *how* the Chicago Police Department, in conjunction with other national forces, summarily executed Hampton. The film tarries between various kinds of footage from a range of players from the events of December 4. A cursory gloss of scenes includes Fred Hampton giving speeches and meeting with local community members; a mock trial ("The People's Trial") to prepare for Hampton's court case regarding the alleged robbery, which turns into the people putting the state on trial; Chicago Police Department officials narrating a case in defense of Hampton's assassination through reenactment and press conferences; a tour through Hampton's bullet-ridden home by a Panther-curator who provides a counternarrative to the state regarding the facts of his murder; and testimonial interviews by Deborah Johnson and People's Law Office lawyer Skip Andrew. The film they produced between 1969 and 1971 took seriously the consensus among radicals at the time: that the police and other state officials infiltrated and destroyed radical organizations that posed a threat to the status quo. In order to arrive at such conclusions, the filmmakers formally sequence the scenes so that the audience is directed toward Hampton's remarkable skill and insight as an emerging leader of the BPP, the excessive abundance of evidence against the state, and the gaps in the state's own narrative designations. This formal strategy of sequencing mobilizes the question of evidence into a broader thematic fold around questions of documenting history.

Film theorist Philip Rosen's "Document and Documentary: On the Persistence of Historical Concepts," an essay on documentary as a mediation through which history, memory, and fiction collide, lucidly weds the formal (technical) qualities of documentary form with its rhetorical implications.[49] As Michael Renov clarifies in his analysis of Rosen's piece, history and documentary film are embedded precisely because within both "meaning arises through a process of sequenciation which is constitutive of historical discourse."[50] Both history and documentary are compelled toward complete documentation and coherent sequencing. Rosen insists:

> If shots as indexical traces of past reality may be treated as documents in the broad sense, documentary can be treated as conversion from the document. This conversion involves a synthesizing knowledge claim, by virtue of a sequence that sublates an undoubtable referential field of pastness into meaning. Documentary as it comes to us from this tradition is not just *ex post facto*, but historical in the modern sense.[51]

In this analysis, documentary articulates a particular knowledge claim because it builds accumulated sequences of filmic moments into a cohesive narrative that attempts to contextualize each fragment. Even though the Film Group did not set out to produce a historical documentary, their film adopts the same sequencing techniques described by Rosen in order to make an argument about Hampton's life and untimely death. The film, however, jumps between coherence and confusion as the newness of the film's contemporaneity cannot lead to the retrospective cohesion of traditional forms of documentary. The balance between scenes of Hampton's life—rich with the quality of "liveness" that Rosen describes as a documentary film's "dream of immediate presence"—and scenes from Hampton's murder exemplify the tension in the film regarding its own genre. By this I mean that although the film is categorized as a documentary film that charts a historical event, its original aim was, in many ways, to offer a filmic testimonial that could visualize and evidence the fact that the state—a malicious actor—killed Fred Hampton. All of the formal sequencing techniques deployed in the film speak to this intended argument.

The film montages a variety of scenes from Hampton's political work. It captures Hampton's 1969 speech upon his release from Menard Prison at the Church of the Epiphany (also known as the People's Church) meetings on behalf of the Chicago BPP to secure a building to create collective housing for the Black working poor in Chicago's South and West Sides, as well as the now well-known Panther-run Free Breakfast for School Children Program that Hampton served at every morning. The film captures the mundane and the spectacular moments that narrate Hampton's life of political subjectivity. In addition to the scenes that document Hampton's vibrant organizing efforts, the film doubles back to moments immediately following his December 4 murder. Most notably, it reveals the logical fallacies of the Chicago police's narrative around Hampton's death by visually sequencing a narrative retelling of Hampton's murder as told by the Panther-curator mentioned earlier. In this way, the Film Group cinematically constructs a visual narrative about Hampton's murder, which culminates into an engagement with how the BPP opened up Hampton's home as an exhibition just days after his murder.

The use of sequencing here suggests that the film struggled to locate its own approximate relationship to the immediate past it worked to picture. Seeing that the subject of the film took a drastic turn within one year (1968–1969), the scenes embrace the oscillation between capturing Hampton's life and the excessive violence of his death. In so doing, the film amplifies an active temporal tension between immediate past and present in order to mobilize a political call to action. Though nonprescriptive or ideologically dogmatic sequencing allows for a kind of spectatorship that asks the viewer to consider the gaps between life and death, the state and the people, the past and the future. As Philip Rosen notes, a "necessary condition of sequenciation of the real" is that the "premise also contaminates the status of survivals of the past" in order to have the viewer infer the "reality of the sequence."[52] The immediacy of the past activates a sense that the sequences presented to the viewer move with a pace of uncanny force. They legitimate popular suspicions surrounding Hampton's murder and sequence the evidence toward another kind of call: one of inference, and what I will later discuss as *politicized looking*. In this spirit, *The Murder of Fred Hampton* is not an example of Trinh T. Minh-ha's proposition that, "in its demand to *mean* at any rate, the 'documentary' often forgets how it comes about and how aesthetics and politics remain inseparable in its constitution."[53] Instead, this documentary's deployment of a particular set of sequences allows for an inference that leans into the entanglement of aesthetics and politics and thereby opens up another condition of possibility for the documentary form as it relates to Black radical aesthetics more broadly. The temporal orientation of the documentary itself is future-oriented; its attention is meant to move the audience toward the revolutionary aims Hampton died for.

Renov qualifies documentary as an "active making" that includes four tendencies in the genre: to record, reveal, or preserve; to persuade or promote; to analyze or interrogate; and to express.[54] For Renov, documentary stands out because the form is recursive: it constantly circles back to the confluence of the nonfiction of the subjects it presents and the nonfiction of the subjects who produce it. The qualifying mark of the form is the way it presents information in order to call attention to a set of claims, often political, such that the audience is encouraged to engage anywhere within the spectrum of asking questions to taking action. These elements are nowhere more visible than in *The Murder of Fred Hampton*, where the filmmakers present images of both Hampton's life and death as a persuasive technique. What is striking about the film, however, is that the presentation of the nonfictional (Hampton's life and death, the state's corruption and bald-faced commitment to anti-Black violence, a presentation of the revolutionary resilience of the Black freedom struggle) is immediate, and therefore the present and past of the film are pressed up against each other. Because of its release only two years after Hampton is slain, his murder is the immediate past of the film, and its audience is left to contend with an aftermath in which they are still a part. This temporal juncture shifts the relationship between the images that are recorded in the documentary and the afterlife of those images for the viewers. In many ways, the *questions* that surround Hampton's death become the subject of the documentary, pushing toward a presentation of Black radical life always already subsumed by premature death. Again, Renov states:

> This documentary impetus transforms the unacknowledged questions that lie beneath all nonfictional forms into potential subject matter: that is, on what basis does the spectator invest belief in the representation, what are the codes that ensure that belief, what material processes are involved in the production of this "spectacle of the real" and to what extent are these processes to be rendered visible or knowable to the spectators?[55]

The unacknowledged questions that structure *The Murder of Fred Hampton* are also what activate its politics. An audience even acutely aware of Hampton's 1969 murder would be faced with the challenge of reconciling that murder with other contemporaneous examples of anti-Black violence. The sequenced scenes between life and death in this documentary only accentuate the protocols of Black radical life: the knowability of violence, the risk that comes with naming and resisting white supremacy, the permanence of fated retribution, and the afterlives of revolutionary life as presented through death. The film folds back on these realities by flickering between scenes and sequencing a narrative that is assured in its revolutionary aims.

Here, we are presented with another prediction: that of Black radical life after death.

By the time the documentary was made, the BPP's image was in full circulation as a militant revolutionary organization, armed and ready for warfare. This image, as detailed in the previous chapter, was transmitted across television sets and in newspapers around the country. In the context of Chicago, the May 1968 Democratic National Convention magnified such an image as Black radicals donned in leather and black berets had joined thousands of protestors downtown. The image of the BPP had become, as Kara Keeling calls it, one of "common sense," even cliché.[56] In her book *Witch's Flight: The Cinematic, the Black Femme, and the Image of Common Sense,* Keeling offers a stunning analysis on the role of the cinema in offering up alternative and resistant modes of picturing Blackness that incorporated this notion of common sense even while refuting the terms from which these images emerged. Keeling's book compellingly suggests that the cinematic is a place where one might wait to see an image of Black life that reflects radicality, even though that image might be fleeting and escape in the very moment it makes itself known.[57] Keeling offers an unprecedented theorization of the power of such Black images on the cinematic writ large. While *The Murder of Fred Hampton* is not necessarily a work of cinema, the film relies on its documentary status to nonetheless offer up extraordinary sequences and images of "black common sense" that trouble the status of life/death and subject/ object.

Deborah Johnson, who has since changed her name to Akua Njeri, structures many of the narrative dynamics of Hampton's murder, though she barely appears in the documentary itself. Her story is accounted for within Hampton's, not without cause, because their fates were enfolded and entangled. Johnson's experience of Fred often takes shape as a narrative exposition that is a testimony to Hampton's revolutionary dedication and the humble force through which he was committed to building revolutionary capacity in Chicago. Johnson's life and own political activism are barely accounted for across various historical documents. While these gaps in recording could easily represent a particular gendered apparatus of historiography, and how Black women's lives seem to appear as mere signposts to their male counterparts, I want to think about these facts toward yet another methodological possibility. Johnson's singular appearance could be thought to move like Kara Keeling's femme as her active presence works to point to the porous absences of narrative that the film's sequencing works to suture. With *and* without her, the film produces a portrait of Hampton's life and death through modes of sequencing that utilize dispersed narrative tactics to call the viewer into a particular kind of looking practice. For me, Johnson's interview in the film (with a toddler-aged Fred Hampton Jr. on her lap) raises the kinds of aporias that Keeling suggests flee in the interval. Johnson's presence calls attention to the limits of narrative and sequence as only partially able to account for the politics delimited in the scenes.

Johnson first appears toward the end of the documentary, approximately an hour and ten minutes into the two-hour film. The scene that precedes hers takes place in her and Hampton's bedroom. A Panther curator narrates, "This is where our Chairman had his brains blown out as he, uh, lay in his bed sleeping at 4:30 in the morning." The scene jumps directly to Johnson, seated on a couch, her left arm wrapped around her toddler son. "Someone came into the room, started shaking the chairman." As she describes what happened next, Johnson raises both of her hands, one of which embraces her young son. Describing the bullets as they entered the bedroom from the kitchen where the police raided, she gestures both hands to give some type of visualization to bullets entering the room. As she does so, her arm raises Fred Jr.'s head as her hands cross over his face. Her hands cross each other as she gestures the act of bullets ripping through the bedroom—"pigs just shooting"—until she moves on to the next detail. This moment strikes me as one of the many ways that Johnson's embodied memory of the scene is presented in the documentary as an isolated sequence. She makes no other appearance in the film, and in this brief two-minute interview, her body and Fred Jr.'s heighten a sense of disarray. What is presented is a series of narrative reflections and bodily gestures—her hands work to accentuate the violence of the scene, her eyes look down and directly into the camera depending on the detail, Fred Jr.'s little body wobbles and sways, a touch between her hands and his, a gargled gasp from the baby's mouth—all of these moments add up to an interruption in the film's otherwise evidentiary commitments. Here, Johnson's experiential narrative exposes an afterlife of Hampton's death that exists within and beyond the sentient. Johnson's account reveals an encounter with a violent scene that is as strangely mundane as it is exceptional. Her general affect doubles onto that of the entire film: an aimed descriptive distance, commonplace understanding of the night's events, and an embodied political recalcitrance that portrays a haunting proximity between life and death (plates 19 and 20).

The play here between Johnson's absence and presence in the film bespeaks this proximity. Her presence interrupts the narrative about Hampton's death by giving us his sentient legacy, the life that succeeded Hampton's own. Fred Jr. embodies a future that Hampton did not live to see. Johnson gives meaning to a legacy beyond one of a reproductive logic; rather, it is one of revolutionary multiplicity. Hers is a presence that encapsulates how "[death], brutalization, and physical violation—acts that previously had inscribed femininity onto the black—were overwritten into heroism and 'dying for the people.'"[58] An anoriginary act of violation, the confluence of violence onto the Black body, is what troubles the rigidity between life and death. To die and to live are thrown into crisis, as Hampton's last few moments of his own life and the embodied presence of his kin/afterlife are brought into being via Johnson's embodied account. It's Johnson's narrative that surges the documentary's end with an entailed focus on what else might exist in the wake of such certainties. Johnson's critical reflections and embodied presence point us to the kinds of activation that may lie in the nonsentient details of the scene, the objects left behind.

"They Came with Murder on Their Minds, You See?"

As part of opening up Hampton's home as an exhibition, the BPP displayed and narrated the bloody scene as a kind of evidentiary proof. As the film visualizes, this act of curation mobilizes quite a radical political articulation. Rather than relying on the state's narrative of Hampton's murder, the BPP preempted impending state repression by providing members of the community with an invitation to come look for themselves. This live curatorial practice was further enhanced and archived when the BPP invited the Film Group to document this exhibition.

While the group has been recognized for their raw, on-the-ground coverage of some of the most turbulent political events in Chicago's history, there has been no scholarly consideration of the Film Group's technique or approach to filmmaking. There are several technological specificities at play in the documentary that are of particular note. At times the filmmakers aim to make the apparatus of the camera disappear and at others they make visible the camera and camera operators, suggesting there were at least two cameras and teams at work. The camera, removed from its tripod and placed on the shoulder of its operator, is shaky and unstable, suggesting a likeness to a person's subjective experience of sight and perspective. Zooms are imprecise and blurry, focus is a real challenge at times, and persons are caught at confusing angles and in poor lighting. To some this might suggest an amateur approach to filming, but both Alk and Gray had significant experience as cinematographers. For one, this approach of removing the camera from a tripod and placing it on the cameraperson's body was a consequence of the locations in which they filmed—often in close quarters, compact rooms, or in crowds.

Secondly, this filming strategy can be experienced as a kind of guerrilla journalistic mode akin to contemporaries like Videofreex, a leftist renegade collective known for its innovating and experimental modes of on-site filming.[59] Videofreex was on the front lines of technological innovation as it often utilized the camcorder or larger format cameras in hand. The result of this operational strategy was a perspective and mode of framing that was more assertive and experiential—viewers had the ability to feel as if they were on site where the action took place. Interviews were prepared but spontaneous, and camera handlers were able to get in close proximity during rallies, barricades, and even occupations. Skip Blumberg, an early member of the group, notes how "in terms of camera skills, it's a constantly curious camera looking, looking, looking."[60] Curiously looking, the camera was deployed to resemble the embodied eye. In a 1969 recording of Fred Hampton, for example, Videofreex members filmed the Panther leader with a wide-angle lens and crawled to try to capture him at different angles.[61] With camera in hand, even if cumbersome, filmmakers were able to gain flexibility and offer up a real-time journalistic experience. This approach is mirrored in *The Murder of Fred Hampton* as the camera acts as a live actor who records in real time a piece of journalistic evidence. Witness and recorder, the camera is removed from the tripod and placed onto a camera operator's shoulder. The enhanced viewfinder now serves as an evidentiary eye, working to capture the intricacies of the scene as the situated human eye would. The camera and its operator become one of the many who came to see the crime scene to gather their own evidence (plate 21).

The footage from the open house shows a line of people, mostly Black, awaiting entrance into 2337 Monroe Street and the voice of a Panther asking visitors not to touch or disturb the objects in the home.[62] "Everything is just how it was," he assures. Then, we are taken to the room in which

Hampton was killed, followed by a thick description of the logical fallacies behind the logistic and forensic claims made by the Chicago Police Department. The camera lens focuses on the wall, which the BPP allegedly shot through toward the police, and this focus is coupled with explicative narration that there were no bullet holes from the inside (where Hampton lay sleeping) toward the outside (from where the police stormed in). Finally, the camera focuses on the Panther previously known only by voice. He stands in front of a wall tagged with the famous Panther slogan "All Power to the People," which reminds us that we are indeed in a curated exhibit space intended to invite us to look (plate 22).

Perhaps the most startling narrative turn in the documentary occurs when we are introduced to Skip Andrew (the same person seen in this chapter's opening image), an attorney for the People's Law Office (PLO) and the Chicago Panther chapter, as he enters a blood-soaked room. In this scene, we are quickly given the remnants of a murder. Andrew slowly raises a previously white, now blood-red, scrap of cloth. We see a bare mattress covered with pools of blood. On the ground, there are broken records, books, and posters lying in tracks of blood. And finally, as the camera moves up, we see dozens of bullet holes. Each bullet hole has a plastic tube protruding out of the hole, measuring the projectile's entrance and exit.

This particular set of scenes parallels the scope of the entire film, which in many ways functions as a piece of evidence in and of itself. The film labors a testimony through juxtaposition. The documentary sequences a contrast between the state's narrative account of Hampton's death and the hard facts from the scene and the broader political context and content of Hampton's life. In this mode of fashioning, display acts as a truth claim, one that aims to reveal, as it was, the disproportionate and extreme violence of the Chicago Police Department's raid. The evidence, as it stands, appears untouched, unmoved in order to lay bare the extremities of anti-Black violence. By inviting in the surrounding community, it could be said that the BPP engaged in a mode of display that worked to delimit any cause for speculation and make evident the extraordinary violence at work in Hampton's murder.

The display of Hampton's apartment includes not only those aspects of the scene that are the evidence and aftermath of his murder but this display also makes visible the contents of the apartment prior to Hampton's death. On December 6, 1969, the *Chicago Daily Defender* printed two crime scene photographs in a full-page feature on the topic of Hampton's death.[63] Both images share similar content, best described by the captions: "Blood stained carpet marks the spot at which Black Panthers fought police and lost" and "Black Panther newspapers lie beside pool of its leader's blood." One photograph focuses in on a blood-tracked carpet, with a pile of papers cramped into the top-right corner of the image and scattered clothing and crumpled loose papers strewn elsewhere. The second photograph is from a disorienting perspective, making it hard to decipher the position from which the camera is pointed. In this image, what is clear is a pool of blood surrounded and overlapped by copies of the *Black Panther* newspaper. Most prominent in the frame is the November 8, 1969, issue, featuring a cover image by Emory Douglas, illustrating how chairman Bobby Seale was bound and gagged by Chicago judge Julius Hoffman for his alleged disruption of court proceedings, a charge that Seale has characterized as his right to self-defense against conspiracy charges for his activism during the 1968 Democratic National Convention, held in Chicago.[64] This overlap between the newspaper cover featuring Seale's case and Hampton's murder demonstrates parallel stories of local and state repression, as both activists overlapped both in their locations but also in regards to legal cases due to their activism. The fact that this newspaper lay in Hampton's pooled blood marks three apparatuses of state repression: criminalization, incarceration, and murder.

In a December 13, 1969, article describing his visit to Hampton's Monroe apartment, *Chicago Tribune* journalist Joseph Boyce noted that in addition to an array of bullet holes that spattered the walls and doors, on the floor of the Panther's bedroom were "boxes containing books. Their topics ranged from how to use a new camera to a biography of Lenin."[65] Seeing that the visual was so crucial to the BPP's politics, and particularly that documentation and encouraged looking were instrumental in the Chicago chapter's exhibition of Hampton's postraid apartment, it is quite telling that the books mentioned by Boyce include an instruction manual on how to use a new camera. This acute attention to lens-based documentary is evidenced by the book itself, which serves as a pedagogical guide alongside other books, pamphlets, and newspapers that act as objects of instruction for a revolutionary life. In this context I argue these objects, as they sit next to the evidence from the scene of his death, come to act as surrogates for

Hampton's body, precisely because they enact the political and come to serve as a catalyst for future revolutionary action.

While the substance of his body—the blood, for one—is exited into the scene, the externalized objects (the records, books, pamphlets, and the like), all intimate remnants of political self-worth, act as Hampton's body itself. We can think back to that seemingly purely sentimental recollection of Hampton as a child and reinterpret it toward another means: "I never saw him when he didn't have a book in his hand."[66] What Hampton at one point always held now could be thought of as holding him. The boundary of his hand and book, where one ends and the other begins, take on another level of significance.

All of these artifacts blur boundaries between inside and outside, as they come to signal the intellectual and political life that Hampton's ongoing presence in the film enacts. Hampton's body is a body composed of objects. We cannot understand his flesh without understanding the political objects left behind. Hampton's body remains despite the violent act; it is just a body far more unknowing in flesh and form. The body in this scene is composed of objects, which offer a very different sense of the body. The fact of Hampton's Blackness is intensified by politics made visible for us by the life of the objects left in his wake.

How is it that although the film offers several scenes of Hampton's political life, his murder scene tells us more about his politicization? The scene is littered with revolutionary propaganda—political posters, manifestos, organizing flyers, pamphlets, and albums. The display of Hampton's apartment is at once a scene about an evidentiary commitment to counter the state's narrative regarding Hampton's death, but so as to keep to the political commitments toward Black liberation, the film also focuses on those objects left behind. It is my contention that the film's apparatus shifts in these moments toward the *political life of objects*—both sentient and not. These objects somehow simulate and substitute Hampton's body in relation to his Blackness. By simulate, I am speaking to how the objects rest in place of Hampton's body. They substitute by making a case for exchange; they work to surrogate Hampton and the political stakes of his life and death. These objects record and grant stimulus *as* Hampton's body would. In what follows, I take on contemporary Black studies' takes of Frantz Fanon as a way to consider what "objects" might mean in relation to a Black radical tradition, one that takes seriously how politics moves within and beyond the binary structures of life and death (plate 23).

A famed leader, Hampton ran the Chicago chapter of the BPP with a commitment to Black self-determination through the institution of various programs, campaigns, and organizational interventions. Hampton paid exceptional attention to political theory, often citing cultural change as a key element in the process of politicization. Like the well-known Oakland chapter, Hampton instituted Fanon's texts as mandatory for membership in the Chicago BPP, as well as for the youth education programs conducted throughout the city.[67] In all of his works, Fanon offers a material history of Blackness as well as insight into how that material history structures both the Black psyche and body. While in *Wretched of the Earth* Fanon specifically analyzes the world of the colonized subject, Black radicals in the United States expressed solidarity and kinship with third-world struggles for liberation. This is especially the case as the condition of colonized subjects detailed by Fanon so closely reflected, and often operated in conjunction with, the violent reality of being Black in America. Fanon's text also calls for self-determination as a practice that engages in militant warfare against colonizers and their various structures of colonization. The BPP viscerally identified with this kind of radical Black self-determination. It is for these reasons that the presence of *Wretched of the Earth* in Hampton's room is of particular significance for this chapter. The book's physical presence is what Fanon, in his earlier work *Black Skin, White Masks*, calls "an object among other objects."[68]

If read performatively, Fanon's theorizations in *Black Skin, White Masks* are given to us in the form of vignettes that wed the written narrative and the visual toward a more cohesive understanding of Black life. He freezes experiential moments of terror, anxiety, confusion, and anger in order to make sense of the structures that produce these affects. These vignettes—at the train station platform, sitting alone in transit, speaking with colleagues—make visible the palpable tensions that saturate Black life. The following engagement with Fanon takes shape around *Black Skin, White Masks* primarily because of its lucid and lasting presentation of the ontological and structural status of Black subjects. This status is crucial for understanding how Black life is constituted by the vexed dynamics of subject and object status, a dynamic the BPP aimed to study in order to undo.

There are many Fanons that exist within and between *Black Skin, White Masks* and *Wretched of the Earth* (not to mention the others who exist in *A*

Dying Colonialism, Towards the African Revolution, Alienation and Freedom, and the various speeches and interviews he gave throughout his life). I turn to two variegated readings of Fanon by Frank Wilderson and Fred Moten, which act as guiding frameworks for my uptake of the anticolonial thinker in relation to questions of Hampton's Black radical body and the object lessons we might take away from his murder.

While both Wilderson and Moten turn to chapter 5 of *Black Skin, White Masks*, they utilize different translations of the iconic text. As Moten points out, a turn to the 1967 Charles Lam Markmann translation of the chapter as "The Fact of Blackness" is what Moten calls "infamously mistranslated."[69] Meanwhile, Moten calls what ends up being a later translation, "The Lived Experience of the Black," a "more literal" one.[70] The gap between the "fact of blackness" and the "lived experience of the black" can be thought to produce tension between the ontological and epistemological considerations of Black life. These translations allow us to ask: What produces "facts" of Blackness? Are those "facts" as immutable as the experiences that are produced by and within them? Can "lived experience" be a "fact" with as much ontological weight? Such variations significantly impact Moten and Wilderson's respective positions in relation to Fanon's theories. Depending on the translation, both scholars tend to approach the rest of *Black Skin, White Masks* with different emphases.

For example, Wilderson's uses of Fanon generally turn to chapter 6, "The Negro and Psychopathology," a chapter that focuses upon various "facts" of white supremacy that manifest as neuroses in the Black psyche. Wilderson reads this Fanon to better engage his own theoretical insights, primarily how Blackness is a nongenerative nothingness, an "affirmation of negation and its destructive force," a "negative political ontology that is manifest as a kind of affirmative nihilism,"[71] or put better by Fanon himself, a "zone of non-being."[72] Wilderson's Fanon is the Fanon of nonontology, fixity, impossibility. Wilderson's Fanon is acutely concerned with an understanding of Blackness as always already understood though white supremacy and the bonds of whiteness by those afforded entry into what Wilderson calls "civil society." For Wilderson, this Fanon clarifies the psychic, material, and political-economic structures that make Blackness an ontological impossibility.

Moten, on the other hand, takes up Fanon's first chapter, "The Negro and Language," which emphasizes "lived experience" as a mode to rethink the politics of language. Using this chapter, Moten makes a case for the kinds of subterranean forms of Black living that are and can be experienced despite the contours of white supremacy.[73] For Moten, Fanon's attention to nothing has generative, though often unrecognizable, potential. For him, the language of pidgin, for example, demonstrates the myriad ways Black people source life forms, styles, and methods of noise despite and within an anti-Black world—this could be shorthanded by Moten's attention to modes of sociality. In Moten's formulation of social life, Blackness is the "name given to the social field and social life of an illicit alternative capacity to desire."[74] In this formulation, Blackness is also of an "other world, the underworld, the outer world."[75]

Based on these varying modes of attention, I conclude that Moten's approach to the question of Blackness tends to study that which *Blackness produces* while Wilderson's approach tends to emphasize that which *produces Blackness*.

Wilderson emphasizes "the fact of blackness" and Moten emphasizes "the lived experience of the black." These emphases offer up two routes to answer the same question: "Can a Black be a subject?"[76] Via Fanon, Fred Hampton's life and death embody how lived experience is structured within the facts of Black life. Therefore, Hampton's status as a subject whose understanding of that position is always impermanent, collective, and imagined elsewhere (with the people, toward revolution, against the state) is vexed as it throws into light a complex relationship between objecthood and subjecthood for Black people. Take the preceding speech from Hampton at the People's Church. Hampton's opening lines embody precisely the compromised status of subjecthood. I re-present these lines here with added emphasis: "Let me say in the spirit of liberation . . . I've been gone for a little while. *At least my body's been gone for a little while.* But I'm back now. And I believe that I'm back to stay." Referring to his incarceration at Menard Correctional Center, Hampton provides a recombination of presence and absence. While his body may have been vulnerable to state violence through methods of incarceration, he remained with the people, in the spirit of liberation. He is both an object and subject of the state as his body is unevenly vulnerable to apparatuses of capture, imprisonment, harassment, surveillance, and death. But as Hampton theorizes in this passage, while he may have been absented for a while, his presence was with the people through other means and in other terms. In this instance, one can infer that Hampton is speaking to the ways his heart and mind were with the people even while his body was taken away. His belief that he's back to stay might take shape through other means. This passage foreshadows the ways in which Hampton's presence, his staying, would be active through the objects left behind following his murder soon after this speech was given. While his body is gone in a more permanent sense, his status might be said to live on in the objects that approximate his own sentient self.

Hampton's theorization helps reckon with the impasse best embodied by Fanon's endlessly generative articulation of being "an object among other objects." The crisis of ontological status brought about by chattel slavery and its afterlives in the United States makes the uneasy relationship between objecthood and subjecthood a long-considered existential quandary. I take Moten and Wilderson's differing positions on the status of Black life as either object or subject of inquiry and push these debates to consider the status of objects found and filmed in Fred Hampton's room. What would it look like to negotiate the Blackness of these objects? How might, borrowing from theories of embodiment, we imagine the corporeal life of nonsentient stuff—from books, to pamphlets, to posters, to records—that both mine and act as surrogate for a revolutionary Black position killed in its sentient form?

If we take Fanon's provocation of being an "object among other objects" and place this lived experience alongside Moten's insistence that "the history of Blackness is testament to the fact that objects can and do resist" and Wilderson's notion (via his read of Saidiya Hartman) of the Black body as an "object of accumulation and fungibility" then we might begin to unpack the disquieting status between Hampton's corporeal nonintegrity and the status of the objects left behind in his wake.[77]

Returning to the documentary, the viewer gets a glimpse of a blood-soaked mattress, upon which sits *The Autobiography of Malcolm X*. This book accompanies *The Wretched of the Earth* as two representatives of a particular political commitment. Left as legacies and remainders of the excessive violence in the scene, Fanon's *The Wretched of the Earth* and *The Autobiography of Malcolm X* are objects whose contents narrate the ongoing structuring force of anti-Black violence. This exhibition provided a narrative sequence that undeniably makes sense of Hampton's murder precisely because it contextualizes it within a history of anti-Black violence. Even further, the political life of the objects left as extensions of Hampton's body alert us to the living and viable threat radical Black practitioners posed to the sanctity of state power. In this way, *Wretched* and *The Autobiography of Malcolm X* are lasting objects (plate 24).

While these objects have been written about as such, what is left un-asked is the question of the visual and aesthetic in relation to the Blackness of these objects. In what follows, I teach how Hampton's own theorization of his body, coupled with a consideration of the aesthetic contours of object status in regards to Black life, open up how these objects surrogate Hampton.

Surrogate Objects

The contemporary state of Black life is structured by the Middle Passage and its attendant transformation of Africans into commodities for trade. This is not an uncommon observation as theorists in Black studies have oft called attention to the uncanny genealogy between Black people and the commodities they were forced to share an ontological and political-economic position with.[78] Hortense Spillers and Huey Copeland both provide a nuanced and complex framework for my consideration of the objects left behind in Hampton's room. Both scholars elaborate on how the object status forced upon Black people during Middle Passage voyage resulted in a transmutation of personhood and objecthood that would have irrevocable and lasting consequences well beyond the formal end to institutionalized slavery in the United States. This vexed status between subject and object takes on even more peculiar contours when we think about the ways that Black life is accounted for in and through objects by Black people. Whether as an indictment of the impact of white supremacist violence on one's status as object under slave law or as a reclamation of the various objects instrumental to the making of Black liberation, I turn to Spillers, Copeland, and Joseph Roach in order to set up the Black life of the objects in Hampton's room.

As Spillers so brilliantly details in her iconic 1987 article "Mama's Baby, Papa's Maybe: An American Grammar Book," what bridges a twentieth-century example of anti-Black racism like the Moynihan report to nineteenth-century practices of institutionalized slavery is the shared genealogy between objects and Black bodies, which can be traced to the Middle Passage where human cargo was accounted for based on its quantifiable relationship to money.[79] This system of valuation translated across varying objects in the ship's hold, from barrels of sugar to Black captives, where worth was determined based on rules of accounting. Thus, the Middle Passage marked an attempted ontological and epistemological equivalence between Black sentient beings and objects extracted for trade. Spillers notes the visual devices that came to crystallize the status between subject and object of exchange were decidedly racial. She argues that hypervisible indications of one's slave status were marked upon the flesh—"anatomical specifications of rupture" as evidenced by lacerations, bruising, bleeding, burning, and other physical signs of harm—that take different shape in the afterlife of the Middle Passage and become signposted through a type of camouflage.[80] In this turn, the visual cues that aligned Black people with objects for trade were once marked upon the flesh violently and are now signaled by the racialization of skin. The repercussions of such historical and symbolic transitions take shape, in part, in and through the ways that objects linger as ontological referents in Black life. This desired and imposed equivalence, though limited in its ability to account for how and when these Black things resist, structurally and visually remains active within the realm of the political and the aesthetic.

Similarly, Copeland's lucid book *Bound to Appear: Art, Slavery, and the Site of Blackness in Multicultural America* generates an abundant framework for the aesthetics of objecthood in Black life. The figure of the slave is of particular importance throughout the book, one that directly engages the transatlantic slave trade as a historical touchstone in the making of the modern world as we know it. Copeland details how a cohort of Black artists in the 1990s "turned to objects, substituting actual things for absent bodies" in order to speak to slavery's ongoing relevance in their collective present.[81] This kind of practice is part of a long Black radical tradition in which Black Americans reconstituted the boundaries and shapes of their status as "commodities who speak." Crucial to this chapter is Copeland's interrogation of how aesthetic strategies offer an opportunity to "apprehend the flesh that undergirds the historical construction of objecthood."[82] This move, as I interpret it, sets the stage for how the construction of Black life throws the notion objecthood, a status attributed to sentient beings who were categorized as such, into crisis in and through the ongoing refusal that produces a series of generative and regenerative manifestations of Black life.

Additionally, objects come to stand in for the Black body in present tense: an anachronistic jolt that spatializes the presence of a figure as an active maker of their surroundings through the things that surround them.[83] This strategy is akin to the kind of role objects play in Hampton's room as captured by the documentary. The objects in this setting work as surrogates for Hampton's body, wherein "actual things" are transmuted, taking shape around Hampton's absence.[84] Unlike the objects in Copeland's study that act as an iterative constant in relation to slavery's present tense, the objects in Hampton's room enact the future of a collective revolution he himself would never live to see. In these works, the objects substitute Hampton's flesh in order to generate the aims of Black liberation. While Hampton's murder spectacularized the limitless power of anti-Black violence, I labor to argue that the documentary film opens up the generatively thin boundary between subject and object status. In this work, the status of the object serves as surrogate for Hampton's afterlife and the revolutionary future promised by his death.

Put differently, these objects carry Hampton's body by other means. In Joseph Roach's *Cities of the Dead: Circum-Atlantic Performance*, he offers up a compelling series of performance histories across Europe, Africa, and the Americas that trouble clean boundaries between the subject and object of a performance's life, death, and afterlife.[85] While Roach's study is primarily one of nineteenth-century acts, his relationship to temporality is promiscuous and daring, showcasing the ways that various thematics, questions, and aesthetic forms appear across historical moments and even into the contemporary. What remains central to his study is a concern with how embodied forms of knowledge making and production transgress proper routes and meanings. Spirits and senses take noble place alongside maps and trade reports. In Roach's study, the question of subject and object is blurred, as is what constitutes "life" under the auspices of colonial and anti-Black violence in a burgeoning circum-Atlantic world. Roach's insights offer generative frameworks for making sense of the objects left behind in Hampton's room, particularly Roach's consideration of the triad among memory, forgetting, and substitution.[86]

In Roach's formulation, communities take up modes of surrogation in an attempt to remember the dead and remain defiant to a normative temporality that encourages a moving past and therefore a forgetting. Surrogation is a process in which "culture reproduces and re-creates itself," because survivors aim to fill the "cavities created by loss through death or other forms of departure."[87] Messy and incomplete, defiant and often a failure, surrogation is an embodied practice that selects and deploys the kinds of memories to carry on into a particular community's future. While Roach himself considers human forms of embodied surrogation, building from Spillers and Copeland, I turn to the political life of the objects in Hampton's room precisely for the ways these objects signal the interplay between subjecthood and objecthood in Black radical life. These objects act as surrogates for a memory of Hampton that exceeds the limits of his life and instead take up the revolutionary promise as spectacularly evidenced by his death.

One way we can make sense of Hampton's murder is through the objects that simulate and surrogate his body. As charted throughout this chapter, Hampton's books, newspapers, and pamphlets often appear and reappear across forms of visual documentation. Whether in journalistic accounts, photographic snapshots, recollections of Hampton's loved ones, or documentary film, books are of particular significance and thread together Hampton's life and death. These objects are sources and resources that account for radical political life. It makes sense, then, to turn to these objects as surrogates that gesture toward, and even perhaps embody, Hampton's legacy.

If Roach's notion of surrogation implies selective memory, then the work these objects perform reveals to us how power operates in relation to Blackness. Because surrogation requires a process through which excess is contained and narrativized through forgetting and substitution, these objects visually contain the excess of anti-Black violence while also making sense of it.[88] These objects activate how anti-Black violence is a structuring force while also making claims to the generative production of practices of living that exist within and against such forces. Like the contested Fanons that shape Wilderson and Moten's respective approaches to Black (non)life, these objects call attention to both what makes Black life unlivable and what makes Blackness a life force. Both of these qualities emerge out of anti-Black violence while they also articulate resistance to that very constitutive violence. These objects act as surrogates for his body while they also force us to centralize the politics that are foundational to Hampton's being.

Violence saturates the scenes in *Murder of Fred Hampton* and act as an indication of the spectacular modes of everyday violence experienced by Black people writ large and exacerbate the lived conditions of Black radicals. Pools of blood, disheveled personal possessions, and bullet-ridden walls declare the excessive nature of Hampton's murder. The objects that preoccupy the camera's lens at once enliven this history and add to the already present terror of Hampton's bloody remains. The book *The Autobiography of Malcolm X* exemplifies surrogation in the film. The camera focuses on Hampton's bloodied mattress and where the famed autobiography rests.

The book, itself a contested and controversial object, comes to represent the kind of revolutionary radical status shared and taken up by the BPP.[89] Malcolm X's 1965 assassination represented a watershed moment in Black radical politics, as his death was considered first and foremost an attempt by the state to suppress his teachings and a strong Black nationalist movement in the United States. In terms of content, Malcolm X's autobiography narrates his personal politicization as well as details a theorization of Black life premised primarily on both the everyday violence of white supremacy and the ways that Black people can and should resist these forms. This status of this object as both commodity and testament signals a revolutionary future that comes to be inhabited by Hampton himself. Put differently, Fred Hampton is Malcolm X's future revolutionary. The uncanny parallels between both their lives and deaths serve as a reminder that a radical Black life is a dangerous state of vulnerability and that what will likely remain, the aftermath of one's likely death, are the objects that narrate revolutionary lives. In the documentary, the apparatus of the lens mobilizes a "curious looking" that focuses on the book's presence on Hampton's mattress. The life that remains amid the presence of death is a revolutionary object. Both objects remain as a kind of political afterlife as they outlive Hampton and continue to theorize and inspire Black radical resistance. These objects always have the potential to threaten and destabilize state sanctity precisely because they are revolutionary in form and content and can therefore spark Black revolutionary praxis in any given historical moment.

While Hampton and Jackson are two of the one thousand Bobby Huttons called for in the previous chapter, Hampton's and Jackson's murders materialize the generative capacity of Black radical death through processes of visualization and surrogation. Hutton's murder and the subsequent Afrotropic circulation of his photographic image contextualized the brutality of his murder in order to politicize and mobilize the masses for revolutionary ends. The call for one thousand Bobby Huttons can be understood as a kind of surrogation, one where Hutton becomes a kind of transmutable figure whose afterlife is scattered and internalized by Black revolutionaries writ large. In a similar spirit, the objects left behind by Hampton live to carry on Hampton's legacy while for Jackson's murder, surrogation takes shape around the visual citations that occur compositionally in political posters. These various iterations of surrogation demonstrate a shared sentiment among these various visual strategies: that the meanings and impacts of these deaths aimed to call out state forms of anti-Black violence while they also encouraged particular forms of looking in order to ensure continued revolutionary action in the future.

As is clear with Malcolm X's autobiography—the scene registers precisely because the objects make clear Hampton's absence—the audience is asked to perform the spectatorial practice akin to the curious looking enacted by the camera, what I call *politicized looking*. This invitation is a critical evaluation: *politicized looking* means that one is invited to slow down the process of image consumption in order to see the conditions through which life, and in this case death, occurs at an uneven, disjunctive, and violent level against Black people. Because, as Roach notes, surrogation "does not begin or end but continues as actual or perceived vacancies occur in the network of relations that constitutes the social fabric," it works only as a process, a process that works within and against the logics that aim to contain it.[90] In this same way, politicized looking serves as a continuum. It is a process in which the looker embodies a revolutionary force that lives within and beyond the objects one looks at. These images lead the politicized looker to Hampton's conclusion: you can kill a revolutionary, but you can't kill the revolution.

Politicized looking clarifies how anti-Black violence is at once gratuitous and mundane. The spectacular nature of Hampton's murder rests on the imperative placed on the viewer to *look for* signs of life and death throughout the film. Sequencing is a filmic tool for the viewer to be able to piece together a picture of Hampton's political life and death, and the objects in his apartment embody a revolutionary afterlife. Filling out the camera's curiosity, the politicized looker understands film as incomplete. The documentary's incompleteness is a generative failure because it requires a looking practice that can fill in its gaps. Politicized looking is a practice that attempts to fill in these gaps and in so doing destabilizes the clean division between presence and absence, memory and forgetting, in order to clarify anti-Black violence via state-sanctioned murder. The exhibition space curated by the BPP and captured by the film enables and invites politicized looking as a means of contextualizing Hampton's death, thus engaging political practice.

For Kara Keeling, the act of looking is political because "liberation, if there is such a thing, is possible in the interval as a present impossibility, an expansion that explodes even the interval in which we wait."[91] This present impossibility can easily be adopted when we look at Hampton's murder scene. The gruesome excretions from Hampton's flesh collide with the political life of the objects in the scene. Politicized looking actively negotiates the present impossibility where "waiting happens without protection, exposed to the examination and expectations of others."[92] Looking *for* is a way to think about the unstable boundary between life and death.

In these images, the objects become the life of the screen. They occupy the space Hampton alerts us to: the space of absence. These objects make all too clear the alarm of absence. When there is nothing there, what are we looking for? Precisely that. We look for the substitutes. We look for the objects that become Hampton's body. Anti-Black violence seals Hampton in Fanon's world as an "object in the midst of other objects."[93] Hampton's objecthood, though, vitalizes a very different sense of Black radical politics. Perhaps the objecthood that Black radicals occupy brings us closer to the object's resistant state. The camera frames the narrative offered by the Panther-curator. While the camera shows the evidence behind his claims, it also frames a particular reality of radical Black life. The objects leak into the frame as the body to look for because Hampton's flesh is nowhere to be captured. The centrality of these "things" heightens the spectacle of Hampton's murder. The camera envisions the remnants of this spectacle while also forcing the audience to ask itself: What kind of threat did Hampton pose to the US government that required the degree of violence inflicted on him? What message does this kind of murder send?

The film frames the message as twofold. On the one hand, Hampton's murder signaled fear and alarm for all radical practitioners—across racial, classed, and gendered vectors of subjectivity. The gruesome document of his murder affirms that the state would go through great lengths to make an example out of anyone who threatened its sanctity. On the other hand, the objects that leak into the frame offer another reading. For those engaged in politicized looking, these objects somehow leave us with the most important message with or without Hampton: the revolution is alive. The revolution is on the brink. The revolution is contained within these things. This revolutionary presence forces a reflection on the material conditions of anti-Blackness within struggles for radical change. The collective of objects that fill the screen live materially and politically. This activation of the material motivates a way of looking that translates into a way of doing, being, engaging, creating. The objects left in Hampton's wake force us to ask: how, then, can we activate an understanding of the body that attempts to account for these historical and material applications?

It is precisely this precarity of radical Black life that allowed Hampton to understand the relationship between dying and living when it comes to revolution. Hampton articulates the call for death as hope: "And I hope that each one of you will be able to die in the international proletarian revolutionary struggle or you'll be able to live in it." The ease with which Hampton is able to hope that his audience will be able to die *or* live in it is no simple matter. Clearly, death preoccupies Hampton's articulation of struggle. The uncertain terrains of revolutionary struggle contain some certainty for Hampton: that death and revolution are inevitable for Black radicals. The significance of death in Hampton's formulation marks the historical difference between bodies. It is this astute way of knowing that makes Hampton's declaration both shocking and mundane. His "hope" is for a more meaningful death—a death on one's own terms, a fully embodied radical Black death. This hope manifests when one takes back one's negation and engages one's death toward a more radical future (plate 25).

Radical Black Legacies

Fred Hampton's murder continued to signal deep mistrust of the state in radical circles. In a historical moment that promised successful revolution, Hampton's murder further ignited Black rage. In his 1970 assessment "The Old Rules Do Not Apply: A Survey of the Persecution of the Black Panther Party," Charles R. Garry—a leftist lawyer who defended several BPP members in the course of his career—catalogues the various ways in which the state targeted the BPP in an attempt to extinguish their political work. Garry indexes the state's sheer variety of tactics, which gives a sense of the comprehensive nature of the state's repressive apparatus against radical Black organizations. From "expended bail-bond premiums . . . money that would never be returned" to "men and women who were harassed and killed," Garry documents how the BPP experienced an exceptional amount of anti-Black violence.[94] Strikingly, Garry notes how "in the over thirty years [he has] been practicing law, [he has] never experienced the type of persecution faced by the BPP. The old rules do not apply to the Black Panther Party. There are new rules, new requirements, new methods of harassment."[95]

In a political moment where the BPP themselves were engaged in a rewriting of history and radical practices toward a new world order, the state too developed new ways to exterminate these practices. The threat of Black radical-political praxis motivated the state to develop new repressive technologies. On the one hand, we can see the murder of Hampton as the undeniable certainty and ease with which the state killed radicals. Though the question of whether or not the state would kill radicals is not a new one, we can see how this practice advanced in the years following World War II known as the McCarthy era. However, it was the depth and comprehensive nature of COINTELPRO as an institutionalized, recorded government program invested in the systematic murder of Black radicals that is particularly striking and "new" as a repressive technology.

If systematic murder can be seen on one side of the repressive spectrum, we can see imprisonment on the other. Incarceration became an increasingly popularized form of state repression in the 1960s and 1970s. The BPP, alongside others, led grassroots movements that popularized resistance in neighborhoods otherwise devastated by police violence. COINTELPRO detailed the process of criminalization and incarceration needed for the state to regain social control. The ongoing incarceration of Black radicals at this time—Huey Newton, Bobby Seale, Angela Y. Davis, and Assata Shakur, just to name a few—aimed to isolate political leaders and exterminate rank-and-file participation by accelerating fear and internal divisiveness within these organizations. Undoubtedly, imprisonment was aligned with the state's aims to destroy the Black liberation movement.

The final chapter looks at the life and death of George Jackson, who spent most of his life in San Quentin State Prison. Jackson's 1971 murder in San Quentin gives us another gruesome scene of anti-Black violence. Jackson's murder illuminates how state technologies of surveillance and censorship give us a sense of the Black body that is marked as carceral. In what follows, I position Jackson's murder as crucial to the emergence of what once-incarcerated Black radical Angela Davis calls the prison industrial complex. It was Jackson's murder that signaled a point of transition for Black radical politics and aesthetics from revolution to abolition.

3

George Jackson's Murder and Fugitive Imaginaries

In the name of love and in the name of freedom, with love as our guide, we'll slit every throat of anyone who threatens the people and our children. We'll do it in the name of peace, if this is what we are forced to do; because as soon as it's over, then we can have the kind of world where violence will no longer exist.

—Huey P. Newton, eulogy for George Jackson, 1971

Time seems to be passing much faster these last few months. Wonder where it's running to, what's building? Will I be able to control the outcome of whatever.

—George Jackson, *Blood in My Eye*, 1972

On August 21, 1971, George Jackson was shot dead in San Quentin State Prison in California. Jackson was killed because of an escape attempt. Historian Dan Berger has provided the clearest, most detailed account of the events that led up to Jackson's death. Berger notes how the "details of the day remain shrouded in confusion: the various theories and countertheories offered at the time and since then inevitably produce a 'Rashomon effect,' in which observers draw mutually contradictory conclusions from the same evidence."[1] With that in mind, Berger goes on to provide a rich series of details, speculative and documented, of the day's events. The story, in its most bare-boned account, reads as follows: around 2:30 p.m. that Saturday, after a visit from attorney Stephen Bingham and legal investigator Vanita Anderson, Jackson had a gun and took control of the Adjustment Center (AC), where certain prisoners were isolated from general population. There are many speculations as to how Jackson secured the gun, and all of the theories are still unproven. Three prison guards and two white prisoners were killed. Likely recognizing that other guards were aware of the escape attempt, Jackson, followed by his comrade prisoner Johnny Spain, ran out of the AC and into the prison yard. As he ran toward the prison hospital, Jackson was gunned down by two tower guards. He was discovered face down and was handcuffed, and he was then turned over to reveal his face; he was left in that position for four hours. George Jackson was one month shy of his thirtieth birthday.[2]

George Jackson was born on September 23, 1941, on the West Side of Chicago. Jackson was the second of five children. His father Lester, a postal worker, and mother Georgia relocated to Los Angeles in 1956 in an attempt to redirect Jackson's teenage years, which were spent in and out of jail and gangs.[3] Jackson's relationship to criminal activity at a young age was formative to his politicization in prison.

Found guilty of a seventy-dollar gas station robbery in 1960, Jackson was given an indeterminate sentence of one year to life. During his time inside, Jackson engaged in a rigorous study of political-economic theory and radical social movements that ignited his own politicization. Jackson's best-selling 1970 publication *Soledad Brother: The Prison Letters of George Jackson* is a collection of letters from 1964 to 1970 written to loved ones, from Jackson's mother to his lawyer. Several of these letters detail Jackson's political and personal approaches to politics, kinship, and social relations. In a letter politically and economically contextualizing his life, Jackson writes:

> Later, when I was accused of robbing a gas station of seventy dollars, I accepted a deal—I agreed to confess and spare the county court costs in return for a light county jail sentence. I confessed but when

time came for sentencing, they tossed me into the penitentiary with one to life. That was in 1960. I was 18 years old. I've been here ever since. I met Marx, Lenin, Trotsky, Engels, and Mao when I entered prison and they redeemed me. For the first four years I studied nothing but economics and military ideas.[4]

What is striking in this account is the ease through which Jackson aligns his entry into prison with the politics he came to inherit. Rather than describing his initial contact with other prisoners, or even prison guards, Jackson foregrounds how he "met Marx, Lenin, Trotsky, Engels, and Mao"—the revolutionary ghosts of Communist political-economic theory whose writing keeps that pantheon alive. Jackson equates his own redemption with his encounter with and study of these radical books and authors. The process of radical consciousness-raising is what guided Jackson to the logics of incarceration within capitalism. These guides served to contextualize his own experience within the juridical-political system. For Jackson, and for many political/politicized prisoners, the study of influential radical texts manifested into their own intellectual writing, thus keeping the premises and promises of these texts alive in excess of their citational uses.[5]

Similar to the political life of objects left in Hampton's wake, the figures Jackson "meets" speak through the objects they create—in terms of both the texts themselves as well as the theories they contain. These objects, fundamental to radical theorizations of anticapitalist struggle, become extended, corrected, and revered in Jackson's own writings. *Soledad Brother* (1970) and *Blood in My Eye* (1972) are both in conversation with, and directly responding to, the more "foundational" Marxist-Communist figures and their writings that Jackson "met" upon his first few months in prison.[6] Within his own writing, Jackson often adopts and reroutes these foundational theorizations to account for the violent reality of Black life, the production of mass criminality, and the incarceration of young Black men in the United States.

Jackson notes that upon meeting "Black guerillas" like George "Big Jake" Lewis, James Carr, W. L. Nolen, Bill Christmas, and Torry Gibson, among others, he turned to political organizing efforts inside Soledad State Prison that were dedicated to creating a burgeoning radical prison population, committed to militancy, political discipline, and revolutionary praxis. He notes that his new collective of Black militants "attempted to transform the Black criminal mentality into a Black revolutionary mentality."[7] This is, perhaps, one of the most iconic and well-circulated Jackson phrases and often stands as testament to his desire to reimagine the revolutionary potential of the social construction of the "Black criminal." What is significant about this political project is primarily how Jackson imagines Blackness in relation to both criminality and revolutionary mentality.

In his vision, the Black criminal mentality is at once a social condition that manifests within the Black psyche and can thus be historically contextualized and transformed politically. For Jackson, the tendency toward criminal acts is conditioned by the harsh reality of impoverishment and violence that accompany being Black in the United States. As Jackson states in *Blood in My Eye*, the "system produces outlaws. . . . the whole growing in spirals that must either end in the uneconomic destruction of the oppressed or the termination of oppression."[8] To make sense of the political and economic conditions that force Black people to lead a "criminal" life, one must understand and combat the ways that racial capitalism creates and protects such structures. In this formulation, Jackson clarifies how capitalism, and its (extra)legal collaborator the state, makes it impossible for Black subjects to be anything other than fugitives. The entire structure is organized around systematically making Black life criminal. Consciousness-raising, for Jackson, would untangle Blackness from criminality and would instead indict the state as the primary generator of criminal acts.[9]

Jackson's time inside led to some of the most prolific writing on the relationship between Black Power politics and struggles inside prison. In the span of his own writings, between 1968 and 1971, the consolidation of power within a burgeoning and strengthening prison system in California reshaped the ways that Black Power could be imagined. Jackson would come to articulate the nuances of such an all-encompassing struggle.

From Black Power to Prison Abolition

In my estimation, much of Jackson's writings, particularly *Blood in My Eye* (which I will discuss at length in the following section), embody the political implications of the revolutionary transition from Black power to prison abolition—a politics of naming that marks the provisional *ends* of the Black Power era as a marker of militant insurrection during the 1960s and the *beginnings* of framing Black Power struggles within the language of prison abolition.

Arguably the most iconic and influential US political force of the late 1960s, Black Power movements concerned themselves with the ongoing struggle toward Black self-determination, liberation, and revolution. The phrase *Black Power* embodies the historical continuity between figures and movements like Nat Turner, Marcus Garvey, Frantz Fanon, and the Deacons of Defense—all of whom unapologetically called for a complete annihilation of white supremacy (and, in most cases, white supremacists) and a total transformation of the existing social order into one more conducive to Black self-determination and liberation. In addition, Black Power also describes organizing models toward Black liberation in solidarity with other third worldist and anticapitalist movements. The general call for "power" aligns itself with a need for more assertive political organizing forms that foreground the relationship between race and capitalism's ongoing and uneven effects. Black Power accounts for several Black radical organizations, from the Black Panther Party for Self-Defense (BPP) to the Black Liberation Army—all of which were invested in active warfare against capitalism and the white supremacist state and moving toward a more egalitarian society in which Black self-determination and liberation are foundational philosophies and practices.

The name *Black Power* is attributed to Charles Hamilton and Stokely Carmichael's 1966 call *for* "Black power," which marked the movement's provisional beginnings and is often represented as a fundamental split from the passive, nonviolent direct action of the civil rights era toward a more disciplined affirmation of Black militancy, self-determination, and self-defense.[10] Likely the most underexamined aspect of Carmichael's call for Black power is the political context and material conditions from which the call arose: "This is the twenty-seventh time that *I've been arrested. I ain't going to jail no more.* The only way we gonna stop them white men from whuppin' us is to take over. What we gonna start sayin' now is Black Power! . . . *Every courthouse in Mississippi ought to be burned down to get rid of the dirt.*"[11] For Carmichael, the need for Black power developed out of political experience with and critique of policing and incarceration. Frustrated with the cyclical civil rights strategy of engaging passively in direct action, getting arrested, and then passively engaging in direct action again, Carmichael articulated the position of a politically emergent generation of young Black radicals. Carmichael's own exhaustion with this strategy is declared by a refusal: he will not go to jail anymore and instead will engage in a politics of "take over." This emergent kind of politics acknowledges the failures of state systems for recognition (the fatigue of getting arrested for civil disobedience as a ploy for media attention) and calls for their complete abolition ("Every courthouse in Mississippi ought to be burned down to get rid of the dirt"). This takeover relies on the destruction of existing legal and extralegal forces in order to construct new political infrastructures. In this conceptualization, Carmichael bridges Black power with what comes into being more directly in the early 1970s as explicit prison abolition politics, whose lineage is fundamentally tied to Black power. Black power was as much a call for more assertive and lasting political actions as it was a symbolic connection to a particular genealogy of a Black historical past.

Historians of the 1960s often associate the Black Power era as loosely between 1966 and 1972, when the first National Black Political Convention marked the unraveling of the radical politics associated with Black Power, toward more reform-based policies advocated by a politically broader (from liberal to radical) spectrum.[12] This general shift, which often gets named as the "end" of the Black Power era, speaks to several issues around the politics of naming in this historical moment. As the term *political prisoner* gained circulation so too did Black radicals' political analyses cataloguing increasingly sophisticated state institutions aimed at repressing Black-led revolution and revolutionaries.

In the November 1967 edition of the *Black Panther*, early in the BPP's history, Huey Newton and Bobby Seale were both listed in the editorial collective as "political prisoners."[13] By 1971, the term *political prisoner* entered a radical vernacular as an unfortunate, everyday term. George Jackson was one of many activists and organizers called by this moniker. We can also add to the roster Assata Shakur, Bobby Seale, Afeni Shakur, Angela Y. Davis, David Gilbert, Geronimo Pratt, Leonard Peltier, and several other political organizers from a broad range of third-world movements, including, but not limited to, the American Indian Movement, Chicano Liberation Movement, and Weather Underground. *Political prisoner* is both a historically specific and activist-rooted term that consolidates the relationship between the context and outcome of one's organizing practice. In other words, *political prisoner* indexes the qualities of then-intensified political insurrection as well as the repressive consequences of political organizing that dared to go outside the bounds of reform-based practice.

As Gregory Armstrong, Jackson's editor for *Soledad Brother*, recounts in his 1972 preface to *Blood in My Eye*:

In prison, commitment to revolution has a special meaning and a special price. To be identified as a revolutionary by the prison authorities means an almost permanent denial of parole, separation from other prisoners, solitary confinement (usually in maximum security wings of the prison), transfers from one prison to another, beatings, bad food. It brings down on you the entire punitive and repressive force of a completely totalitarian system.[14]

Armstrong details the stakes of being known and named as a political prisoner. The material consequences enforced by state officials—"almost permanent denial of parole, separation from other prisoners, solitary confinement . . . transfers from one prison to another, beatings, bad food"—structure everyday life. These conditions clarify the then-relatively new understanding of the prison as a site of punishment *itself* rather than isolation toward rehabilitation. The self-designated status of political prisoner makes one increasingly vulnerable to the coercive regime of state-sanctioned punishment and torture. The shifts that I am interested in here, and that Jackson's works so readily interrogate, are the explicit and residual bonds between the prison and anti-Black racism. In his 1970 preface to Jackson's *Soledad Brother*, written from Brazil, French philosopher and playwright Jean Genet dramatically articulates the intimacy between prisons and anti-Black racism:

But I have lived too long in prisons not to have recognized, as soon as the first pages were translated for me in San Francisco, the very particular odor and texture of something written in a cell, surrounded by walls and guards, poisoned by hatred, for what I did not yet know with such intensity was the hatred of the white American for the Black, a hatred so extreme that I wonder whether every white man in that country, when he plants a tree, doesn't see *Negroes* hanging from its branches.[15]

The "particular odor and texture of something written in a cell" alarms any romance of writing—it is Jackson's status as a political prisoner that impacts his living conditions, the materiality of his everyday, the intensity of those who hate him, the racial epidermal schema that positions him as Black in relation to a white world.[16] Genet vividly captures how deeply rooted American prisons are in anti-Black racism. For Genet, and indeed for Jackson, the white world—its institutions, guards, cells, trees—are all born out of and sustain anti-Black violence.

Jackson's murder in 1971 simultaneously signaled the unraveling of a particularly politically insurgent era and the beginnings of a burgeoning prison system more explicitly wedded to corporate capitalism.[17] Among the many revelations that Jackson's assassination reveals is the precision with which the prison system secures its best interests through unyielding murderous practices.[18] Therefore, performances of state violence—in this case incarceration, policing, surveillance, and varying degrees of murder—are extended and durational performances of anti-Black violence. In this spirit, I adopt and adapt performance studies scholar Patrick Anderson's uptake of the state as the "the continuous production of designated insides and outsides, rules of identification and abjection, practices that define belonging and enforce exclusion."[19] Prison, as but one institutional arm of the state, is crucial to this continuous production, as it is a site where performances of violence maintain the edges and centers of state power. In the case of the prison, this durational performance occurs unevenly though intensely. This intensity, coupled with an unparalleled forceful system, gave rise to what we now refer to as the prison industrial complex.

The prison industrial complex represents the shared investments and interests of state and industry, both of which consolidate power in an around the expansion of the prison industry. By Jackson's 1971 murder, the California prison system was in the process of transformation, building up for one of the most contracted growths in history. According to preeminent abolitionist scholar Ruth Wilson Gilmore, the state responded to the so-called social crisis of "mid-sixties radical activism, both spontaneous and organized" that "successfully produced widespread disorder throughout society."[20] In addition, the economic panic of the early 1970s occurred at the "same time radical activists were assassinated, went to prison, disappeared underground, or fled into exile."[21] This social crisis resulted from the state repression of radical activists as well as the ongoing structural impoverishment of Black neighborhoods and other communities of color. For Gilmore, Nixon's 1968 platform of "law and order" aimed, to borrow a phrase from anthropologist Allen Feldman, to "individualize disorder" into "singular instances of criminality that could be solved via arrest or state-sanctioned killings rather than fundamental social change."[22] This tactic aimed to fortify the function of police and prison officials by gathering a rhetorical and material justification for the growth of carceral institutions. However significant this social crisis appeared to be, the state was simultaneously expanding and sustaining its value and profit in the form of various surpluses—finance capital, land, surplus labor, and state capacity.[23] These elements of surplus, effectively put to work by the state, offered a solution to the crisis posed by social unrest: the expansion of prison growth to formerly agricultural California towns that could house the so-called criminals created by the social crisis while also booming these rural economies by transforming them into prison towns.

The state's success in implementing this political and economic experiment in California quickly spread across the United States, which gave rise to the rapid expansion, growth, and infiltration of prisons into the everyday lives of mostly Black people. Deemed the *prison industrial complex*, this political and economic phenomenon is of increasing relevance to the transition from Black Power to prison abolition that I aim to trace in this chapter. This watershed political and economic investment in prison and prison population growth took place during George Jackson's incarceration and subsequent murder—an event memorialized in the Black Power era as a moment of troubling crisis within Black radical politics because of how significantly this murder represented an "end" of the possibilities posed by the promise of revolution. In addition to the political and economic influence of prison expansion on the transition from Black Power to prison abolition, we must also account for the rhetorical shift that called attention to the historical affinities between the Black freedom struggle and abolitionist politics.

The rhetorical shift from Black Power to prison abolition repeats and reconsiders the genealogy between abolitionist politics and Black histories. In other words, the history of abolitionist politics first appears in response to the bondage of Black men and women under chattel slavery, a historical moment that couples historical Black Power discourses and abolitionist discourses. The reiteration of this historical and discursive link emerges in the late 1960s and early 1970s within Black radical writings and political organizations. These connections between slavery and incarceration are of utmost importance for this chapter, as Jackson's political theorizations always posit continuity between the condition of Black people in the 1960s and their direct historical linkage to slavery. Prison abolition, then, continues that historical genealogy as it marks the prison as the fundamental site of Black political struggle toward liberation and revolution.

Prison abolition reshapes the conversation about prisons in order to "shift our attention from the prison, perceived as an isolated institution, to the set of relationships that comprise the prison industrial complex," which include the "symbiotic relationships among correctional communities, transnational corporations, media conglomerates, guards' unions, and legislative and court agendas."[24] Angela Y. Davis reframes the way prisons are usually perceived of as merely one entity in an all-inclusive and all-expanding terrain of institutions, commercial investments, representational economies, and, finally, state and nonstate actors. Put simply, prison abolition is "both a practical organizing tool and a long-term goal" of "eliminating prisons, policing, and surveillance and creating lasting alternatives to punishment and imprisonment."[25] The theoretical and political implications of such a goal ask for a conceptual disassociation of discourses of crime from punishment as they also radically disassemble understandings of the state's role in creating and maintaining the fiction of law and order. Stated explicitly, prison abolition works toward seeking and creating alternatives to prisons and the socioeconomic and representational processes that criminalize those most vulnerable to state violence. In this way, it is both a theory and practice aimed toward a more egalitarian and restorative approach to rethinking harm and its effects. Crucial to the prison abolitionist vision is the ongoing study and critique of prisons, policing, and surveillance as they unevenly condition everyday life within the United States.

In his engaged reflection upon US social movements, and prison abolition in particular, Frank B. Wilderson III is cautious of anti-Blackness within these political articulations. Within his critique, Wilderson notes how

> coalitions and social movements—even radical social movements such as the prison abolition movement, bound up in the solicitation of hegemony so as to fortify and extend the interlocutory life of civil society—ultimately accommodate only the satiable demands and finite antagonisms of civil society's junior partners (i.e. immigrants, white women, and the working class), but foreclose on the insatiable demands and endless antagonisms of the prison slave and the prison slave-in-waiting. In short, whereas such coalitions and social movements cannot be called the outright handmaidens of white supremacy, their rhetorical structures and political desire are underwritten by a supplemental antiblackness.[26]

In his analysis, Wilderson alerts us to how even the most radical forms of resistance harbor "rhetorical structures and political desire" that may affirm anti-Blackness. Within these coalitions is a mistaken understanding that Black people are legible in hegemonic terms—who can "win" or "seize" variations of state or capitalistic power via civic society—and thus prison abolitionist struggles can petition hegemonic structures for political ends. Wilderson offers a corrective to this logic by suggesting that prison abolition radically positions itself alongside Blackness by moving toward death—"If this is not the desire that underwrites one's politics, then through what strategy of legitimation is the word 'prison' being linked to the word 'abolition'?"[27] In this "dance of social death," Blackness and prison abolition may avoid certain failure within conditions of hegemonic petition from which "they try to do work of prison abolition, the work will fail, for it is always work *from* a position of coherence . . . on *behalf* of a position of incoherence of the Black subject, or prison slave."[28] It is from this conceptual antagonism that Blackness and prison abolition recalibrate "death"—metaphorically and materially—toward political ends. For Wilderson, those political ends are death, unthought, and the complete annihilation of the world as we know it. For George Jackson, those emergent political ends are revolution—for which Black radical death is a crucial component. Though both political theorists are invested in seemingly divergent political ends, both meditations on Blackness and prison abolition are premised on an understanding of the prison industrial complex as an ultimate site of dereliction, confinement, and social death.

Articulating a Black Revolutionary Mentality

With this in mind, we can reinterpret George Jackson's aforementioned desire to "transform the Black criminal mentality into a Black revolutionary mentality."[29] The figure of the Black criminal has revolutionary potential because *the Black subject exists always as a fugitive.*[30] Criminality conditions Black life—the only way to imagine and activate another reading of Blackness is to engage in revolution and the total destruction of the existing social order. The implications for Black subjects are best illuminated by Jackson's life—a life that was not guaranteed freedom but instead understood captivity as his condition for living.

Dylan Rodriguez compellingly intervenes in famed theorist Michel Foucault's notion of the disciplinary construction of the prison.[31] Deeply critical of the notion of hegemony as crucial to carceral logic, Rodriguez considers the prison for its totality of coercion in place of the balance between coercion and consent. Calling this nature of total coercion "state terror," Rodriguez notes:

In the space of the prison, violence overdetermines, discipline and surveillance articulates as coercion, forming a physical, visceral, and psychic context that funnels and focuses oppositional political subjects. . . . Where the disciplinary hegemony of the free world presumes the malleability—and thus, the final conformity—of bodies and subjects, the prison seeks to burn off deviant excess, punishing and effectively exterminating those who lie beyond the constructed limits of the normalising regime.[32]

Rodriguez articulates how Foucault's understanding of discipline and surveillance mutate into violence and coercion. Violence and coercion become the carceral logics of the prison, thus replacing the relatively subtler presence of discipline and surveillance. The prison is a site of totality for Rodriguez. Because "the surfaces of these deviant bodies compose a particular border that reflects and refracts the institutional border of the prison," conditions of confinement for these "deviant bodies" seal and intensify everyday conditions of discipline and surveillance.[33]

Those everyday technologies primarily concerned with normalizing such deviants as a method of reentry into society transform into technologies of invisibility, torture, and civic death when considered within the prison. Rodriguez's argument leads us to an understanding of imprisonment, rather than a limited punishment that eventually transitions the incarcerated back into society, as the goal of prisons. Because violence and coercion become the philosophy of prison itself, punishment becomes a permanent state of being. Within this space, any articulation of presence—every momentary rupture of being within this space of totality—translates into an articulation of resistance. Articulation, in this case, can be understood as a confirmation of one's presence within prison, positing one's capacity to resist the state's desire for invisibility and annihilation.

According to Dylan Rodriguez, articulation is always a form of political antagonism. Control over the incarcerated body is a guaranteed means for the prison to secure its own totalized power. As Rodriguez reminds us:

Totalising control over the prisoner's body—its mobility, location, contents, behaviours, gestures—consistently surfaces as the core logic of prison discipline, and it is the way in which the allegedly disciplinary apparatus relies on the constant application of physical and psychological violence—in essence, a sometimes sophisticated, often vulgar technology of human torture—that coercively re-shapes the body's form and content.[34]

In this space of bodily restriction and policing, the act of articulation is a form of refusal under a regime of direct coercion. Strikingly, articulation renders the "prison wall permeable through a discourse of collective, counter-state political agency" and thus "produces possibilities beyond reform and state accountability" toward more abolitionist visions of a world without prisons.[35] Articulation resists the state's desire and need to use direct coercion and totalizing violence in order to silence dissent among the incarcerated. For Rodriguez, and indeed in my own work, when political prisoners articulate a radical analysis and practice, the underlying premises of invisibility, silence, and eradication begin to erode. The conceptual unraveling of the logics of incarceration (as a precursor to their eventual material destruction) is a crucial component of political antagonism and prison abolition.

More recently, Nicole Fleetwood has similarly theorized the meanings and impacts of carceral cultural productions in her book *Marking Time: Art in the Age of Mass Incarceration*. Groundbreaking, this book makes its arguments about the impact of the prison industrial complex via featured artworks by imprisoned and nonimprisoned artists. Fleetwood argues for the centrality of art-making practices as modes to challenge questions of subjectivity, collectivity, violence, isolation, and creativity in ways that focus on those very people who live at the margins of visibility. These artists become theorists throughout the book, offering fresh, new insights into otherwise well-worn debates in aesthetic, political, and social theory. She notes how "prison art practices resist the isolation, exploitation, and dehumanization of carceral facilitates" toward what can be called "carceral aesthetics, which refers to ways of envisioning and crafting art and culture that reflect the conditions of imprisonment."[36] Fleetwood's notion of carceral aesthetics seems very much influenced by Jackson's writing, and indeed I believe the political prisoner would very much fit Fleetwood's definition of a prison artist. Fleetwood's notion of carceral aesthetics ultimately focuses on "practices of relationality, creativity, and discernment that do not aim to reproduce or preserve prisons, but to visualize the end of human captivity, devaluation, dispossession, and the carceral logics that tether bodies to penal systems. In this regard, carceral aesthetics builds upon prisoners' rights movement, the black radical tradition, and other dissident cultural and political movements for freedom."[37] Jackson's theorizations could be understood as a framework to understand the artists and practices that Fleetwood covers in her book, as his writing very much generates the kind of aesthetic forms she offers up.

Jackson's publication record is a direct political articulation of resistance and political antagonism. Arguably, the late 1960s and early 1970s were political moments in which the efficacy of prison logics was sedimented into industrialized models of incarceration. In other words, state technologies for what I believe Rodriguez effectively identifies as "state terror" were being perfected at the very time Jackson published his works. Jackson's politically antagonistic 1972 publication *Blood in My Eye* demonstrates how mechanisms of state-sponsored terror operated against visions of revolutionary liberation.

Blood in My Eye was completed days before Jackson's murder in San Quentin State Prison. *Blood* is a treatise on revolution—a manuscript awaiting manifestation. Jackson's writing centers around *how* revolution will look and *why* it must be activated as a total transformation of the foundations of capitalism, which required a Black revolutionary death. The book is organized into four sections: "I. Blood in My Eye," "II. The Amerikan Mind," "III. After the Revolution Has Failed," and "IV. The Oppressive Contract." These four sections detail both the pragmatic and conceptual logics of revolution. Jackson also indicates the relationships within psychological, social, and material manifestations of capitalism. He does not stop at naming the problems; Jackson also details the force and conditions of necessary resistance. The title page of the first chapter makes visible the allegiances and agreements needed to trust Jackson's project: "We must accept the eventuality of bringing the U.S.A. to its knees; accepting the closing off of critical sections of the city with barbed wire, armored pig carriers crisscrossing the streets, soldiers everywhere, tommy guns pointed at stomach level, smoke curling Black against the daylight sky, the smell of cordite, house-to-house searches, doors being kicked in, the commonness of death."[38] At play in this introductory manifesto is the relationship between action and theory (or praxis).[39] Jackson visualizes the visceral impact of revolution in all of the banality of the "commonness of death." Revolution is imagined as engaged and sustained warfare—mobilized both against and through repression, toward the eventual aim of ending US imperial and capitalist power. Significantly, Jackson's description does not evade the violence of revolutionary means. We are given images of warfare—imagery that is both familiar and distant to his audience. These descriptions are familiar because of the precision through which he describes scenes reminiscent of a then-ongoing Vietnam War, which was responsible for the politicization of many in the United States precisely because of the circulation of images through popular media such as *Life* magazine. The parallel in Jackson's description between "barbed wire . . . armored pig carriers . . . soldiers everywhere . . . tommy guns pointed at stomach level" and the promise of "house-to-house searches, doors being kicked in, the commonness of death" simultaneously describes the then-current events of the Vietnam War and the promise of sustained military presence when revolution makes its way onto American soil. In many ways, this description attempts—to borrow from radical vernacular—to "bring the war home" by calling attention to the material realities and promises of revolution.

The manifesto is nonnegotiable. The dynamics at play in *Blood* rely on an unrelenting commitment to the generative potential of Black radical death. Jackson goes on to specify:

> As a slave, the social phenomenon that engages my whole conscious-
> ness is, of course, revolution.
> The slave—and revolution.
> Born to premature death, a menial, subsistence-wage worker,
> odd-job man, the cleaner, the caught, the man under hatches, with-
> out bail—that's me, the colonial victim. . . . I've lived with repression
> every moment of my life, a repression so formidable that any move-
> ment on my part can only bring relief, the respite of a small victory
> or the release of death. In every sense of the term, in every sense
> that's real, I'm a slave to, and of, property.[40]

With both clarity and ease, Jackson identifies the reality of Black life in the United States. Invoking Marx's reading of the master-slave dialectic, Jackson associates the slave's consciousness as bound to the promise of revolution.[41] With this promise comes both the reflection on "premature death" and the "release of death," two understandings of revolutionary death as understood from within carceral conditions.[42] Similarly, both pre-mature death and the release of death are two temporal logics. In one, to be Black signals a kind of prefigured social death (premature death) into which one is born. In the other, the release of death signals the end of one's life and the feeling of release or liberation. This release signals an end to one's experience of social death at the same moment in which some kind of liberation is achieved. In the case of premature death, one's life is situated within broader systemic structures that facilitate how Black subjects experience their exploitation. However, it is not the promise of release that facilitates the need for revolution. On the other hand, it is that the capacity for revolution exists within premature death. For Jackson, capitalism and the exploitation of labor are central to this notion of premature death.

Premature death, for Jackson, refers to the uneven conditions of alienation and exploitation that structure Black life. Within this claustrophobic space, one experiences a psychological and material containment so severe that these structural conditions guarantee premature death. The release of death, however, is activated toward revolution. The release of death marks a kind of liberation but one that encapsulates the generative potential of Black radical death. This death—always present and always inevitable—is visualized as release from under capitalism by way of death *toward* a more radical social order. Jackson's *Blood in My Eye* can be understood within a rich lineage of Black aesthetic traditions in which the questions of death and freedom are collective encounters, theorized through the relationship between the subject and the collective.

Jackson's writings illustrate historical continuity between slavery and its afterlives in relation to his own experience and thus provide a crucial theoretical labor for this chapter. In his discussion on Frederick Douglass and the literary production of slave narratives, Paul Gilroy suggests that the centrality of death in the pursuit of freedom undertakes new philosophical meanings:

> What appears in both stories to be a positive preference for death rather than continued servitude can be read as a contribution towards slave discourse on the nature of freedom itself. It supplies a valuable clue towards answering the question of how the realm of freedom is conceptualized by those who have never been free. This inclination towards death and away from bondage is fundamental.[43]

For Gilroy, slave narratives contextualize autobiographical ruminations on the centrality of death in thinking through the Black freedom struggle. In other words, thinking through death generates a means of imagining freedom. The form and function of literary articulation allows for an increasingly intensified means of Black radical knowledge production aimed toward death and liberation. As Gilroy reminds us, the horrors of slavery produced an albeit disjointed kind of collectivity manifested through Black literature that dared to centralize anti-Black violence in every notion of the Black experience. As Gilroy argues, "It is important to note here that a new discursive economy emerges with the refusal to subordinate the particularity of the slave experience to the totalising power of universal reason held exclusively by white hands, pens, or publishing houses."[44] In this way, writings produced out of slavery's lasting afterlife invest in the "act or process of simultaneous self-creation and self-emancipation."[45] I would extend Gilroy's argument that Black autobiographical writings engage in a process of self-emancipation to include the process of collective emancipation—a process that Jackson directly engages with in *Blood in My Eye*. In Jackson's writings, the relationship between the individual and collective liberation is not a question at all. In fact, Jackson's commitment to Black radical death in pursuit of freedom relies upon an understanding of the Black subject as always already bound to Black collectivity. We can link Jackson's understanding of the individual as always collective to Gilroy's assertion that slavery collectivized Black experience and, in doing so, made thinking of Black freedom impossible without thinking of Black radical death.

In this way, *Blood in My Eye* is both an archive and a call to action. It is an archive for its rich historical study of Black struggles for liberation from slavery to Jackson's present moment. The book's call to action is about furthering Black liberation through revolutionary militancy. Because the text itself is revolutionary dialogue and engagement, Jackson predicts the failure of any forthcoming revolutions in order to mobilize a durational struggle—one that foregrounds the worth of Black revolutionary praxis. In other words, Jackson predicts the potential failures of revolution in order to open the parameters of *lifetimes of struggle*. What better way, then, for the state to squash Black revolutionary praxis than to strip a person of their lifetime? What better way to spectacularize the totality of the prison's apparatus than to display the expendability of the radical Black body both inside and outside prison walls? In a system dependent upon sight as a primary apparatus of control, how does the lack of visibility of Jackson's murder, and ongoing state censorship, shape any revolutionary potential that might emerge out of his death?

Mythologies of Sight: Excremental Expendability and Jackson's Corpse

A crucial mechanism of control within the prison system's regime of terror is its perfection of sight. Extending Michel Foucault's theorization of the centrality of sight as a means of social control, the prison system relies upon modes of surveillance, bureaucratic documentation of observation, and an acute power over prisoner visibility by others.[46] Visibility and invisibility govern many of the ways that prisoners are made to endure racial terror inside prison walls. Prison officials maintain power over visibility by limiting prisoners' access to the public and compulsive practices of observation and recording that log a prisoner's every movement, meal, recreational activity, and the like. I believe this is why speculation and conditions surrounding Jackson's death take on peculiar exceptions in relation to the following section. As aforementioned, state narratives of Jackson's murder are inconsistent and contradict themselves. Prison Information Group (Groupe d'information sur les prisons [GIP]), a French political education collective that included philosophers Michel Foucault, Jean Genet, Gilles Deleuze, and Jean-Paul Sartre, published writings that illuminated the anti-Black violence and state-sponsored terrorism that eventually led to Jackson's murder in 1971.[47] A November 1971 publication on Jackson's death notes how

> for a number of weeks, American newspapers have published articles about Jackson's death. Many divergences exist between all, or almost all, of these articles. Impossibilities and contradictions appear at every stage. One article claims that the events started at 15:10, another at 14:25. One article describes the revolver as a 9mm; another as a .38 caliber. One article reports that Jackson wore a wig; another claims he did not. On Saturday, the whole event was described as a thirty-second blaze; on Monday, it became a long massacre of thirty minutes.[48]

These journalistic inconsistencies evidence larger systemic censorship of the details surrounding Jackson's murder. Along with these journalistic contradictions, there was also a failure to account for the visual conditions of Jackson's murder. These lapses in the state's presentation of events and the glaring lack of visual evidence have methodological ramifications that affect how we might even begin to look for the conditions of Jackson's death. These facts required a methodological approach that could meet such challenging terms, which is why I turn to methods in the historiography of slavery and its afterlives as a way in to these archival absences. Ultimately, I turn to artists who offer up alternative debates surrounding the archive and its limitations. The artists covered in this chapter mobilize the speculative as a set of encounters with the impossible set of possibilities that may unfold if we linger in the unknown.

In her gripping essay "Venus in Two Acts," historian Saidiya Hartman expands on concerns detailed in her first groundbreaking book *Scenes of Subjection* that have to do with accounting for Black life, from slavery to Reconstruction in the United States. In the essay, like in her book, Hartman offers an account of the violence of the archive, not only as a description of the general condition of historical research when it comes to those searching for signs of Black life but also as a way of opening up the theoretical implications of conducting such research from the position of a historian. Hartman, in the pursuit of writing about Venus and her friend, two young Black girls on a slave ship who appear in the captain's legal indictment for murder, writes, "I chose not to tell a story about Venus because to do so would have trespassed the boundaries of the archive. History pledges to be faithful to the limits of fact, evidence, and archive, even as those dead certainties are produced by terror."[49] There's too much to say about Venus, her friend, and Hartman's stunning and careful ability to account for them both. I will say that with poetic precision, Hartman poses a central concern that has influenced my own approach to Jackson's murder.

While there are likely internal, confidential documents that include photographic records of the crime scene, there is little visual evidence from Jackson's murder that has been made public. The question of visual evidence ties Jackson's murder to those of Hutton and Hampton. There is no real visual evidence from Hutton's murder, which paradoxically took place publicly and quite spectacularly. Recalling chapter 1, this lack of legible forensic and visual evidence from the crime scene is partially what motivated the *Berkeley Barb*'s cover image, which creatively aimed to call attention to such a questionable lack. On the contrary, the crime scene from Hampton's murder was filled, almost abundantly so, with forensic and visual evidence. Seizing the opportunity to record such evidentiary facts in demonstrating the state's extreme and violent murder of Hampton, the BPP opened up the slain Panther's home for tours and invited Gray and Alk's documentary film team in so as to ensure the local, national, and even international circulation of these evidentiary images. Jackson's murder scene was indeed an even more extreme example and as such points us to the limits of the visual entirely. Because the prison operates because of a complete prohibition of public access, the kinds of brutal forms of quotidian and spectacular violence that take place inside often remain invisible to those on the outside. Hence, the question of visual evidence feels so far out of reach in the case of Jackson's murder that visuality and sight itself are desired though unreliable, if not completely impossible, sources of information.

I have seen one photograph from the murder scene. Archival chasing has left me empty-handed. What is recounted is filled with what I call mythologies of sight. First-person accounts, blacked-out institutional documentation, objects memorialized in the prison museum, and activist accounts all signify anxiety about the details surrounding Jackson's murder. If writing a visual account of Jackson's history necessitates fidelity to the archive, then I would have stopped before I began. Because of archival inconsistencies, or even outright fallacies (as TGIP catalogued), I turned instead to how artists approached these limits in relation to questions of recovery and speculation.

In the introduction to their sweeping 2015 issue of *Social Text*, dedicated to "the question of recovery," the editors offer an incredibly generous roadmap into the role of the archive in relation to accounting for Black life vis-à-vis the practice of chattel slavery:

> Acknowledging that the archival form itself often precludes recovery, some scholars have transformed archival lack into a methodological tool, which exposes the transformation of human beings into property that set black subjects outside the realm of history. Indeed, the archive often records blackness only as an absence of human subjecthood, as when the enslaved enter the historical record as a number, a mark, or a notice of death. And yet, scholars such as Jennifer L. Morgan and Stephanie Smallwood, for example, argue that "the impossibility of recovery is inextricable from the moral imperative to attempt it." These attempts have often entailed forms of critical speculation that challenge what types of evidence count when it comes to making claims about the lives of the archive's dispossessed.

On the same road, in many ways cleared by Hartman, the editors here also account for the archive's violent limitations. They turn to scholars who have enacted "forms of critical speculation that challenge what types of evidence count" rather than those who might aim to extend archival reach or fill in archival gaps. This turn toward the speculative is what I have chosen to emphasize with the artists discussed in this chapter. The speculative, in this register, is about informed creative guesswork, in which an artist takes up research that includes all roads of information available to them on a given case. This includes not only present-tense information but also the historical, material, and political contexts and data from which one might begin a speculative approach. Black arts archives often embody such speculative practices in light of the problematic limits of archival work but also because of the realms of possibility that might emerge from a critical visual uptake of the speculative. Artists had to make educated guesses, and these guesses took shape on paper as a means of visualizing the conditions of Jackson's murder.

With this status in mind, the question of visibility returns in the context of the afterlife of Jackson's murder. As accounted by Dan Berger, prison organizing "utilized what could be called a strategy of visibility" as a mode of resisting the ways that prisons rely on rendering prisoners invisible, removing "people from view and access, thereby subjecting them to untold and untellable forms of violence."[50] To expose the brutality of violence by making it visible offers potentialities for the Black freedom struggle. Even while any project for visibility has pitfalls, attempts to visualize George Jackson's death offer a nuanced analysis in direct conversation with a broader historical Black art genealogy. This project privileges sight as an instrument for negotiating the dilemmas raised by images of death during the Black Power era—particularly the political stakes of visibility of the radical Black body in relation to histories of anti-Black violence.

In many ways, visibility constructs, affirms, and confirms. Fred Moten suggests this process elicits a "responsibility to look every time, again, but sometimes it looks like that looking comes before, holds, replicates, reproduces what is looked at."[51] Similar to the modes of politicized looking encouraged by *The Murder of Fred Hampton*, looking, as theorized by Moten, motivates the looker toward active engagement with the question of responsibility, replication, and reproduction—all of which are crucial elements in the political posters discussed in this chapter. These posters, reproduced and replicated across the nation, were made to live temporary lives wheat-pasted on walls, carried in demonstrations, and hung in living rooms. These posters were never meant to live in archives and are ephemeral objects in and of their own right. The use of political posters and their ready-made need for reproduction and replication also politically record the responsibility to account for Jackson's death—one unseen and only imagined.

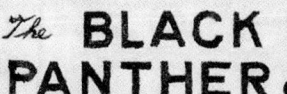
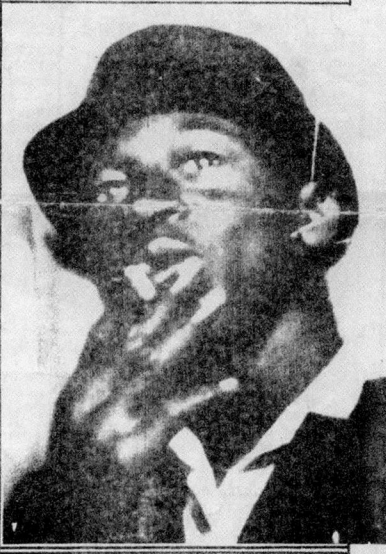

Plate 1   *Black Panther*, volume 1, April 25, 1967.

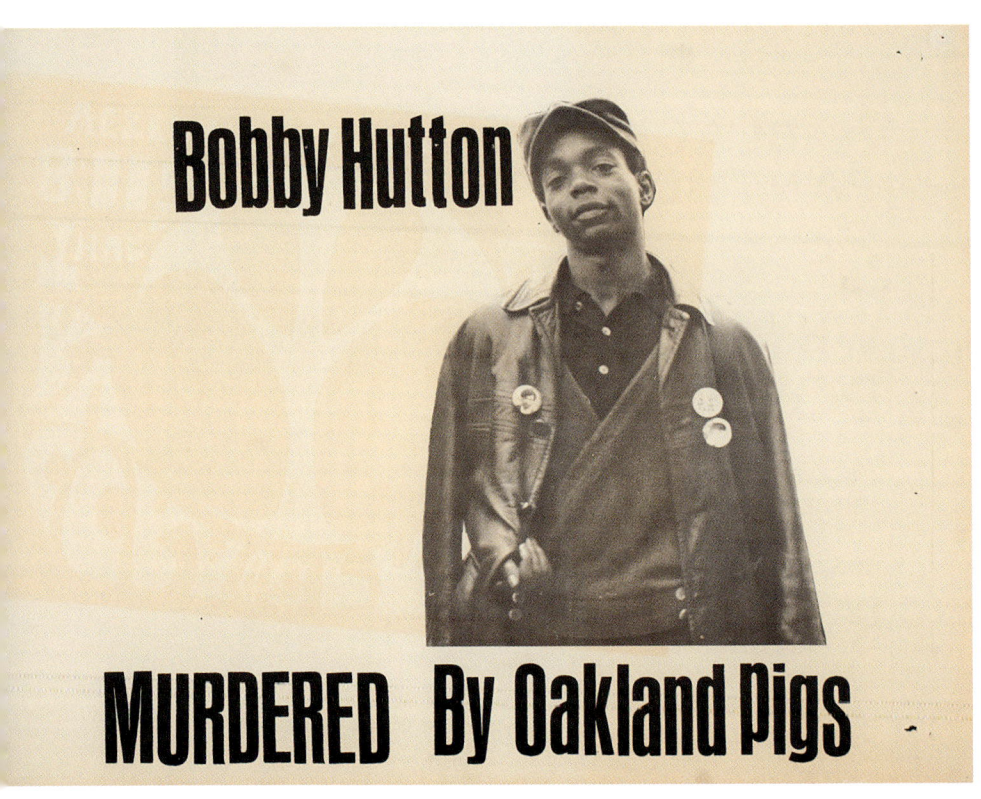

Bobby Hutton

MURDERED By Oakland Pigs

Plate 2 (above)   Bobby Hutton Memorial March flyer, ca. 1968, offset.
Image courtesy of Lincoln Cushing and the Lisbet Tellefsen Collection.

Plate 3 (right)   "Black Panther Party Member Bobby Hutton Carries
a Loaded Shotgun in Front of the Oakland Police Station in
This Undated Photo." Ron Riesterer/staff archives, *East Bay Times*.

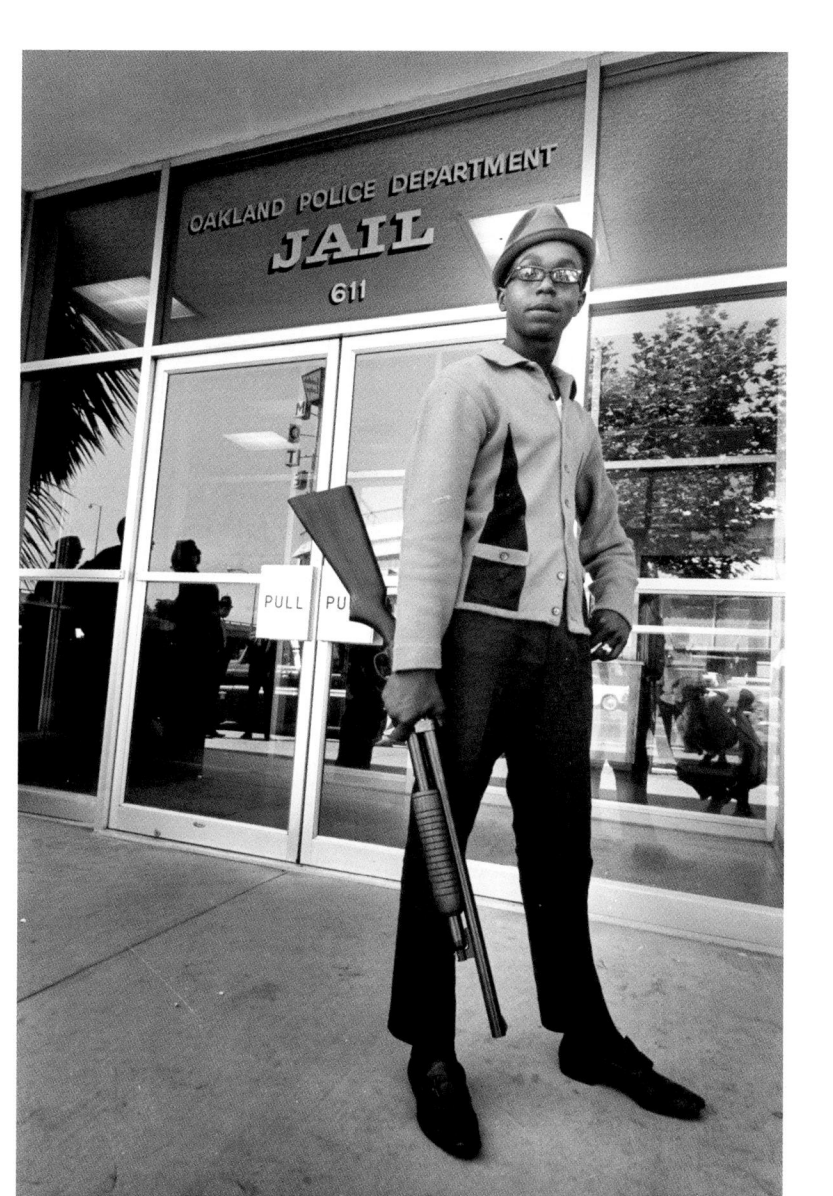

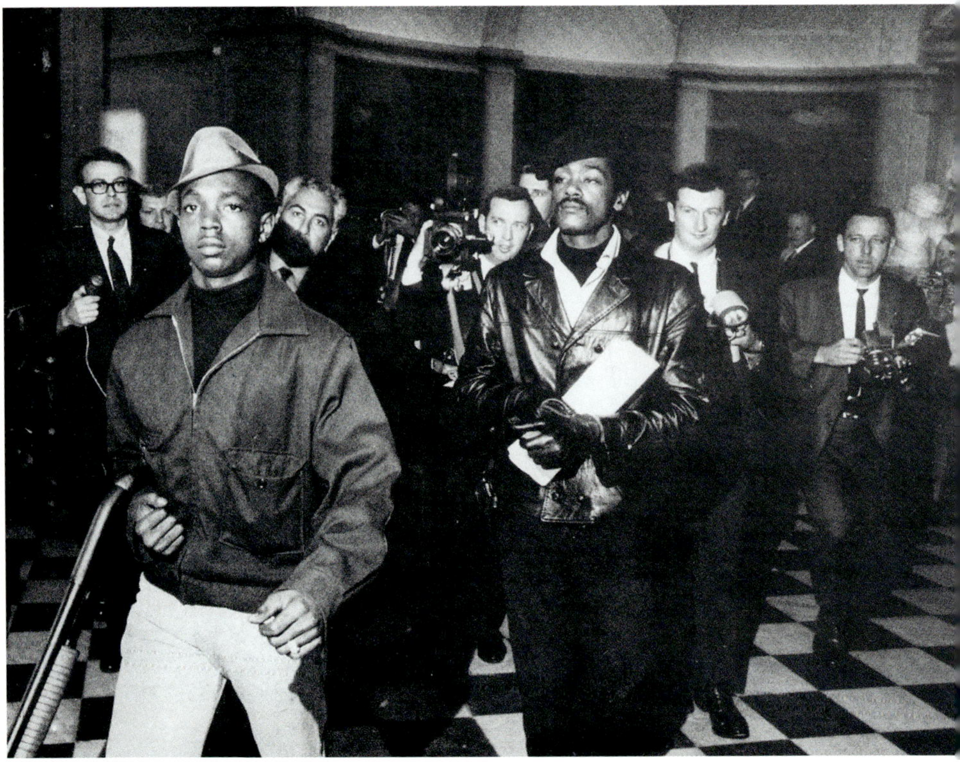

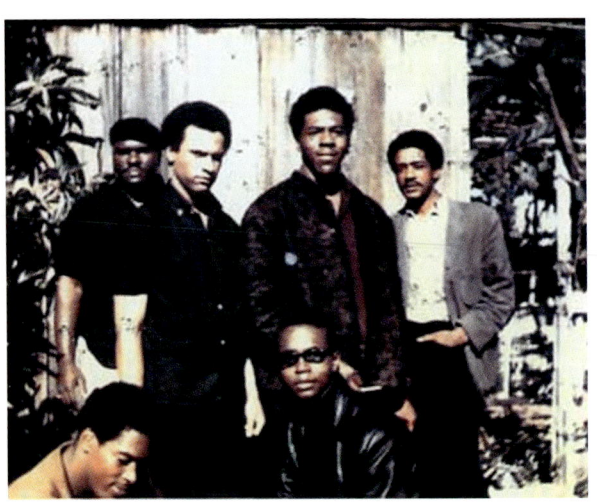

Plate 4 (top left)   Wade Sharrer, "Black Panthers Bobby Hutton, Bobby Seale Storm Capitol w Guns." *Sacramento Bee*, 1967.

Plate 5 (bottom left)   Black Panther originals (*clockwise from top left*) Big Man, Huey, Sherman Forte, Bobby Seale, Lil' Bobby Hutton, and Reggie Forte.

Plate 6 (below)   Bobby Seale and Bobby Hutton, detained at Oakland Police Department while their guns are checked. Photo by Ron Riesterer, 1967.

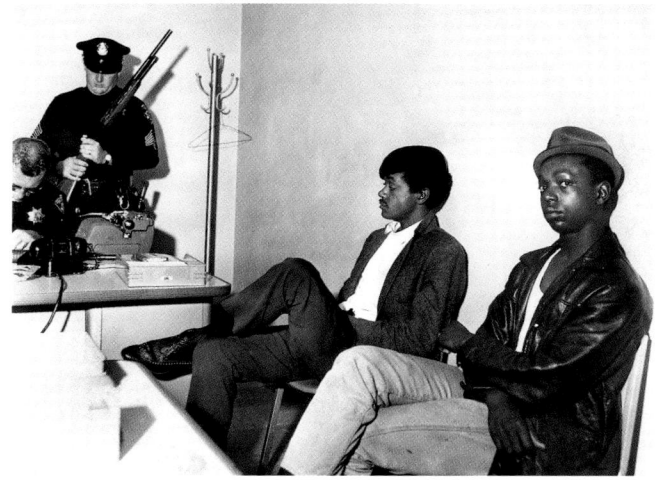

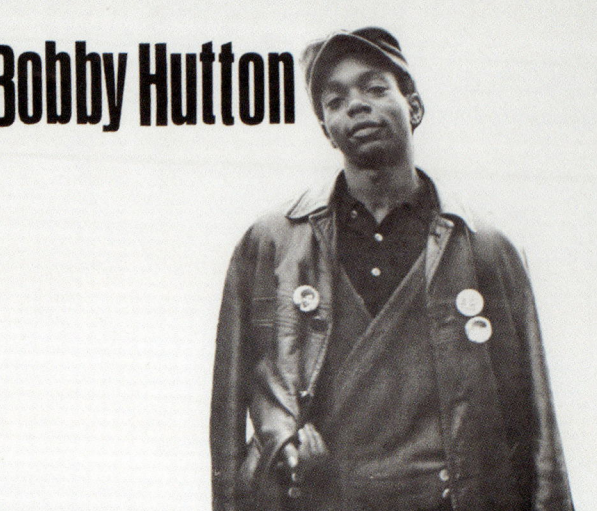

Plate 7 (above)   Bobby Hutton Memorial March flyer, ca. 1968, offset.
Image courtesy of Lincoln Cushing and the Lisbet Tellefsen Collection.

Plate 8 (right)   *Berkeley Barb*, April 12, 1968. Image courtesy of Raquel Scherr.

IN COLD BLOOD

HOW THEY KILLED HIM --story below

Berkeley Barb

VOL. 6 No. 15 ISSUE 139 (PUB. FRIDAYS) April 12 – 18
2886 TELEGRAPH AVE., BERKELEY, CALIF. 94705 841-9470

204

15¢ BAY AREA   **20¢ ELSEWHERE**

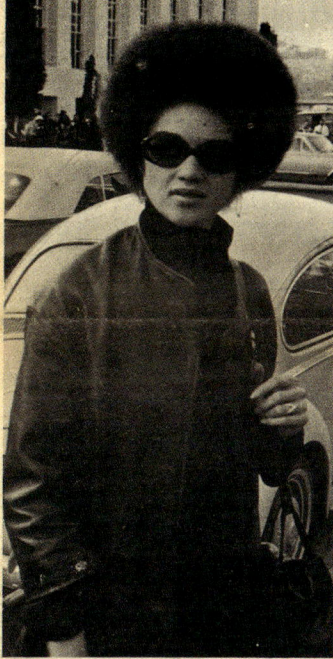

Photo by Reim

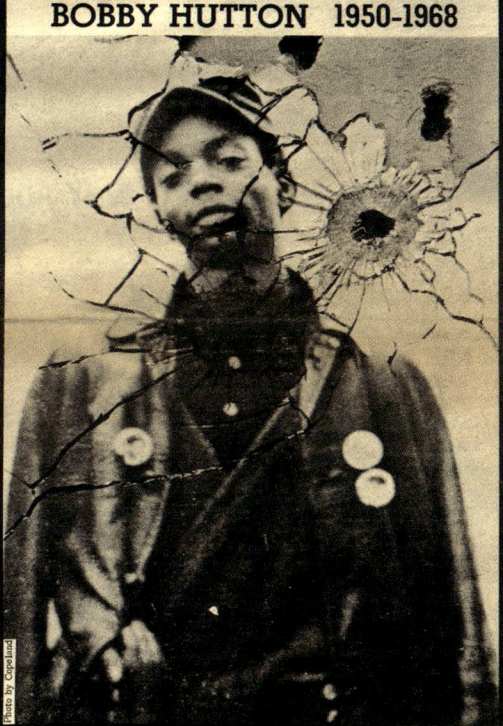

BOBBY HUTTON 1950-1968

Photo by Copeland

EXCLUSIVE
CHARGES COPS SPRUNG TRAP

Kathleen Cleaver, weary but somehow tireless, came to the BARB offices Wednesday night to talk about the latest police attack on the Black Panthers, in which young Bobby Hutton was gunned down and her husband was yanked off to prison.

She made it clear that each attempt by police to chop down the Panthers' leadership has only made their black liberation movement grow larger and more determined.

"The support we've received for Eldridge Cleaver is tenfold what we received when Huey Newton was shot, and we thought that support

see page 11

The first one out was Bobby Hutton.

He emerged, his hands in the air, from a burning tear-gassed basement where eight of his Black Panther brothers were still holed up. He stepped into the bright searchlight. Oakland police shot him dead.

Bobby James Hutton, Black Panther treasurer, is now a martyr of the fight for

see page 3

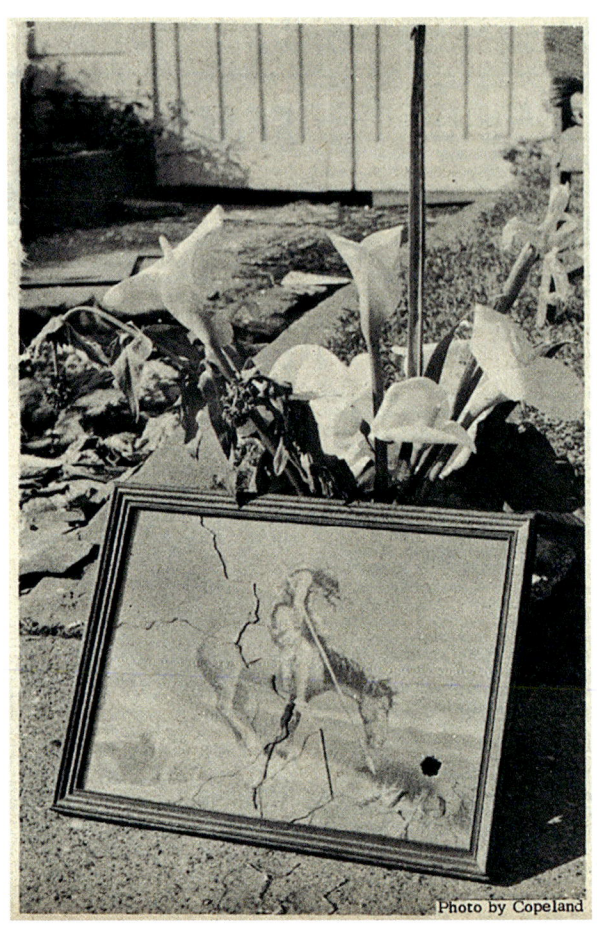

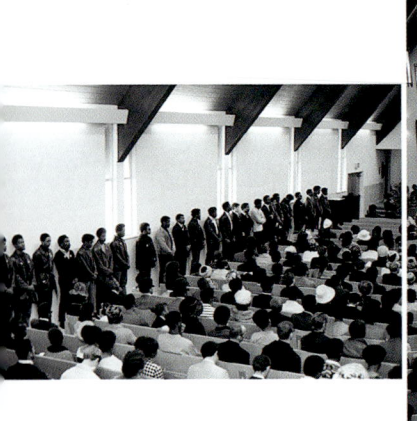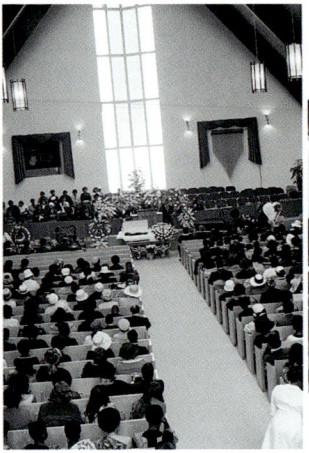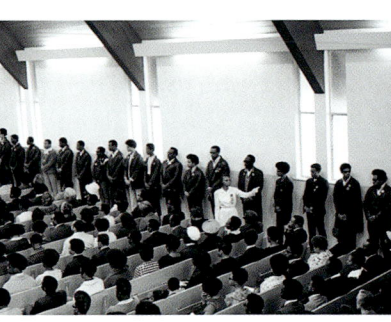

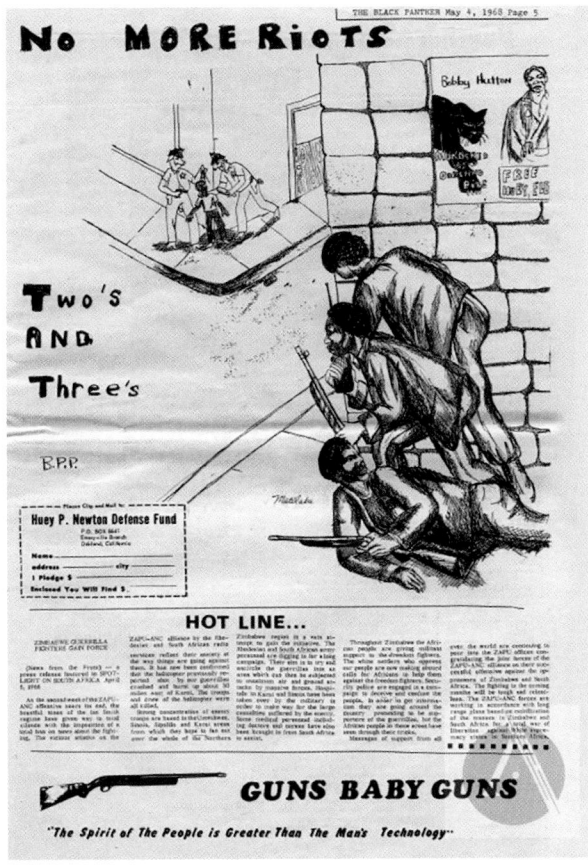

Plate 9 (top left)   *Berkeley Barb*, April 12, 1968, detail. Image courtesy of Raquel Scherr.

Plate 10 (bottom left)   "Funeral for seventeen-year-old Panther Bobby Hutton, known as 'Lil' Bobby,' at Ephesians Church of God. Hutton was killed by the Oakland police on April 6, two days after the assassination of Martin Luther King. Berkley, April 12, 1968." Stephen Shames.

Plate 11 (above)   Joan Tarika Lewis drawing, May 4, 1968.

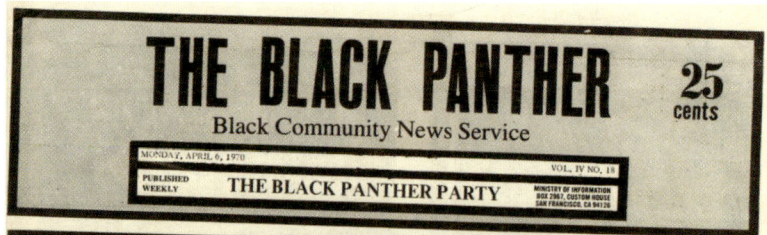

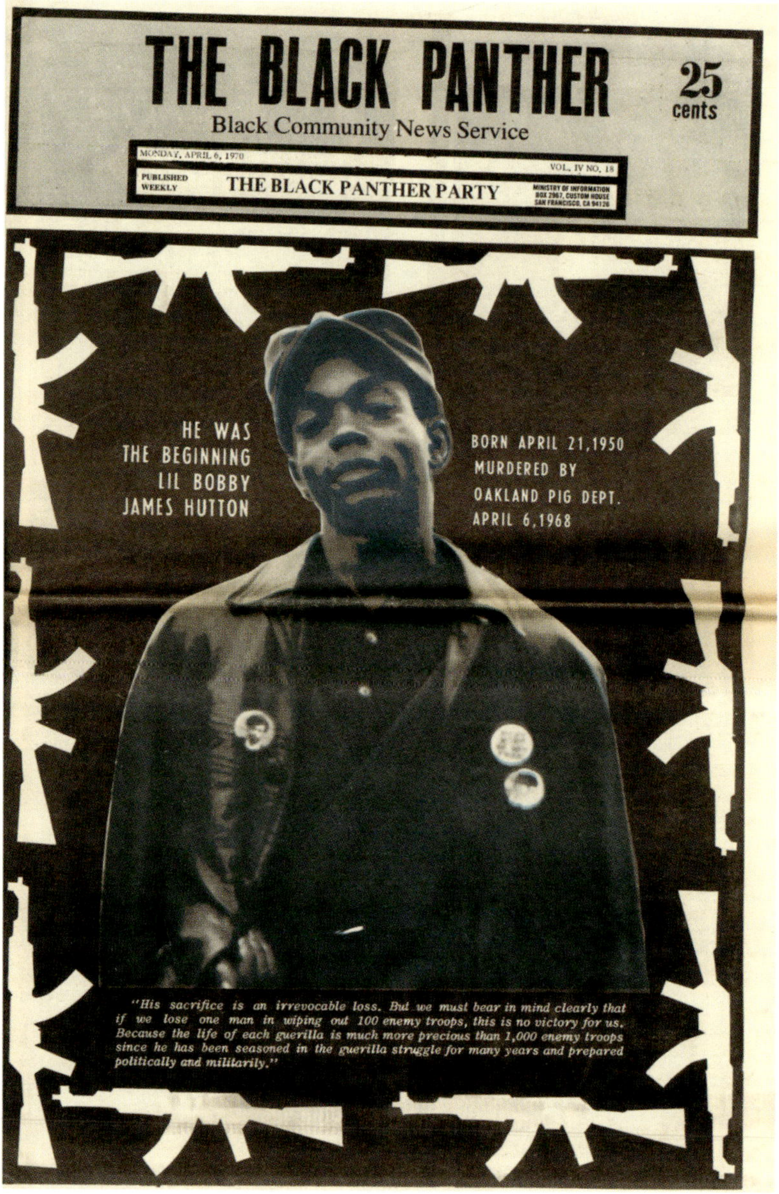

Plate 12 (above)   *Black Panther*, April 6, 1970.

Plate 13 (right)   Emory Douglas, April 3, 1971.
© 2020 Emory Douglas / Artists Rights Society (ARS), New York.

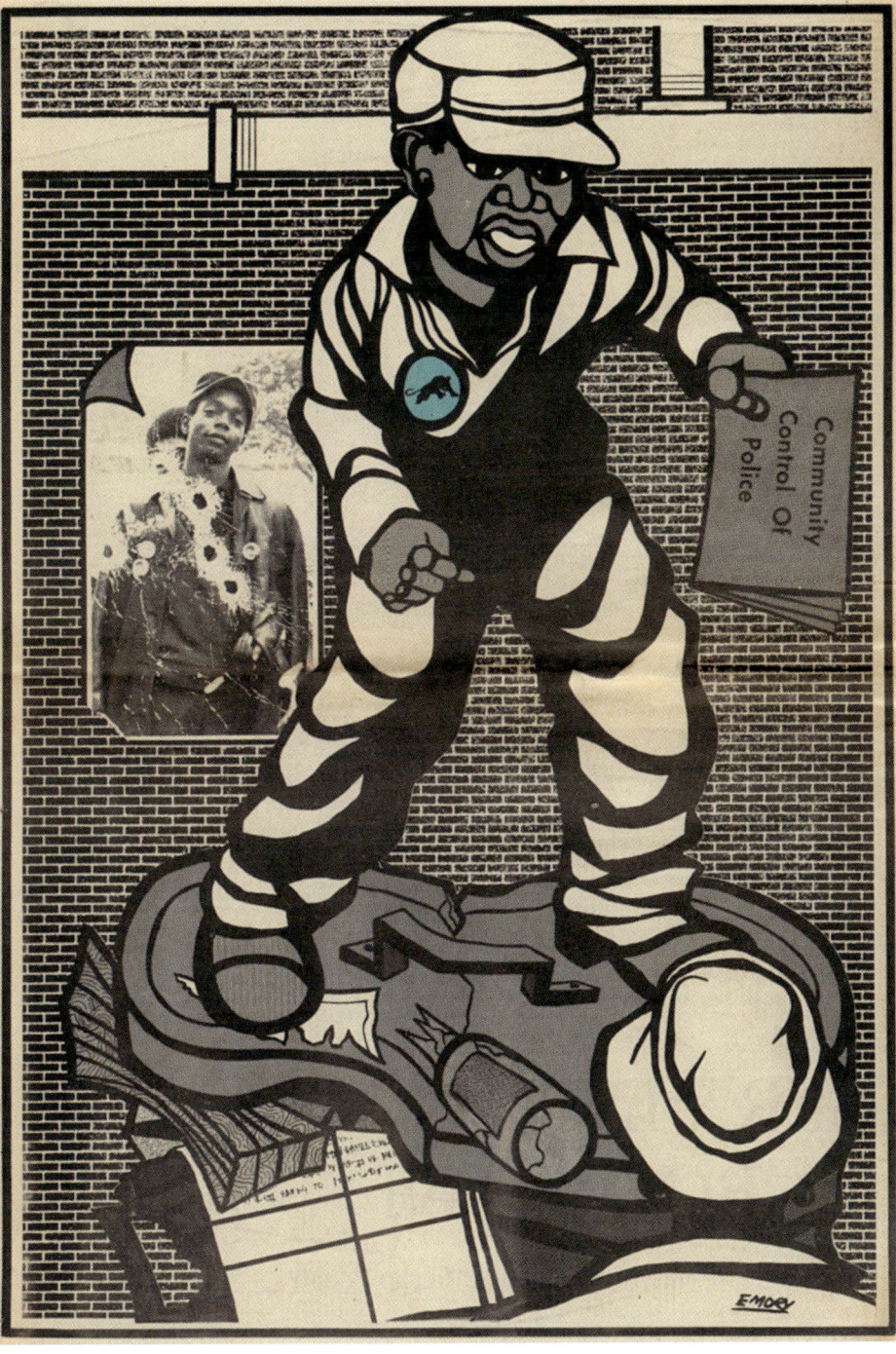

Panthers Ambushed--One Murdered

The Minister of Information, Eldridge Cleaver, is behind bars for life as a result of an attempted assassination on his life by the Oakland Police Department, the Gestapo strongarm of the racist power structure.

Eldridge Cleaver, Bobby Hutton, and eight other brothers were ambushed by the Oakland pigs on April 6, 1968... a set-up to put Eldridge Cleaver in prison for life and to wipe out the leadership of the Black Panther Party.

As a result, Bobby Hutton is dead, brutally murdered by a volley of pig bullets as he surrendered with his arms above his head.

The Minister of Information's parole was immediately revoked, and he is now imprisoned for three years, and faces life imprisonment on the charges stemming from the ambush. Cleaver was shot, has numerous buckshot wounds in his legs, was severely burned by tear gas on his chest and in his eyes. Police transported Cleaver from Oakland to Vacaville State Medical Facility "for security reasons" under machine gun guard, chained to a wheelchair, and heavily drugged.

Bail for Eldridge Cleaver was set at $63,000 even though it is strictly nonfunctional bail since

peared on the scene thoroughly equipped with riot helmets, OVER-KILL weapons, tear gas bombs... AND had notified the local racist press, who were on the spot as evidenced by their pictures and falsified radio reports from 10pm throughout the night.

The pigs fired off at least 1500 rounds of ammunition and shot numerous tear gas bombs into the residence to force Cleaver and Bobby Hutton out as well as randomly dangering the safety of other ghetto dwellers on the same block by firing aimlessly into their houses. When this tactic failed, the pigs and members of the Oakland Fire Department set fire to the house and forced the two to surrender.

Driven out by the burning flames and the stifling fumes of the tear gas, Bobby surrendered first, staggering out with his hands up – DEFENSELESS, UNARMED, OVERCOME BY FUMES – putting himself at the evil mercy of the pigs who waited until they recognized him and then gunned him down, killing him instantly and riddling his lifeless body with bullets.

The Minister of Information, who had had Hutton take off his clothes in the basement, to determine the

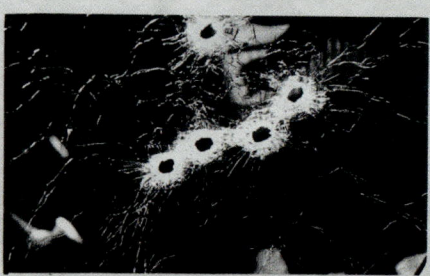

POLICE MURDERED A MAN, IMPRISONED A MAN, JAILED SEVEN OTHERS, RUINED THIS HOUSE AT 1218 - 28th ST, OAKLAND, AND SHOWED THE COUNTRY AND THE WORLD THE EXACT NATURE OF THE RACIST OPPRESION IN THE U.S.

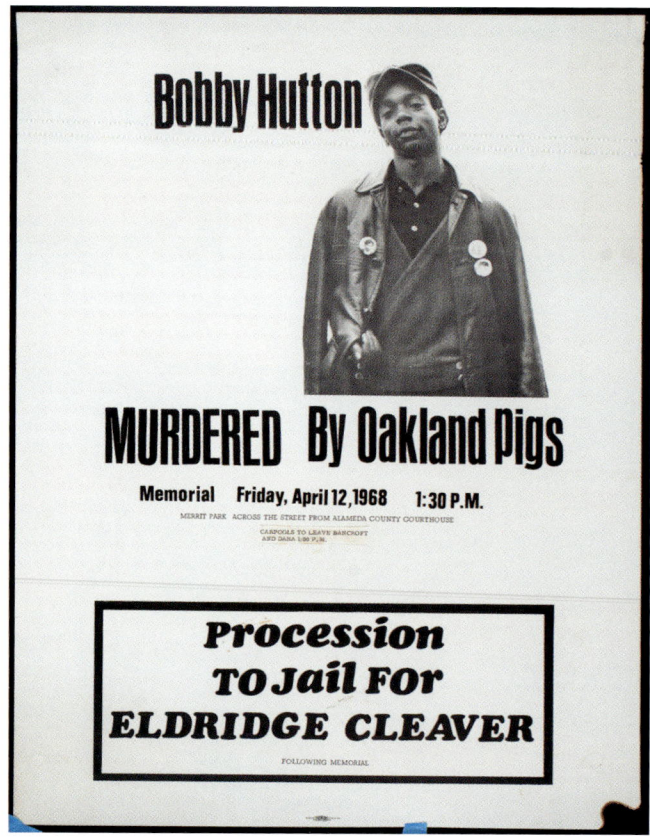

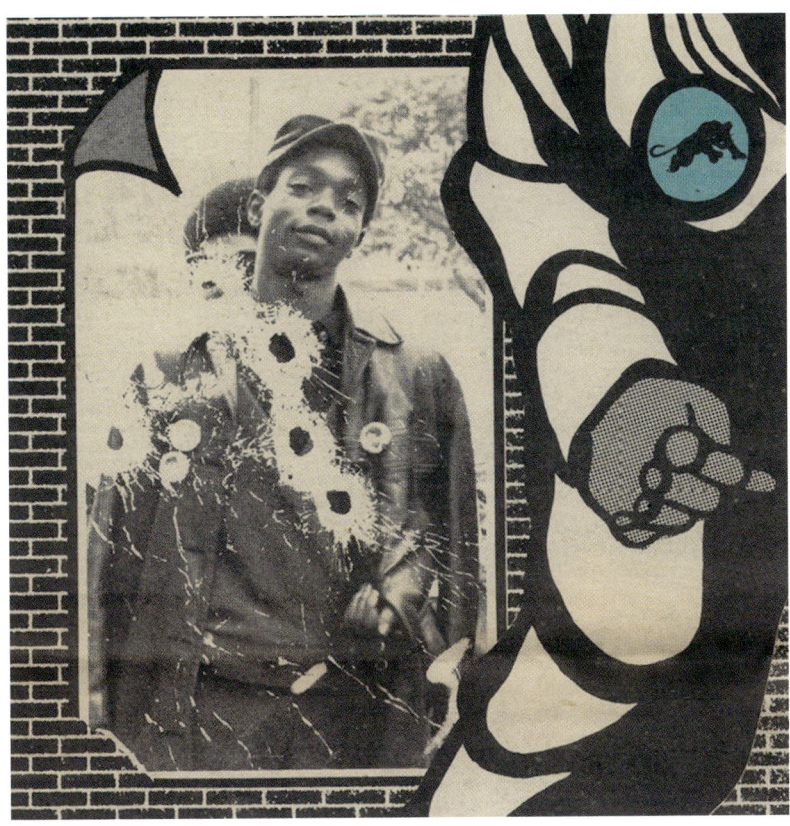

Plate 14 (top left)   *Black Panther*, May 4, 1968.

Plate 15 (bottom left)   Bobby Hutton Memorial March flyer, ca. 1968, offset.
Image courtesy of Lincoln Cushing and the Lisbet Tellefsen Collection.

Plate 16 (above)   Detail, Emory Douglas poster.
© 2020 Emory Douglas / Artists Rights Society (ARS), New York.

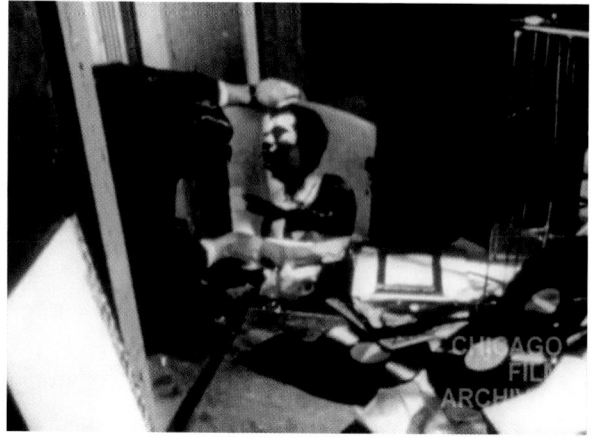

Plates 17–25 *The Murder of Fred Hampton* film stills, 1971. The film stills are printed here with generous permission from filmmaker Mike Gray and the Chicago Film Archives. *The Murder of Fred Hampton* is distributed by Facets Multimedia and can be purchased through its website.

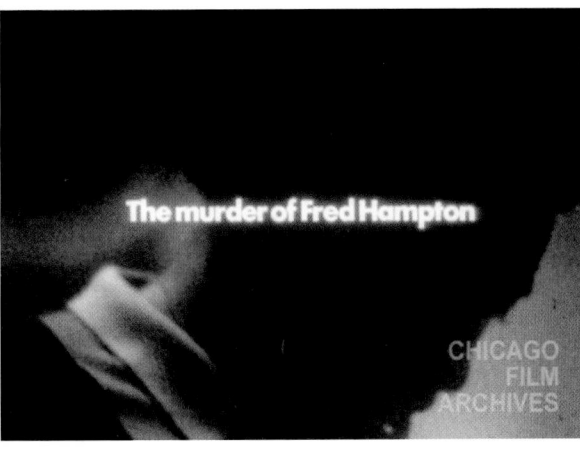

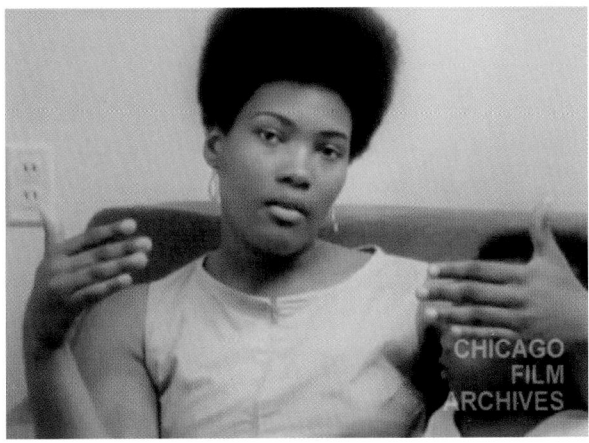

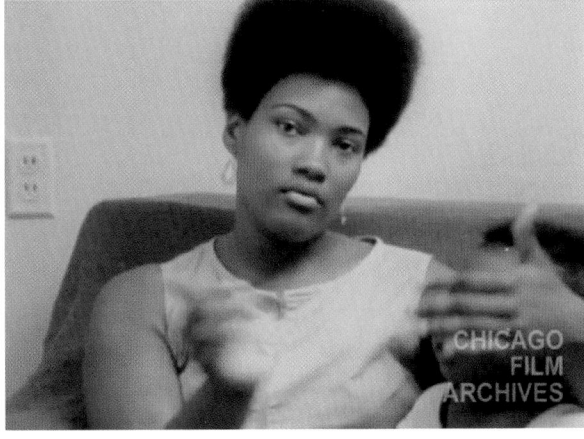

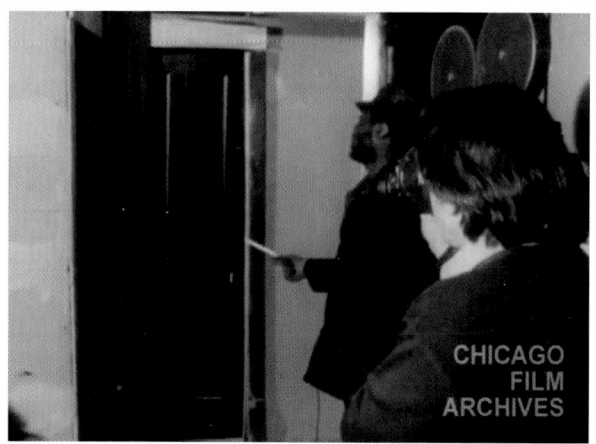

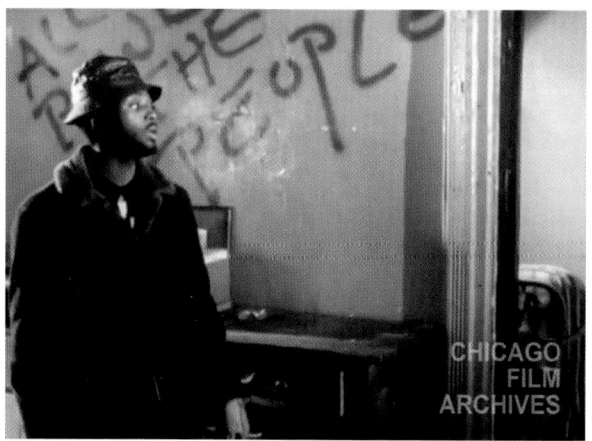

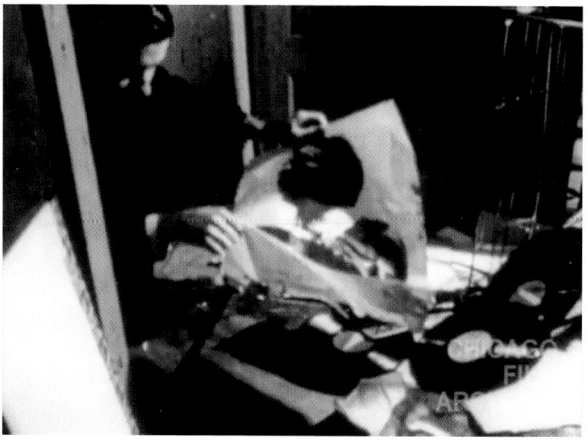

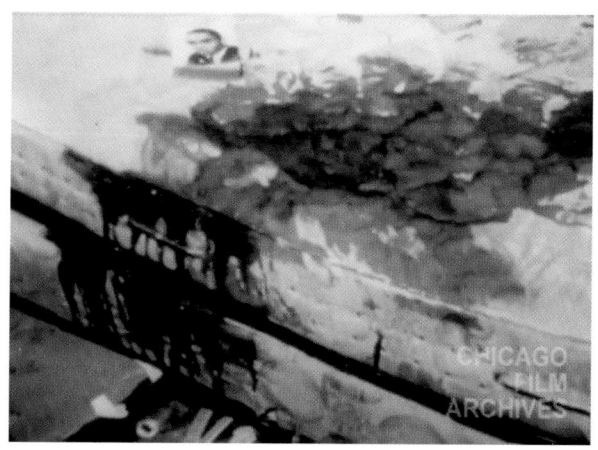

AND I HOPE THAT EACH ONE OF YOU WILL
BE ABLE TO DIE IN THE INTERNATIONAL
PROLETARIAN REVOLUTIONARY STRUGGLE

OR YOU'LL BE ABLE TO LIVE IN IT.
AND I THINK THAT STRUGGLE'S
GOING TO COME.

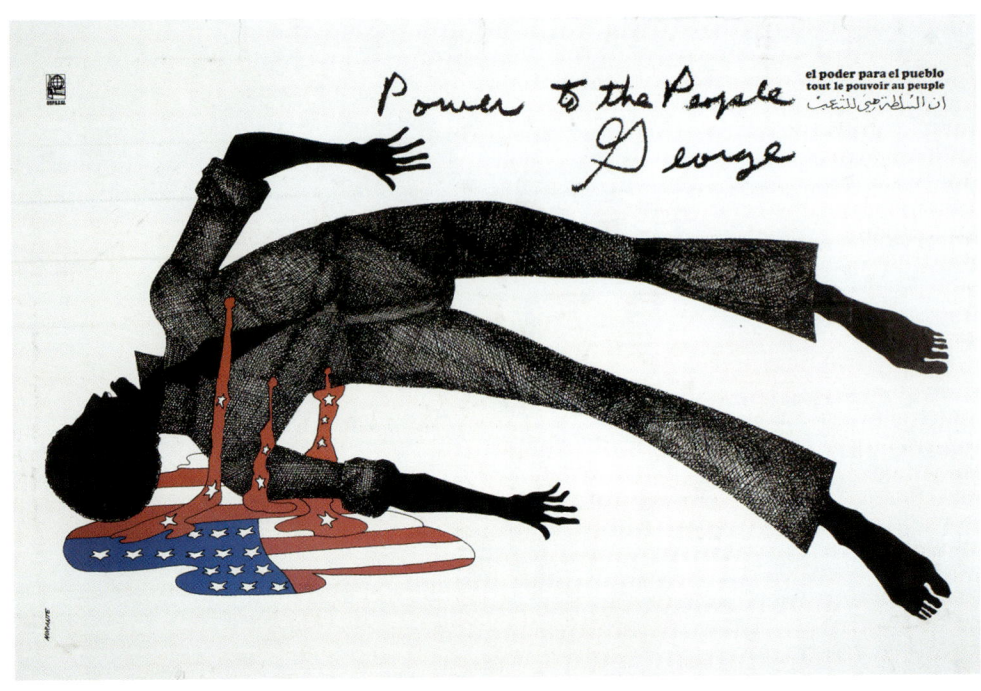

Plate 26 (above)   Rafael Morante (OSPAAAL), *Power to the People George*, 1971, 20 in. × 28.5 in., offset. Image courtesy Lincoln Cushing/Docs Populi.

Plate 27 (right)   Elizabeth Catlett, *And a Special Fear for My Loved Ones* (formerly *The Negro Woman*), published 1947, printed 1989.

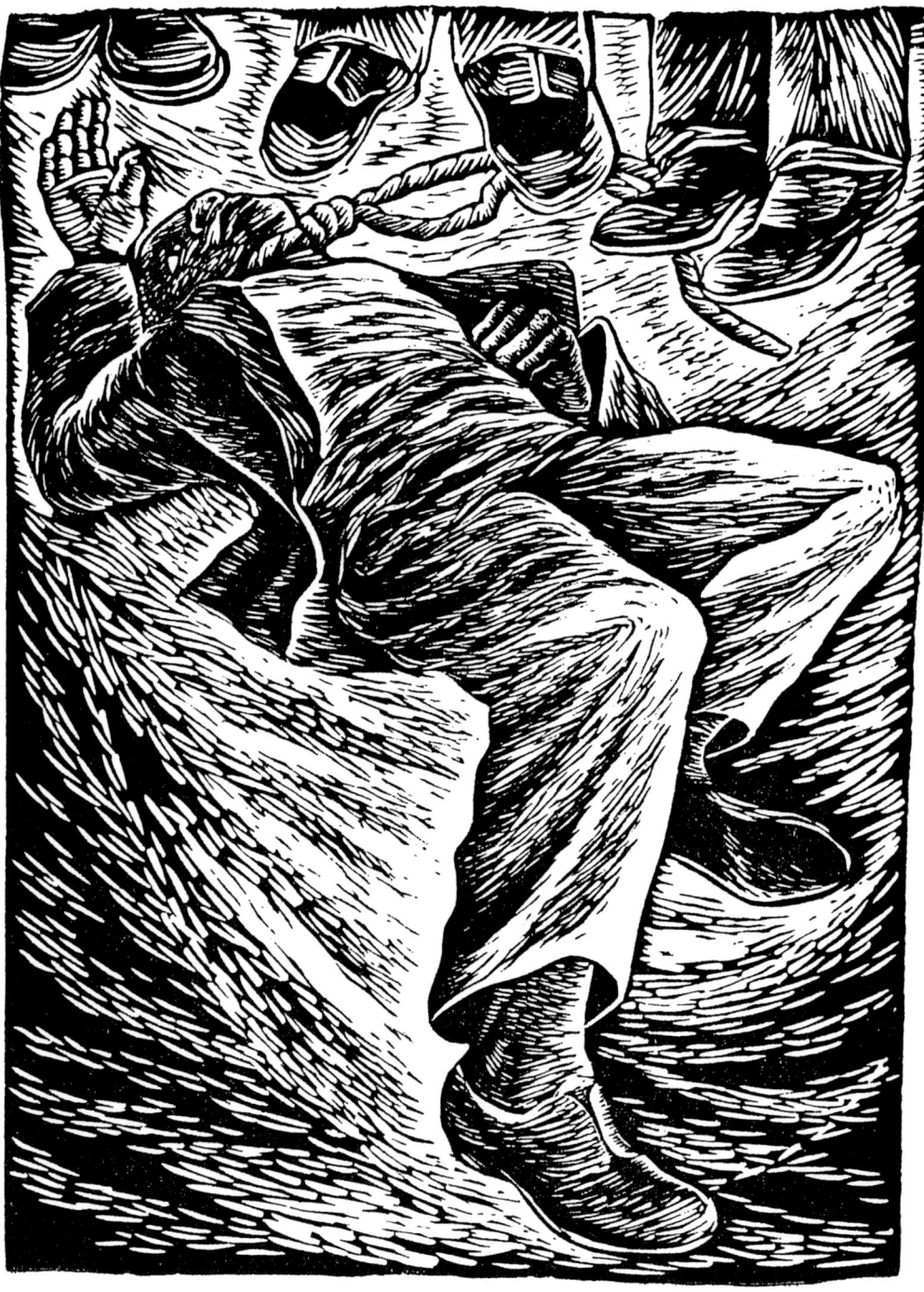

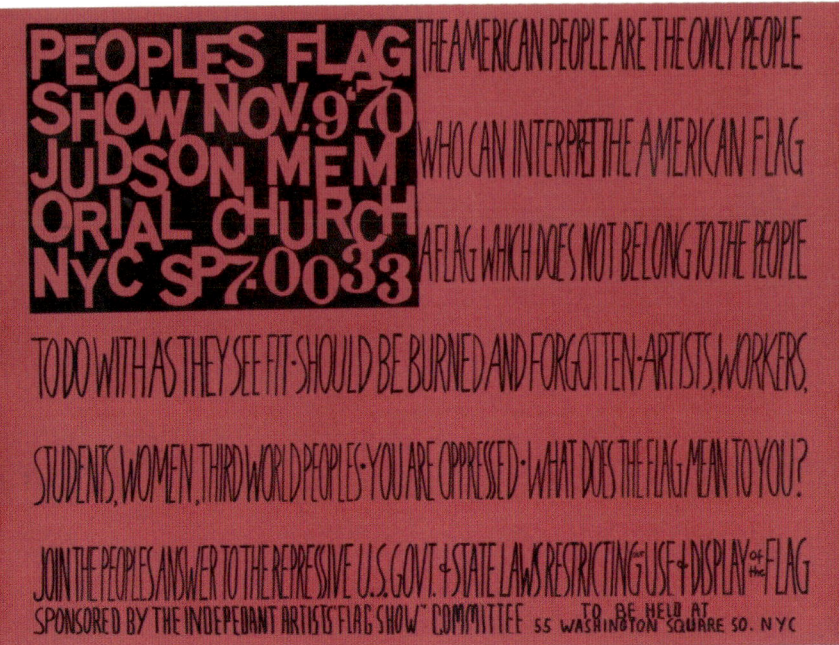

Plate 28 (above)   Faith Ringgold, *People's Flag Show*, 1971,
offset lithograph, 18 in. × 24 in. (45.7 cm. × 61 cm.).
Museum of Modern Art, the Abby Aldrich Rockefeller Endowment for Prints.

Plate 29 (right)   David Hammons, *Injustice Case*, 1970, print,
body print (margarine and powdered pigments), and American flag,
sheet, 63 in. × 40 1/2 in. Museum Acquisition Fund (M.71.7),
Prints and Drawings Department, Los Aneles County Museum of Art.

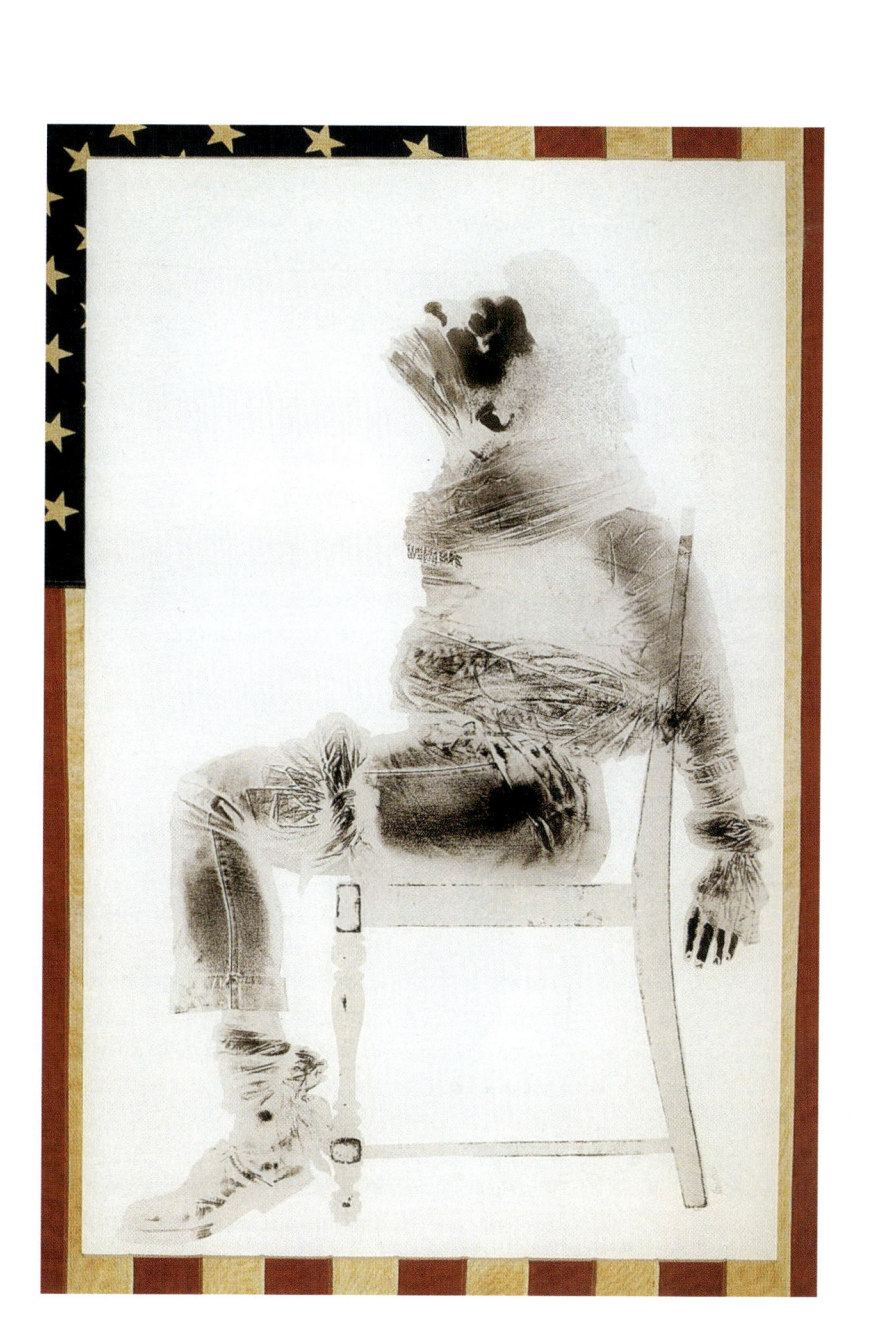

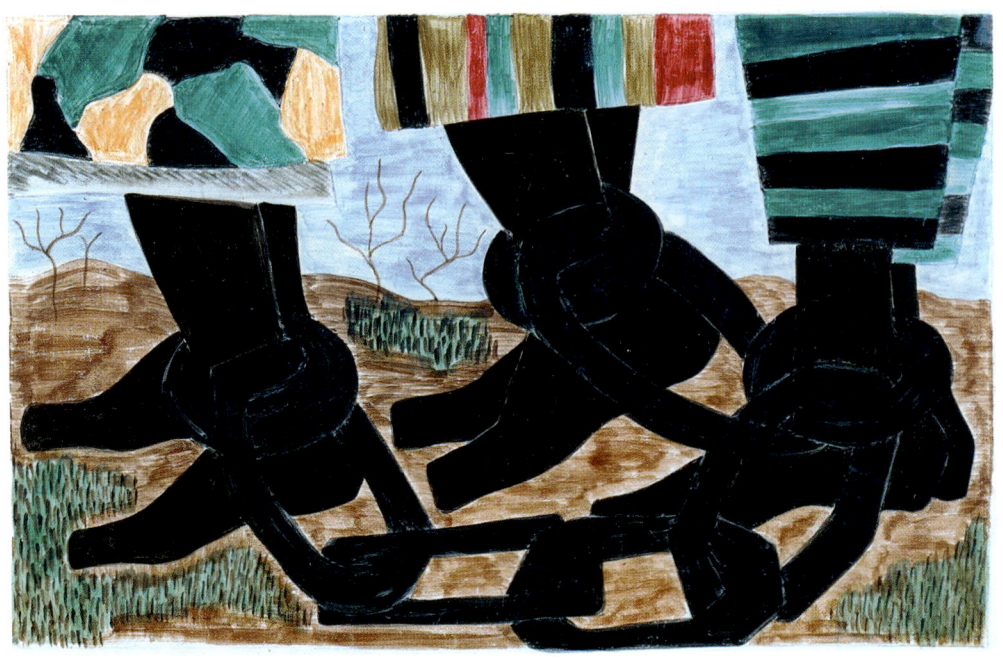

Plate 30 (above) Jacob Lawrence, panel no. 9, "Harriet Tubman dreamt of freedom ('Arise! Flee for your life!'), and in the visions of the night she saw the horsemen coming. Beckoning hands were ever motioning her to come, and she seemed to see a line dividing the land of slavery from the land of freedom," *The Life of Harriet Tubman*, 1940, casein tempera on hardboard, 12 in. × 17 7/8 in. (30.5 cm. × 45 cm.). Hampton University Museum, Virginia.

Plate 31 (right) Jacob Lawrence, panel no. 10, *The Life of Harriet Tubman*, 1940, casein tempera on hardboard, 12 in. × 17 7/8 in. (30.5 cm. × 45 cm.). Hampton University Museum, Virginia.

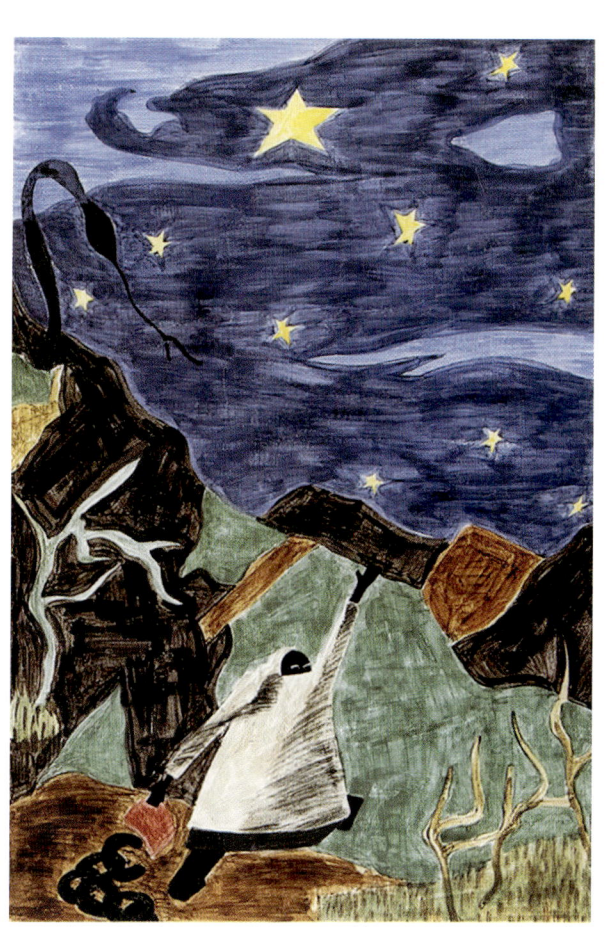

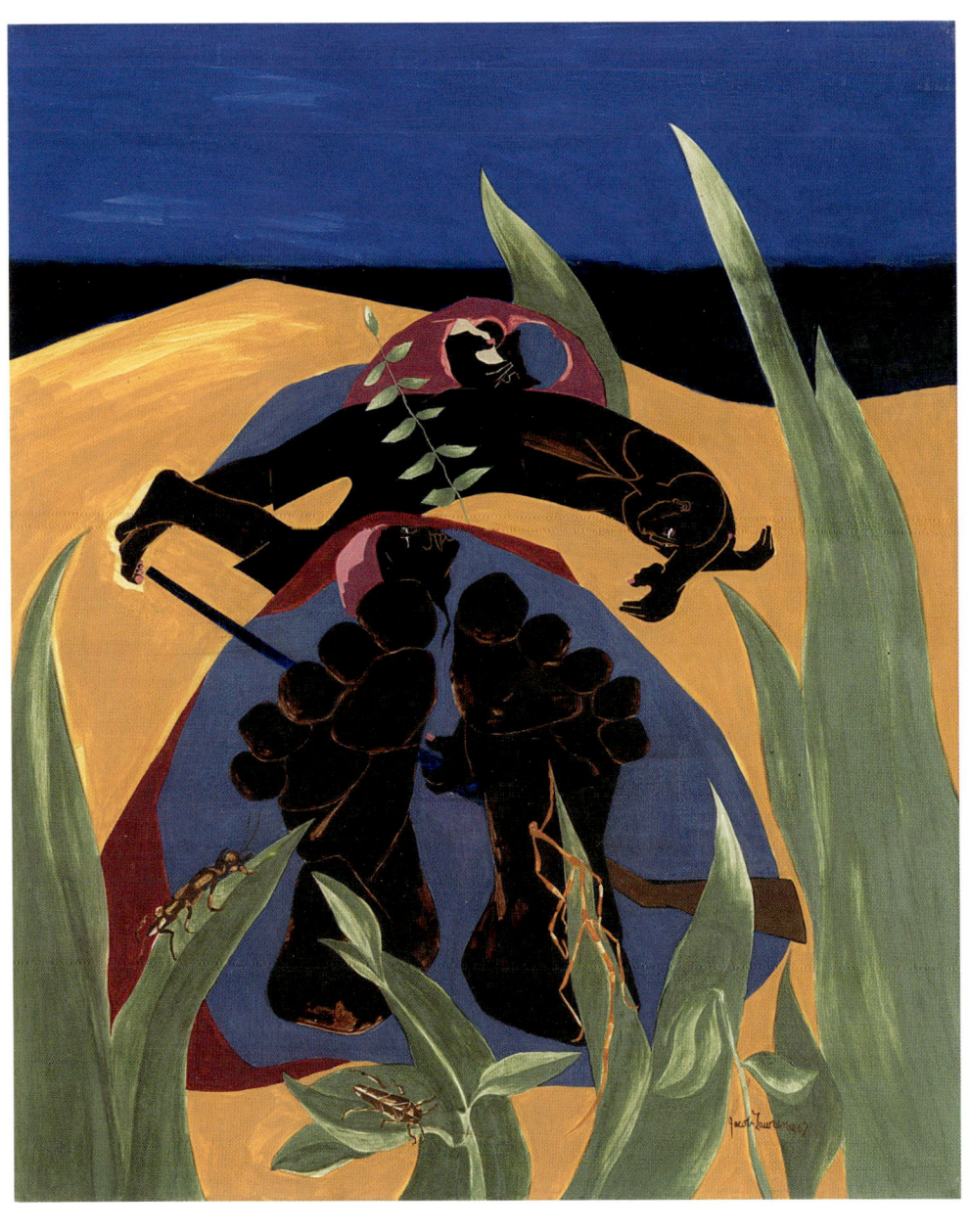

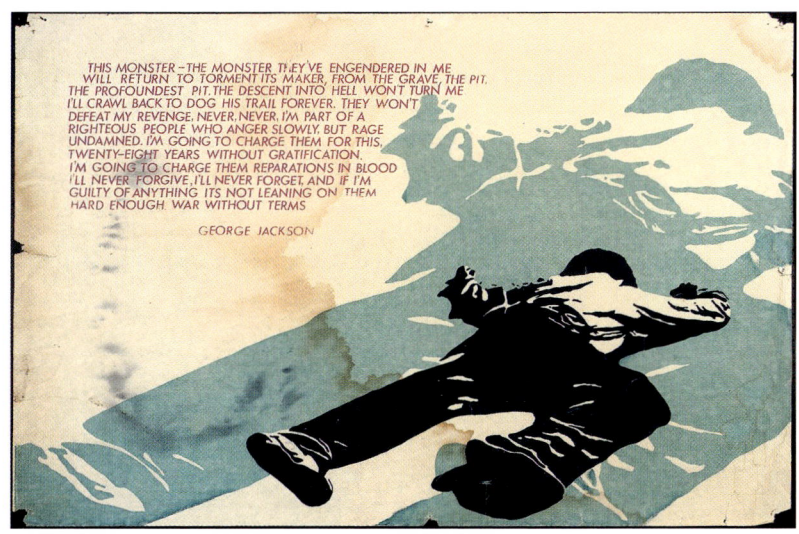

Plate 32 (left)   Jacob Lawrence, "Daybreak—A Time to Rest,"
The Life of Harriet Tubman, 1967, tempera on hardboard,
30 in. × 24 in. (76.2 cm. × 61 cm.). Anonymous gift,
National Gallery of Art, Washington, DC.

Plate 33 (above)   Doug Lawler/East Bay Media Collective,
This Monster, 1971, paper screen print, 20 in. × 30 in.
All of Us or None Archive, gift of the Rossman Family,
image courtesy of the artist and Lincoln Cushing/Docs Populi.

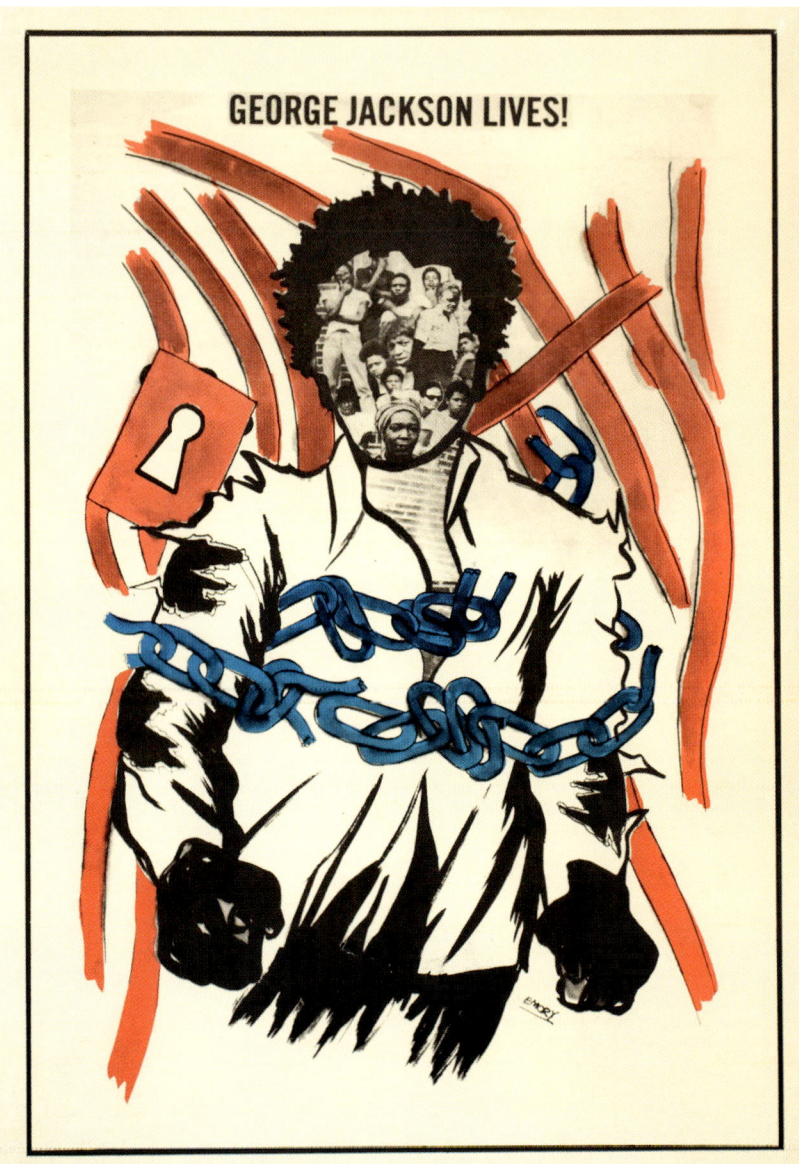

GEORGE JACKSON LIVES!

BLACK PANTHER PARTY CENTRAL HEADQUARTERS   8501 EAST 14th STREET OAKLAND, CALIFORNIA 94621

TO: L. S. NELSON, Warden   DATE: September 3, 1971
San Quentin State Prison

FROM: N. R. SNELLGROVE
SA/CDC

SUBJ: Books taken from cell of George Jackson, A-63837, following
Adjustment Center incident at San Quentin. S.P. of 8/21/71.

1. TO BE FREE by Herbert Aptheker
2. AFRICA: THE WAY AHEAD by Jack Woddis
3. THE EMPIRE OF OIL by Harvey O'Connor
4. A HISTORY OF PAN AFRICAN REVOLT by C. L. R. James
5. REVOLUTIONARY PRIEST by Camilo Torres
6. BLACK SKIN WHITE MASKS by Frantz Fanon
7. THE NEW INFORMATION PLEASE ALMANAC ATLAS AND YEARBOOK - Editor
Dan Golenpaul
8. THE MYTH OF BLACK CAPITALISM by Earl Ofari
9. WHO RULES AMERICA by G. Williams Domhoff
10. MAO TSE-TUNG - Foreign Languages Press, Peking, 1967
11. A DOCUMENTARY HISTORY OF THE NEGRO PEOPLE IN THE UNITED STATES -
Edited by Herbert Aptheker
12. ANTI-DUHRING, REVOLUTION IN SCIENCE by Frederick Engels
13. THE POVERTY OF PHILOSOPHY by Karl Marx
14. FIDEL CASTRO SPEAKS - Edited by Martin Kenner and James Petras
15. HOME TO CATALONIA by George Orwell
16. READER IN MARXIST PHILOSOPHY - From writings of Marx, Engels,
and Lenin
17. THE AGE OF IMPERIALISM by Harry Magdoff
18. AMERICAN NEGRO SLAVE REVOLTS by Herbert Aptheker
19. MATERIALISM AND THE DIALECTICAL METHOD by Maurice Cornforth
20. DIE NIGGER DIE! by H. Rap Brown
21. INSURGENT MEXICO by John Reed
22. PHILOSOPHY OF WORLD REVOLUTION by Frank Marek
23. PRE-CAPITALIST ECONOMIC FORMATIONS by Karl Marx
24. HISTORICAL MATERIALISM by Maurice Cornforth
25. SOME CHANGES by June Jordan
26. THE TRUMPET OF CONSCIENCE by Martin Luther King, Jr.

Plate 34 (left)   Emory Douglas, *George Jackson Lives!*, 1971.
© 2020 Emory Douglas/Artists Rights Society (ARS), New York.

Plate 35 (above)   Inventory of books in George Jackson's cell,
San Quentin Prison, 1971.

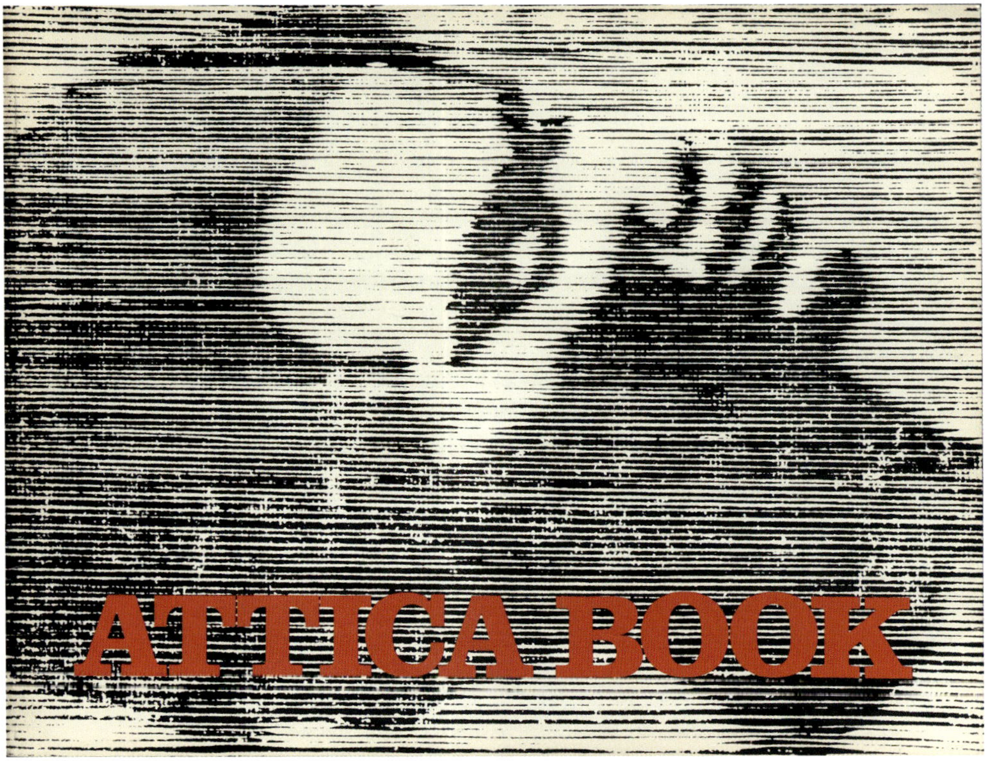

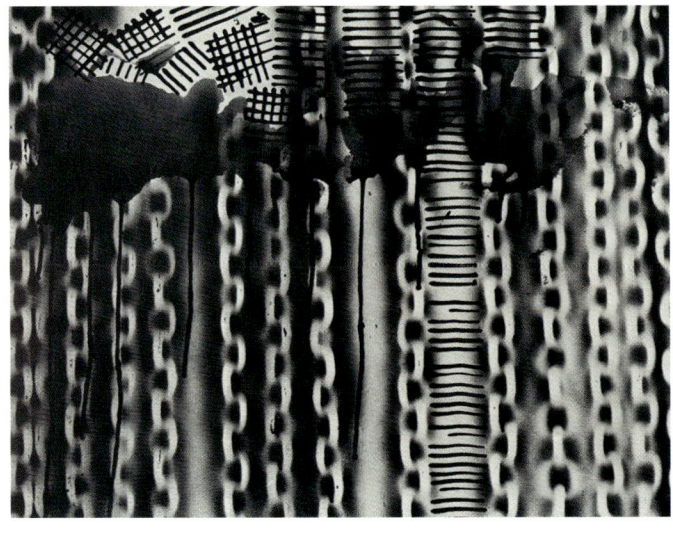

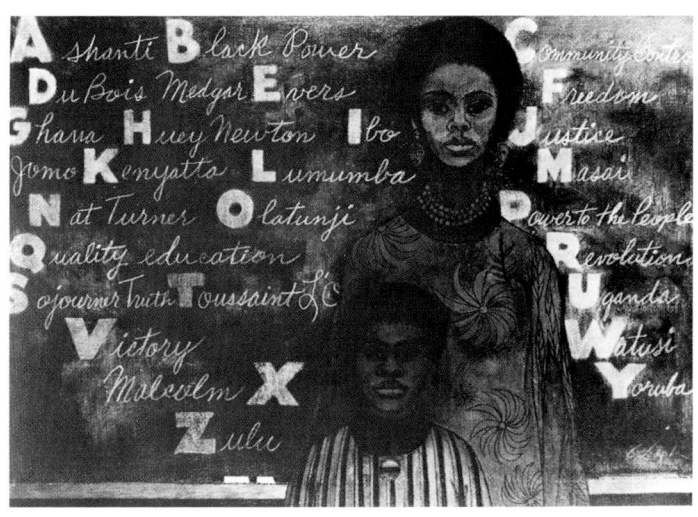

Plate 36 (top left) *Attica Book*, edited by Benny Andrews and Rudolf Baranik. Illustrations; 11 in. × 14 3/16 in., 1972. Book courtesy of Thom Pegg.

Plate 37 (bottom left) Mel Edwards, title unknown, 1971.

Plate 38 (above) Cliff Joseph, *Blackboard*, 1972.

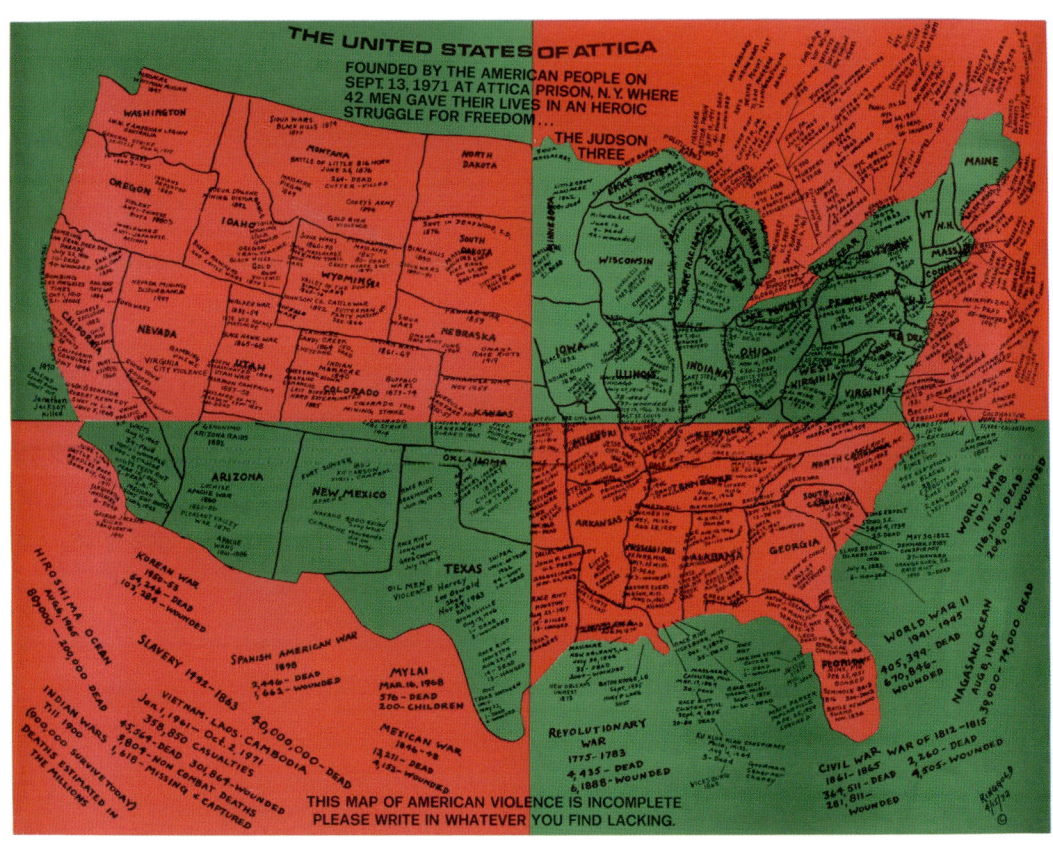

Plate 39 (above) Faith Ringgold, *The United States of Attica*, 1972, offset poster, 21 3/4 in. × 27 1/2 in.

Plate 40 (right) *Black Panther*, September 18, 1971.

THE BLACK PANTHER

INTERCOMMUNAL NEWS SERVICE 25 cents

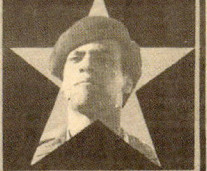

VOL. VII No 4   Copyright © 1971   by Huey P. Newton SATURDAY, SEPTEMBER 18, 1971

PUBLISHED WEEKLY   **THE BLACK PANTHER PARTY**   MINISTRY OF INFORMATION BOX 2967, CUSTOM HOUSE SAN FRANCISCO, CA 94126

MASSACRE AT ATTICA

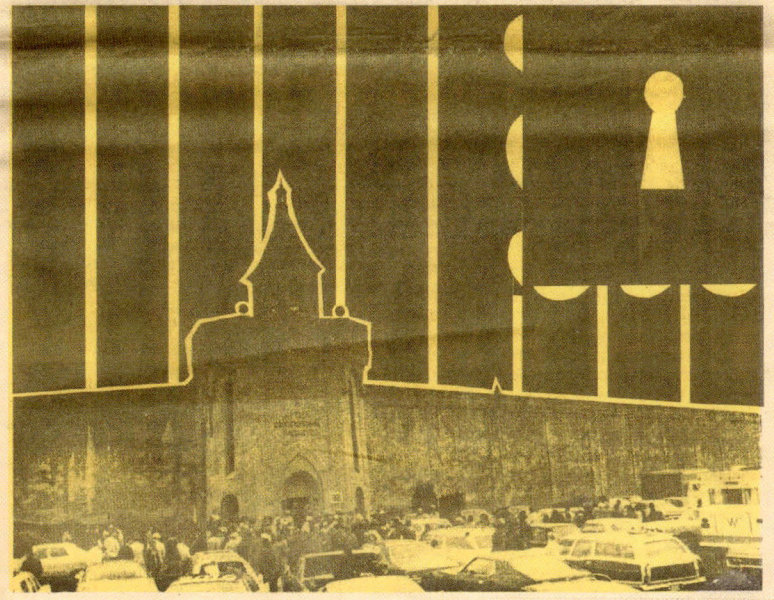

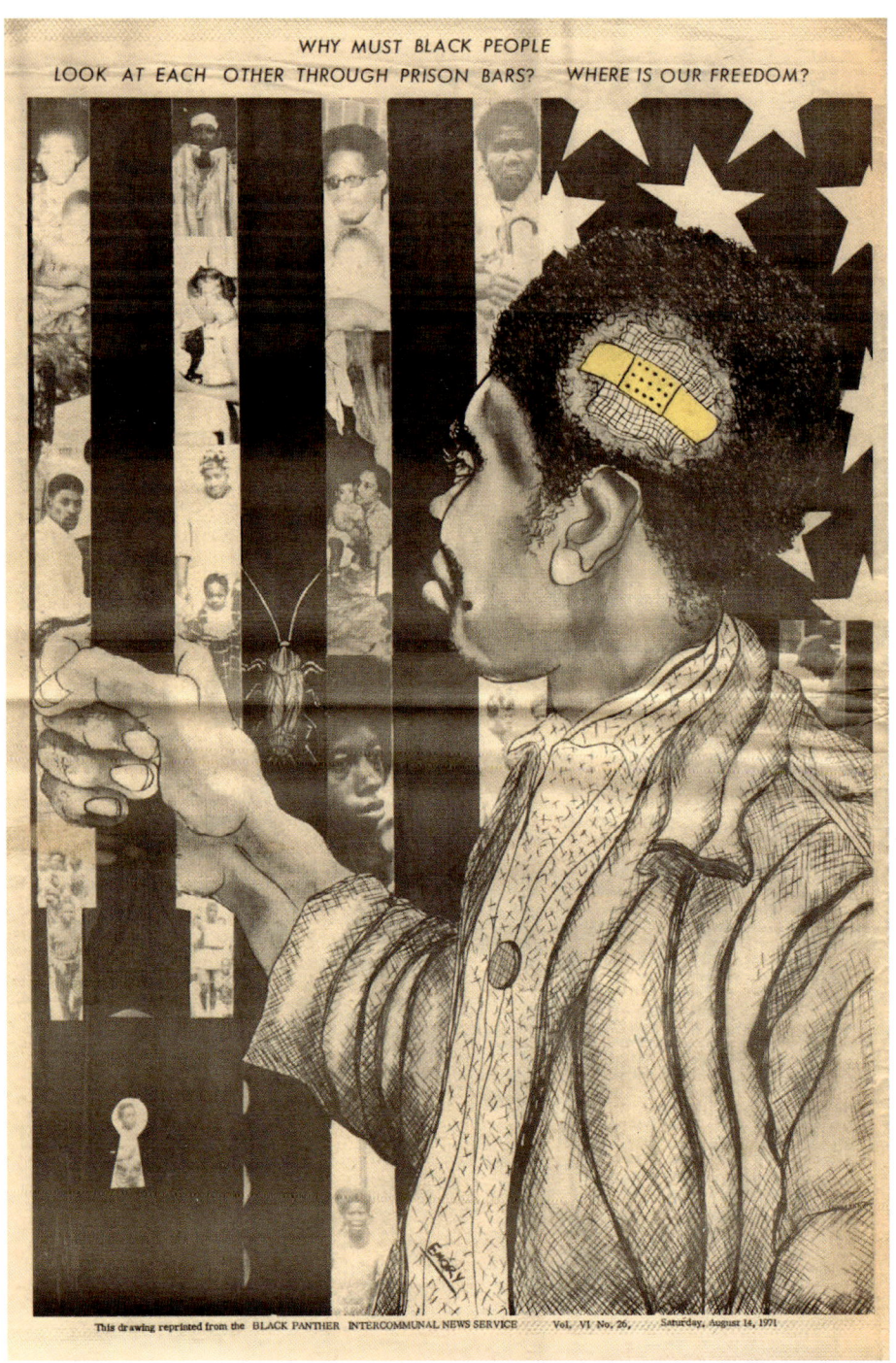

Plate 41   *Black Panther*, August 14, 1971.

Radical Visions: Political Posters and Fugitive Imaginaries

The genre of art objects broadly categorized as political posters are rarely included in art history studies as legitimate objects. As curator and collector Lincoln Cushing acknowledges, political posters tend to be an "awkward orphan in the world of art history."[52] Historically, the genre of the political poster can be traced to the late 1800s, though the production of political posters in the 1960s sedimented them as both "much more political" and a "vital propaganda channel that continues today."[53] In this chapter, *political poster* accounts for art objects developed out of relationships among artists/artist collectives, radical political movements/organizations, and processes of production that propagandize ongoing struggles against the state and capitalism, as well as racialized and gendered forms of oppression. It is from within these relationships that political posters take shape as dynamic cultural productions that enable and fortify visual and narrative declarations between political struggles and social movements. In the Bay Area alone, the majority of political posters preserved and collected by private and public institutions are of, by, or for the Black Panther Party.

In the case of Jackson's murder, political posters are among the few public visual remnants that graphically imagine the conditions of his death and therefore illustrate a particular understanding of Black radical life. Because political posters are "propagandistic pretenders," "crassly commercial," and "lowly multiples on bad paper," they defy high cultural associations with "artwork" in order to reveal realities experienced by the disenfranchised masses.[54] In this way, the "fusion of aesthetics and function" in these posters produces a sense of the visual and material conditions of the political prisoner's murder while also positing a kind of fugitive imaginary that signals Black radical life. The historical context, manufacturing details, and aesthetic decisions deployed in these political posters often reveal radical collective experiences that give us particular insight into Jackson's murder.

The term *fugitive imaginaries* gestures toward an understanding of Blackness still locked in antagonistic tension between the state and any notion of freedom. After all, a fugitive is never free but is always seeking refuge in hiding, always in breach of the law, always threatening the efficacy of the police state. Speaking to the social chromaticism of Black (fugitive) life, theorists Stefano Harney and Fred Moten poetically meditate on how the "work of blackness is inseparable from the violence of blackness."[55] Blackness, in their formulation, is presented as "something ungovernably, fugitively living in us," though that "us" and that "something" are far from reductively essential and innate to Black people.[56] Indeed, the pair insist that ungovernability extends even to "those understandings of blackness to which black people are given" because even the concept of Blackness resists fixity "since fugitivity escapes even the fugitive."[57] Instead, Blackness "still has work to do" to "discover the re-routing encoded in the work of art," to see how violence that forms Blackness is "where beauty and technique come back."[58] This emphasis on the aesthetic, erratic, ungovernable qualities of Blackness offer up a notion of fugitivity that relies on an encounter with Black radicality that is criminal, defiant, and utterly resistant. This is where my notion of fugitive imaginaries dovetails with Harney and Moten's salient theorizations: the aesthetic forms that present Jackson's Blackness also work to account for his fugitivity and eventual death as a means toward the Black freedom struggle. Fugitive imaginaries offer up a new encounter with Jackson's aforementioned desire to transform the "Black criminal mentality into a Black revolutionary mentality."[59] If Jackson's assertion that Black subjectivity is always a kind of Black fugitivity within the state and capitalism's anti-Black organizing logics, then the very notion of fugitive imaginaries open up the condition of possibility of thinking Black freedom. Fugitive imaginaries allow a way of thinking about revolution and Black freedom as these visions are enacted vis-à-vis Black radical death.

The following section addresses two political posters made and distributed in 1971 by two different artists and artists' collectives: the first is by Rafael Morante (Organization of Solidarity with the People of Asia, Africa, and Latin America, OSPAAAL) entitled "Power to the People George," and the second is by Doug Lawler (East Bay Media Collective, EBMC) entitled "This Monster." Both of these pieces aesthetically and politically situate Jackson's murder within a tradition of radical responses to anti-Black violence.

Fugitive Imaginaries in "Power to the People George"

Against a stark white backdrop, "Power to the People George," is scribed in lucid cursive. Next to the script, stacked translations of the slogan appears in three different languages: Spanish, "el poder para el pueblo" ("power for the people"); French, "tout le pouvoir au peuple" ("all power to the people"); and finally, underneath, Arabic, السلطة للشعب وليس للقائد ("the power is for the people, not for the leader").[60] The name "George" only appears in the English translation "Power to the People George." Black ink outlines a stationary body, laid horizontally from left to right, across the page's landscape. On the left-most side, the Black ink silhouettes the figure of a head, mouth open, facing up, with arms and legs also bare and black in silhouetted form. The body lays sprawled out and spans the print from left to right in a bowed arc shape. Dressed in a jumpsuit, sketched in gray cross-hatched patterns, sleeves rolled three-quarters of the way up. The pants billow out to bell-bottoms—a fashion style made popular in the late 1960s and 1970s. His feet are bare, toes pointed toward the edge of the paper's right-hand border. Blood, colored red, white, and blue, pours from three distinct openings in his torso. The blood spills into a puddle, the contents of which are arranged schematically as the American flag. Not only a painting, not only a drawing, not only a declarative political text—this print captures the significant possibilities within the political and artistic genre of the political poster (plate 26).

The poster is offset, a style of printmaking that is most notably used to mass-produce posters for popular distribution. During the offset process, an original inked image is transferred onto a plate, from which it is printed onto a surface. This type or artistic process allows artists or, in this case artist collectives, to produce and distribute a large quantity of posters relatively quickly.

Distributed by OSPAAAL, composed of "representatives from eight communist and socialist organizations and four leftist states" who aimed to solidify "the idea of cooperation and coordination amongst leftist liberation movements and socialist states."[61] Posters like "Power to the People George" appeared as free tear-outs in the organization's publication *Tricontinental*.[62] Artists who worked with OSPAAAL produced hundreds of images for *Tricontinental*, including, most notably, iconic posters of Cuban revolutionary Ché Guevara. Rafael Morante penned this poster in 1971, in the immediate wake of Jackson's murder.[63] While in Cuba, Morante was an active member of the Instituto Cubano del Arte e Industria Cinematográficos (ICAIC), created days after the Cuban Revolution as a way to demonstrate the value of revolutionary arts and culture.[64] Coupled with his ICAIC affiliation, Morante would have encountered works by internationalist, radical Left publications in the Americas like *Freedom Ways* and *Taller de Gráfica Popular*, both of which featured prints and graphic illustrations by prominent Black American artists like Elizabeth Catlett and Charles White.[65] Morante studied graphic design, painting, and lithography at the School of Visual Arts in New York City before returning to Cuba around 1962.[66] During his time there, it is highly likely that he encountered works by White, who had since left New York but who continued to exhibit at the American Contemporary Art Gallery between 1957 and 1963, when Morante would have been in residence in New York City. These speculative glimpses into Morante's biography are offered to open up how the artist would have likely been versed in Black radical aesthetic traditions as a part of a method of establishing visual associations in his works.

In many ways, Morante's poster speaks to the ways in which Jackson's internationalist politics inspired global social movements of the time. For example, the simple translation of "Power to the People" into multiple languages represents both the internationalist spirit of Jackson's political praxis and the poster's ability to translate globally across social movements in several different countries. Known primarily for its mass production of political posters and other visual cultural productions, OSPAAAL influenced global social movements of the 1960s and 1970s because of how these objects contributed to an already burgeoning culture of resistance. While their signature posters often commemorated the life and legacy of Argentine revolutionary Ernesto "Ché" Guevara, OSPAAAL produced and distributed thousands of political posters that mostly celebrated revolutionary social movements all over the third world, primarily those of anticolonial, feminist, and Indigenous rights movements. By depicting his gruesome death—a kind of commemoration that argues his death is emblematic of American political life—OSPAAAL commemorates Jackson's life.

Aesthetically, this poster remarks on the latent visual ambiguity Jackson's body represents. This ambiguity displays the figure as every unknown Black victim of violence and also the unique and particularly American experience of his death. The visual ambiguity of Jackson's subjectivity combined with the poster's commentary on Black radical death in America collide to make a claim surrounding mythologies of sight surrounding Jackson's murder.

In this poster, the figured corpse presented before us is Jackson, indicated by the cursive caption. The caption labors because it relies on particular facts that spectators are assumed to know: (1) the phrase "Power to the People" is notably associated with the Black Panther Party specifically and the Black Power era more broadly, and (2) "George" refers to George Jackson, whose murder in San Quentin sparked rage across global liberation movements at the time. These informational fragments serve to make meaning of the corpse figure inked horizontally on the poster itself. Along with this fragment of narrative text, Jackson's corpse is figured in silhouette— a form that gives us insight into a particular history of anti-Blackness.

Silhouette, as a form, can historically be traced to the eighteenth century as a popular form of portraiture primarily made available to those with upper-class backgrounds or those with limited class mobility. The form itself focuses on the profile of its subjects and captures the shape of the face and figure without necessarily allowing the spectator to identify its subjects by face, expression, clothing, etc. On the one hand, silhouettes allowed access to the realm of representation where a portrait could secure representational future and legacy. On the other, the ambiguity of the silhouette—the fact that you have the outline of someone's face without the specificity of their facial features—leaves room for the figure to be easily misinterpreted as someone else, if associated with anyone at all. As art historian Carol Mavor notes in her insightful coupling of contemporary artist Kara Walker with inventor and early photographic innovator William Henry Fox Talbot:

> William Henry Fox Talbot called the images thrown upon paper by his little camera obscuras "fairy pictures," an enchantment that led him to photography, what he would call "the art of fixing a shadow." Likewise, the silhouette's history is associated with shadows of racism, magic, and the invention of photography. John Caspar Lavater's late eighteenth-century silhouette machine (used for physiognomy) was a seed of the evils of the *racing* of photography.[67]

Mavor historically links the silhouette with other early technologies of racism in order to make sense of how and why attempts to reconstitute the form itself are always clouded with anti-Black meaning. By declaring the silhouette akin to the "evils of the racing of photography," Mavor effectively couples these technologies as race-based tactics of exclusion, representational confinement, and legitimating factors of anti-Black violence.[68] This is why, therefore, the use of silhouette in Morante's poster mandates a closer look or, rather, a *politicized looking* that brings to bear histories of anti-Black violence.

As an extension of this historical form, in this figure there is no facial resemblance to Jackson, no echoed gesture recreated from popular photographs of Jackson himself, and no otherwise verbal or narrative quotes from the deceased that might, at least figuratively, alert us visually to resemblance between the figure and Jackson. On the contrary, the inked figure is a silhouette, wearing clothes that are not specific to place, labor, or class differentiation. Though his sleeves are rolled up, which could represent several kinds of work, we have no other stylized indication of the body's labor. In that same vein, we have no visible indication of the figure's gender. How the body is gendered is left unmarked, thus composing a figure whose gender and class markers are rendered illegible while the body labors Black subjectivity throughout. Because of a fundamental censorship of photographs and other visual evidence from Jackson's murder scene, the silhouette genealogically links Jackson's corpse with the countless number of Black people whose murder was also censored or erased from institutional histories. In doing so, we are given a historical account of solidarity between eras. The use of silhouette visually cites Black visual forms while also making claims to both the sheer volume and anonymity of individual victims of anti-Black violence. By figuring Jackson through the use of silhouette, Morante turns the frame onto how Black subjectivity is conditioned through programmatic violence. Jackson's figure becomes an open space of identification through anti-Black violence and therefore enables a notion of subjectivity that historically engages with histories of lynching. In this dramatic staging, the body in the poster likens itself to the body in Elizabeth Catlett's 1946 linocut "And a Special Fear for My Loved Ones," which aligns itself with generations of Black subjects who remain uncounted victims of racist violence. In this way, George Jackson is historically placed in a genealogy of others whose death is historically charged within sustained anti-Black violence (plate 27).

This kind of representational ambiguity around questions of gender and class disappear into the way in which the figure illuminates the condition of Black radical life. We can think of Morante's artistic choices as negotiating questions of Blackness in America (one argument for the decision to use Black ink for the corpse). He effectively enables us to recall (if not remember) histories of lynching.[69] Drawing on a mid-century tradition of radical graphics and printmaking, I believe Morante's formal choices can be contextualized within this particular moment, when the tradition of artist as cultural worker was crucial to leftist political movements. OSPAAAL definitely came out of this tradition, as artists were considered to be cultural workers whose artistic productions were part and parcel of a global commitment to radical critique and revolution. Their works were considered propaganda to galvanize a people against global injustice and toward more revolutionary forms of world-making. The works produced out of this long tradition share not only in the principles of political content but also in terms of formal qualities and conceptual approaches.

Of particular relevance to "Power to the People George" is printmaker and sculptor Elizabeth Catlett's 1946 linocut "And a Special Fear for My Loved Ones," which rhymes formally and politically with Morante's figuration of Jackson's body.[70] "And a Special Fear for My Loved Ones" is the penultimate print in the artist's fifteen-piece series *The Negro Woman*. The print I turn to in this analysis is housed in the Art Institute of Chicago and is numbered 13 of 50. In the bottom left corner of the print, written in pencil, presumably by the artist herself, reads the work's edition number and title, followed by a signature "ECatlett, '47." In contrast to Morante's poster, "And a Special Fear for My Loved Ones" is oriented in portrait versus landscape and figures a young Black man, laying on his back, right hand raised, and eyes gazing above him. In Catlett's print, the perspective reshapes the viewer's relationship to figure and ground. His entire body cuts the plane of the image diagonally, creating a distortion where the figure's right foot and left knee graze the edge of the picture's frame. Contrasting lines highlight shadow and texture and compose the figure's clothing: nonspecific trousers, shirt, and jacket. A noose grips his neck, the loose end of the rope dangling by his side. To his left, we see three pairs of boots and trousers. It is unclear if the figure's feet and ankles are floating above as if also lynched or if they are surrounding the main figure in an ominous act of danger and violence. The entire print features a fury of striking marks, some sharp, jagged lines and other thicker, fluid shapes that appear to hold, cradle, or furiously sway the subject. There is both movement and stillness in this work, as the stark contrast of black and white leaves no area of the print undefined. Historian Melanie Herzog has noted how both "past and present fears are invoked here," thus speaking to the continuity of anti-Black violence and the lasting impact of the image presented.[71] This understanding of Catlett's print is similar to Jaqueline Goldsby's reading of antilynching political cartoons, where Black artists "could use the drawing techniques of line, proportion, and point of view to determine what and how the viewer experienced the scenes staged in the cartoon's visual field."[72] There is a similar uptake in Catlett's print, where the viewer is encouraged to pay attention to the intensity of the figure's contortion, the rapid crosshatching that resembles movement, and the overwhelming uncertainty that comes with watching a murder attempt. Thus, the act is "no longer a timeless atrocity that bore no relation to (then) present-day cultural politics, lynching is figured as a symptom of modern American living."[73] In this sense, Catlett brings us into a present-tense relationship to the image while also activating histories of anti-Black violence.

I turn to both of these images together precisely because of how they imagine anti-Black violence as a graphic mode of bodily contortion that has devastating impacts on the ways that violence and death are figured within a Black radical tradition. For one, in Catlett's image, the figure's status as dead or alive is left unanswered. The dependent identifiable clues that might help a viewer decipher (open eyes, loose rope) are unresolved: Are his eyes open because he's alive or is this a scene of a corpse whose eyes remain open after the act? Was he freed and saved from immanent death by lynching or was he cut loose post-mortem? These details complicate the image's emphasis on death while also leaving unassailable the fierce terror of anti-Black violence. Catlett's decision to present the figure contorted, seemingly on the ground, highlights the notion of physical impact and raises the possibility of bodily contusions and comminuted fractures. The graphic detail—the level of texture, perspective, and the body's angular stature—connect to Morante's use of cross-hatching, contortion, and lack of gravity to depict Jackson.

Morante's image deploys the contorted body to gesture to the broader history of anti-Black violence as intensely manifested through acts of lynching. Jackson's body's strange position—legs and feet hip-width apart, right arm bent, left arm straight, and sitting in the pool of American flag–colored blood—is made even more uncanny in relation to Jackson's head. Thrown back, mouth slack-jawed, Jackson's head bends at a severe ninety-degree angle facing left. Both Jackson's neck and Catlett's subject's neck are crooked, forcing the head toward an awkward angle. The neck's snap is indicated in the angular, a snap that is most clearly linked to the lynching act. And while Jackson's neck is not secured by a noose like that of Catlett's subject, the bodily contortion presupposes a genealogical link. The angles and bends of limbs, the body's horizontality coupled with its obvious position not in rest but struggle places Jackson's death in relationship to those known and unknown in a broader history of anti-Black violence.

Jackson's body appears as if floating in a nonspace. The only signifier that grounds the location of the violence is the pool his own spilt blood forms, itself dressed in the colors and loose shape of the American flag. It is important to note that while the colors and shape signal the context of Jackson's murder, the terra firma is formed out of liquid—a fugitive substance that registers a particular solidity even while resisting fixity. The use of silhouette, bodily combined with the American flag–colored blood, place this work with concurrent approaches by Black American contemporary artists. To take a slight detour, I find it compelling to shape Jackson's death alongside these concurrent practices in order to further place the instructive uses of death in Morante's print.

By 1970, the use of the American flag was commonplace as a resistant form in popular culture. In November, Faith Ringgold, along with artists John Hendricks and Jean Toche, organized *The People's Flag Show* exhibition at the Judson Memorial Church in New York City.[74] Ringgold designed the exhibition's poster, which adopted the structure of the American flag and supplanted its stars and stripes with an informational and political text written by her daughter Michele Wallace.[75] The flyer was reminiscent of the political poster genre, as the text decidedly adopts language common to leftist movements: "ARTISTS, WORKERS, STUDENTS, WOMEN, THIRD WORLD PEOPLES YOU ARE OPPRESSED WHAT DOES THE FLAG MEAN TO YOU?" Ringgold, herself an artist-organizer with the 1970s Art Workers Coalition, deploys radically attuned language and call and response as ways to directly place issues facing artists as part of a broader realm of struggle identified by popular social movements. The use of the flag here, as redirected into a flyer for a gathering, serves another kind of political function: one that substitutes the stars and stripes for declarative text calling for action. This understanding of a desired collective action and intended public mirrors that of Morante's poster. In a similar move, though without text, David Hammons too repurposes the flag to speak to ongoing modes of anti-Black violence (plate 28).

The same year that Ringgold and her colleagues organized *The People's Flag Show*, David Hammons produced quite possibly his most notable body print, "Injustice Case." This work, a 63-inch-by-40.5-inch body print composed of margarine and powdered pigments, is one of a series of body prints that Hammons completed in the 1970s. These works have been considered in light of the complex and vexed relationship between skin and race in the Black American experience, highlighting Hammons's adept ability to call attention to the processes of racialization as a kind of engagement with the surface, the visible, and various modes of flattening that accompany physical and representational violence.[76] For these works, Hammons used his own body as a matrix, greasing his skin with margarine or oil and pressing his body onto the paper. He would then apply loose pigment onto the paper, allowing it to stick to the greased impressions. "Injustice Case" was not Hammons's first experiment with featuring the American flag in his body prints. This work was, however, directly linked to Hammons's work to then-current events, specifically in relation to the BPP. "Injustice Case" was a direct response to BPP chairman Bobby Seale's 1968 "Chicago Eight" trial in the aftermath of the Democratic National Convention. As mentioned in the previous chapter, Judge Hoffman ordered that Seale be bound and gagged in court. Hammons, having followed Seale's case and working within the broader context of Black Power activism in 1960s Los Angeles, constructed this print in the wake of Seale's 1969 case. In this print, we see the impressions of a figure sitting on a chair. The figure's wrinkled jeans and creased shirt appear in tandem with the rippled folds of a cloth that binds arms, thighs, hands, neck, and mouth. The fabric's texture appears as one of many contrasting textures in the work. The figure's skin appears smooth on the face and hands and is of darker contrast than the rest of the body. Hair pillows like clouds and appears faint in the Afro style. The figure's arms are tied behind the chair, head is thrown back, and mouth is gagged. The entire print resembles an X-ray and alludes to silhouette. The print itself is centered on the American flag, which offers a border and frame to the print itself (plate 29).

"Injustice Case" and "Power to the People George" share emphasis on state violence against Black radicals. Both works emphasize the ways that US modes of anti-Black violence are structured by national ideology. While Morante's print is not placed within a frame, the uses of the American flag by both artists signpost how the conditions of violence experienced by both BPP leaders are framed by and for anti-Black violence and place these occurrences within this broader history. Strikingly, these two prints also share in their presentation of the Black radical body. Both offer bodies that are both general and specific. The direct use of silhouette in one and the adaptation of silhouette through bodily impression on the other present figures that are identifiable based on the narratives surrounding each work but are general enough in their presentation of the body in order to offer up the possibility of identification or affiliation between figure and viewer. This kind of shared aesthetic strategy points to how both works mobilize violence as a mode of political education, reconfiguring these scenes as unflinching indictments of the state and extending out possible felt impressions onto their viewers.

In addition to picturing anti-Black violence, "Power to the People George" also imagines conditions of Black freedom. As a final close look at this poster, I want to focus on the disproportionate scale of Jackson's silhouetted feet, which take up a significant amount of the right half of the image. Because Jackson's bare feet are rendered at such a scale, they locate for us a Black artistic visual language that simultaneously mobilizes abstraction and figuration to create a composition of the radical Black body that contains within it the relationship between the violence of captivity and a quest for freedom.

Because of the use of silhouette here, Jackson's body is saturated in Black, the depths of which add to the severity of his feet's particular disproportion. The feet figured in this image direct our vision to the borders of the page, as the toes on Jackson's left foot graze the edge of the paper. Dangling over the paper's white plane, Jackson's feet seem ungrounded, untethered, as if hanging from the weight of his body. In fact, if we imagine the poster reoriented ninety degrees, we can see a vertical gravitational pull toward the edge of the page, which immediately recollects images of lynching victims who often share in the positioning of the head/neck and are, too, barefooted. Both the appearance of a floating body and the dimensions of his feet also draw our attention toward the use of silhouette as an account of Jackson in the particular context of his death while also abstracting specificity in a way that leaves the figure open enough to be that of any revolutionary. The emphasis on bare feet here also proportionately rivals more direct emphasis on the violent act, thus making the feet the site for imagining both violence and freedom. By exaggerating Jackson's limbs— that part of the body responsible for movement, transport, escape—the poster makes visible how Jackson's murder exists within a long history of anti-Black violence. In so doing, the work insists we should not consider this event immobilizing. Instead, his bare feet also invoke the runaway slave—a figure of Black resistance, like Jackson himself.

Limbs appear as a familiar trope within slave narratives, often to illustrate how runaway captives imagined their battered and torn bare feet as signs of their resilience and commitment to liberation. This narrative attention to feet is echoed across Black art history, which allows us to reconsider the compositional power of the image in mobilizing radical looking practices that see feet for their fugitive qualities. I turn to how feet, often composed to signal various scales and visions of Black freedom, demarcate the fugitive possibilities of escape within regimes of anti-Black terror within a suite of works by Jacob Lawrence.

Lawrence's 1940 series on Harriet Tubman, the abolitionist celebrated for her lawlessness, and the Underground Railroad, which facilitated the fugitive practice of escape under the cover of night, best captures a more figurative emphasis on bare feet. In this biographical series, Lawrence sequenced key moments in Tubman's life across thirty-one captioned panels, acting as a kind of "picture book."

Lawrence's paintings employ modernist attachments, including the flatness of each figure and scene as well as the use of unconventional geometries and settings. In his depiction of his subjects, Lawrence moves us through the partial or whole figure whose specificity is often obscured, even silhouetted. In the same spirit of Jackson's poster, which utilizes silhouette to materialize the relationship between specific and abstract, Lawrence's paintings make themselves available to a populist impulse, in which there is always room for the Black viewer to see themselves in the image.

As we can gather from the images presented, Lawrence also emphasized feet in several of the panels. Shackles, which bind the feet to a particular place of confinement, mark the condition of captivity in some panels while others highlight the escape from restriction into open yet ominous pastures leading to nowhere in particular. However, Lawrence is careful not to give us the false promise of the purely pastoral. Instead, these open fields are saturated in dark blues and blacks, magnifying the unknown and treacherous futures that escape brings. Lawrence's paintings give us a landscape fraught with the terrors of violence and uncertainties of freedom (plates 30 and 31).

In a late addition to the series, added in 1967, entitled "Daybreak—A Time to Rest," Tubman is lying on her back and gazing at the sky above while embracing a rifle. Her feet, which take over the canvas and our vision, are disproportionately scaled, even deformed, in relation to the rest of her body. Large and grotesque, calloused and worn, Tubman's feet are the painting's subject (plate 32).

Lawrence deforms the plane, the scale of the body, and our vision through his figuration of Tubman's feet. Deformation is a strategy crucial to Black artistic practice, and here the strategy operates to enliven the fugitive qualities of escape practiced by Tubman herself.[77] Her feet tell us something the rest of her body does not. The underside of her bare feet—where her skin meets the ground—mobilizes the intensity of her lawlessness, of her status as an accomplice, if not conduit, for enslaved fugitives committing illegal acts of escape. Our vision is consumed by her fugitivity—running from the very law that mandates her captivity. This visualization of Black liberation is tinged with the very capture that mandates escape. Tubman's feet, then, are the vessels that make escape the means for Black liberation.

Knowing that Jackson's attempted prison escape warranted his murder, his feet come to signal the dangers of enacting one's own freedom. After all, his feet led him to his death. Mirroring tales of runaway enslaved persons who attempted to enact their freedom and thus risked immanent death through escape, the feet in "Power to the People George" galvanize resistance. To take one's freedom through escape, through the use of one's feet, is to activate a vision of Black freedom that understands death as a likely possibility but risks life to pursue a radical collective future.

Jackson articulated this sentiment in a letter written on May 26, 1970. Using the fragmented body as a metaphor for collectivity within revolutionary struggles, Jackson writes:

> There are no principal parts. You conceded that with the "all or none." It means that the small toe is as important to the human organism as the heart. It must be that way: the small toe is essential to balance, and its loss could precede or let's say presage the loss of the foot. *Without footing the movements of the head and heart become less efficient,* the remainder of the organism could survive without the arm but it should never be surrendered without making the strongest possible protest, I won't stand for any loss at all. The instant that my toe is taken, I will lose my head.[78]

Jackson's poetics offer up a composition of the body that considers the relation between all parts. Elsewhere, Jackson refers to the head and heart as the twofold structure for revolutionary struggles, which requires an activation of the rational and irrational, cerebral and physical, the practical and the soulful. In this passage, the head and heart are restaged in their relationship to the body, only to be abstracted more generally to speak of the Black freedom struggle. To be warned of the loss of one's foot or to be "without footing" is to slow down the momentum of the Black freedom struggle. To move toward a vision of freedom is to depend on one's little toe as much as one's head and heart.

In this image, the unresolved questions that surround Jackson's death transform into a political declaration of solidarity and Black radical resistance. The uncertainty around the sequence of events that led to Jackson's execution, and the state's subsequent visual and verbal censorship, though intended to silence awareness of the gruesome scene, instead manifested exponentially in political organizations and publications at the time of his death. Attempting to reconcile the carceral conditions of Jackson's life and the brutality of his murder, many radicals transformed the vague details of his murder into political fodder aimed to collectively respond by expressing political solidarity.

The 1971 piece "This Monster," by the EBMC, similarly configures the conditions of Jackson's murder in a political poster. However, as opposed to Morante's poster, which foregrounds anti-Black violence as the foundational structuring force of Black life in the United States, this piece offers a call to arms as visualized through Jackson's own words. In a subtle, visual move, EBMC member Doug Lawler, who was responsible for producing this particular work, intensifies the tension between Black life and death in order to leave the question of revolutionary insurrection as a continuing political project (plate 33).

Doug Lawler (East Bay Media Collective) and "This Monster"

The EBMC was founded by Doug Lawler sometime in the mid-1960s.[79] At first, the collective included four artists in total. When the *Berkeley Tribe*, a newspaper started by dissidents from the *Berkeley Barb* (the same newspaper responsible for the Bobby Hutton issue covered in chapter 1), dismantled in 1972, the EBMC took over their offices, which increased the collective's production and distribution capacity.[80] Prior to this merger, the EBMC ran a pretty small operation but produced a host of posters that were distributed widely across the Bay Area. The collective's most circulated poster, an antiwar poster called "Bring the War Down," made the collective enough money to purchase an offset printing press, which offered the opportunity for more collaborations across radical organizations.[81] In contrast to OSPAAAL'S global reach, the EBMC was a regional force and often worked in conversation with local radical organizations to coordinate political messages. The EBMC collaborated with the BPP, including assisting with cover design and sharing their stock image library with the organization.[82]

Internal processes of the EBMC, from ideation, to brainstorming, to sketching, to production, to circulation mirrored common radical collective processes in the 1960s. The collective deliberated proposals together and made decisions through consensus. Refusing the capitalist notion of singular artistic authorship, the EBMC chose not to assign artistic author-ship to individual posters. This was part of their production process, which was collaborative; therefore, any credit for works should be listed under the collective's name. Similarly, the collective's production processes are in harmony with the political aims of their distribution tactics.

In an interview with the artist, Lawler notes that early distribution methods included pinning and wheat-pasting posters across the Bay Area as a kind of guerrilla-style tactic. With careful consideration, he made sure to emphasize that the posters were incredibly detailed and time consum-ing and many required multiple runs because of the amount of color and graphic detail featured in the works.[83] For Lawler, this attention to the aesthetic dimensions of the poster was desirably for the people, and their status as aesthetic objects was in harmony with the direct political mes-sages they made publicly visible.

Jackson's murder was of national note, in no small part because of the acclaim of *Soledad Brother*, his brother Jonathan's takeover at the Marin County Courthouse, and Angela Y. Davis's subsequent court case the year prior, all of which brought George's name into an everyday conscious-ness.[84] Locally, the impact of Jackson's murder was devastating, as many radicals in the Bay Area looked to Jackson and the BPP as homegrown he-roes whose praxis informed many of the organizing efforts regionally. The poster by the EBMC comes to mark both the regional and national impact of Jackson's life and death through the use of Jackson's own writing and a doubled image of his slain body. These aesthetic strategies mobilize a fugi-tive imaginary that takes shape at the level of both print and text.

"This Monster" is a 20-inch-by-30-inch paper screen-printed poster. My reference for this chapter is a copy of the poster that is a part of the *All of Us or None* archive at the Oakland Museum of California. Watermarked, torn at the corners, and filled with push-pin or staple holes, this object is the perfect example of how these posters were intended for use. The object is printed on thin, affordable paper while the formal details of three colors of ink, intricate application methods, and meticulous typeset reflect a shared commitment not to sacrifice aesthetic sophistication for cost.

Beige colors the floor. Positioned diagonally, just right of center in the image, with shoe bottoms facing us, is a dark blue graphic of a body. The left leg is angled and bent while the right leg is straight and even. Arms are sprawled out, raised to ear level but spaced from the body. We see no face; just hair. Superimposed and shadowed in a lighter blue is the same graphic of a body but magnified to take up the entire right-hand side of the land-scaped image. In this superimposition, feet cut off the page while the head remains two inches from the page's border. In dark-red ink and all capital-ized letters is an excerpt from George Jackson's *Soledad Brother*. The follow-ing excerpt from the original letter appears in the poster in all caps:

> "This Monster—The Monster They've Engendered In Me / Will Re-turn To Torment Its Maker, From The Grave, The Pit, / The Pro-foundest Pit. The Descent Into Hell Won't Turn Me / I'll Crawl Back To Dog His Trail Forever. They Won't / Defeat My Revenge, Never, Never, I'm Part of A / Righteous People Who Anger Slowly, But Rage / Undamned. I'm Going To Charge Them For This, Twenty-Eight Years Without Gratification. / I'm Going To Charge Them Repara-tions In Blood / I'll Never Forgive, I'll Never Forget, And If I'm / Guilty Of Anything Its Not Leaning On Them / Hard Enough. War Without Terms. / George Jackson"

The text somehow spectacularizes the juxtaposition between the superim-posed graphic and the more solid, smaller graphic body. As if the narrative haunts the body, the text forces a spectatorial reexamination of how the body lays to make certain the figure is of Jackson's corpse. I examine this image as it illustrates the political work of death in Black radical thought, particularly as Jackson envisioned that work and its direct revolutionary consequences.

The formal technique of superimposing Jackson's corpse figures the gravity of his murder scene. Superimposition works so that Jackson's body somehow echoes itself—a repetition that mobilizes certainty in re-sponse to the state's unwillingness to release information about Jackson's murder. The visual history of superimposition is often understood as an early cinematic technique utilized to introduce apparitions and ghosts into a scene.[85] In this formulation, superimposition labors to embody representations of "spirited" others (ghosts) within a reality composed of living bodies. We can see how this argument resonates with this par-ticular poster of Jackson, precisely through the use of superimposition as a means of ghosting Jackson's corpse onto itself. It is a self-referential rep-etition that mobilizes the centrality of Jackson's murder within the legacy of his politics. In this poster, his life (text) and death (image) collide, re-vealing insight into Black radical life and the generative capacity of Black radical death.

Written among several unaddressed letters in March 1970 and signed with a simple "George" features a letter with some of Jackson's most rage-filled prose. Likely because of its uncensored condemnation and trenchant resolve for reparations, this particular letter captures Jackson's commitment to revolutionary action. Nestled in this letter, feet appear and perform a collective function once again, this time to shake the ground as a warning sign to a "they," the state, white supremacists, and others that secure white power:

Tuesday, March 24, 1970 (evening)

This monster—the monster they've engendered in me will return to torment its maker, from the grave, the pit, the profoundest pit. Hurl me in to the next existence, the descent into hell won't turn me. I'll crawl back to dog his train forever. They won't defeat my revenge, never, never. I'm part of a righteous people who anger slowly, but rage undammed. We'll gather at his door in such numbers that the rumbling of our feet will make the earth tremble. I'm going to charge them for this, twenty-eight years without gratification. I'm going to charge them reparations in blood. I'm going to charge them like a maddened, wounded, rogue male elephant, ears flared, trunk raised, trumpet blaring. I'll dance in his chest, and the only thing he'll ever see in my eyes is a dagger to pierce his cruel heart. This is one nigger who is positively displeased. I'll never forgive, I'll never forget, and if I'm guilty of anything at all its not of leaning on them hard enough. War without terms.[86]

Unflinching and poetic, Jackson offers vivid descriptions of self-defense unfettered by the mandates of a "proper" politic or by protocols that condemn rage as a revolutionary force. Here we are given a self that is thoroughly collective, a memory that is lasting and precise, and a life that is ready to end for reparations. There is a consistency in Jackson's account of revolutionary violence. He offers a vision, a strikingly descriptive one, of the stakes and need for that violence. His resolve, tenacity, and fearless declaration of his own fatal dedication might be why this letter provided the title and text for the 1971 poster made in the immediate aftermath of Jackson's murder.

By August 1971, Jackson's text circulated with a kind of frequency that he himself could not, thus allowing for collective engagement with the political prisoner's voice. The use of text from *Soledad Brother* highlights the ways in which Jackson's life and death trespass the boundaries of the prison cell or the home library. His words become fugitive as they come to mark a relationship to Black life and death always considered outlawed by the state. Jackson's unflinching analysis of racial capitalism, combined with his emotionally adept prose, makes his voice burst off the page of the poster. The composition's red coloration, capitalization, and placement hugs his body, almost appearing like a pool of blood shaped by words that shout, not whisper, from the page. The force of this passage is a call to break the law, to wage war against the state, for a kind of fugitivity lived by Jackson and other Black radicals day to day. By choosing to juxtapose this passage with the doubled image of a slain Jackson, the artists mobilize the question of afterlife as a circulation of Jackson's words and the uptake of the invitation of those calls to action.

Because Jackson's writing appears as a haunting reminder of his life, it intensifies the superimposed figures of his corpse. Marked with the conditions of his death, the text reimagines the conditions of his death (and life) as cause for rebellion. It is within the stylistic choice of how to represent that final phrase:

WAR WITHOUT TERMS

No punctuation, no final period to cap the sentence, no indication that the thought has reached its end. Punctuation impacts meaning in consequential ways.[87] Performance studies shocker Jennifer Devere Brody has written extensively on the centrality of grammar in performativity, as punctuation is crucial in making or breaking an effective performative occurrence. The "materiality of punctuation" contains the "tenets of 'close reading' and good editing in which each mark on the page matters."[88] In this way, the presence, or in this case absence, of punctuation is crucial for meaning in any given text. In this minutia of detail, Lawler reimagines Jackson's death as a declaration, a call to arms. This juxtaposition between the ellipses of textual insinuation and the graphic alarm of Jackson's corpse argues for continuation—a war without terms—so that the radical possibility of a new political future can be realized and Jackson's death might take on new meaning. In this same spirit, "This Monster" visualizes Jackson's dead body as a way to engage revolutionary praxis.

Although both posters animate fugitive imaginaries surrounding Jackson's murder, they do so without relying on institutional visual or narrative help. Artists are called upon to do something about this erasure, silence, and archival absence. In this way, both posters deploy understandings grounded in the political use of Jackson's death—a similar strategy the Panthers practiced following Bobby Hutton's murder. From Hutton to Jackson, we see the generative use of Black radical death toward revolutionary political means. Interestingly, the Morante and Lawler posters embark on an understanding of Black radical life and death through the activation of fugitive imaginaries. Both posters embody these imaginaries as Jackson's afterlife and an invitation to take up his call.

After Death: The Sentence Continues

This section offers two different responses to Jackson's murder and call for "a war without terms." One takes place in the immediate aftermath of Jackson's death, at his funeral in fact, and the other overseas in Paris. While both differ from each other significantly, they share understandings of Jackson's murder and the political afterlives of his death.

On August 28, 1971, exactly seven days after Jackson was gunned down in San Quentin State Prison, thousands of BPP members and allies gathered outside of St. Augustine's Episcopal Church in Oakland, California. Already clad in requisite black, Panthers lined San Pablo Avenue to accompany and protect the arrival of Jackson's casket. Draped in the national BPP flag—a powder-blue cloth with the illustration of a Black panther screen-printed on the textile—pallbearers carried Jackson's casket from the street to inside the church.

Newton's eulogy was republished in a special edition of the *Black Panther* newspaper dedicated entirely to Jackson's legacy. In it, Newton strikes at the heart of Jackson's death: "In the name of love and in the name of freedom, with love as our guide, we'll slit every throat of anyone who threatens the people and our children. We'll do it in the name of peace, if this is what we are forced to do; because as soon as it's over, then we can have the kind of world where violence will no longer exist." This piercing call for revolutionary violence in the name of love and freedom is, indeed, a version of war without terms. Newton was not alone in his unflinching commitment to Jackson's revolutionary love. Angela Y. Davis, who was an illustrious philosopher and activist whose analysis of prisons reshaped the Black freedom struggle's expanse into a protracted struggle toward prison abolition, expressed a version of revolutionary love undoubtedly inspired by Jackson's war without terms: "I can only say that by continuing to love him, I will try my best to express that love in the way he would have wanted—by reaffirming my determination to fight for the cause George died defending."[89] Love, in her formulation, must be expressed by continuing to live as Jackson did, continuing to pursue that which killed him: freedom. Both Newton and Davis insist on a version of love that pursues a life that is worth dying for. Davis ends her statement with Jackson's own words. Tellingly, she chooses the very passage chosen by the EBMC, only her excerpt ends at, "We'll gather at his door in such a number that the rumbling of our feet will make the earth tremble."

Feet once again activate the revolutionary, fugitive fervor represented by Jackson's life and death. By ending her dedication with these lines, we might reinterpret Jackson's phrasing here to suggest a continuity, an activated presence that takes shape around life after death. The afterlife of Jackson's death lives within those who take his place as revolutionaries.

Also included in this issue of the *Black Panther* was an Emory Douglas poster titled "George Jackson Lives!" Like Morante, Douglas's poster mobilizes the colors red, white, and blue to reference the American flag. But here, the red colors the prison cell and lock, wrought iron bent and wavy signaling a destruction. The blue colors the chains that once gripped the figure, now newly shattered and in the midst of falling to the ground. White is the ground of the image and the shirt of the former prisoner, whose newly achieved freedom raises a question of the subject's identity. Line drawing and silhouette reappear here to outline the shape of the figure, likely George Jackson himself. Unlike Morante's work, however, Douglas takes care not to leave the visage of a general depiction of a slain Black subject. Here, Douglas remobilizes his famed technique of photomontage to once again offer up the relationship between the individual and the collective.[90] A faded brick wall stock image is used to shape his neck and chest, which peeks from an open shirt. Photographs of over a dozen Black people take the place of Jackson's face. What strikes me about this aesthetic choice is the markedly poignant formal extension that decentralizes Jackson in his particularity and instead opens up the collective function of his death. Many make George Jackson and George Jackson makes many. This kind of Black aesthetic remixing of illustration and montage embodies what freedom might be after Jackson's death. The viewer witnesses the moment right *after* he frees himself, a momentary freedom dependent on all those that (in)form him. But most likely, Douglas proposes that it is up to everyday Black people to live out Jackson's commitment to Black liberation, to take up the cue for a Black revolution, and to storm out such that earth trembles (plate 34).

Jackson's declaration of war against the US government and capitalism leads us directly to the reality of Black radical life and the fugitive imaginary necessary toward engaging revolutionary praxis—two realities on which 1970s poststructuralist French philosophers wrote extensively in the aftermath of Jackson's murder. I turn to the works of Jean Genet, Michel Foucault, and others because they inch us closer to an articulation of American Black life (from the perspective of French white subjectivity) that rhetorically takes seriously the insurgency of Black radical praxis in a way that little American historical work does. On November 10, 1971, the French radical collective Prison Information Group (Groupe d'information sur les prisons [GIP]) published its third pamphlet within a series about prison expansion from a revolutionary abolitionist perspective.[91] The third pamphlet, entitled *The Assassination of George Jackson* (*L'Assassinat de Georges Jackson*), included a preface by French playwright Jean Genet.[92] In that preface, Genet—an ardent supporter of the Black Panthers—delivers a searing indictment of the state as the main arbiters of the murder of Black revolutionaries. It is within this critique that Genet repurposes a declaration of "war without terms." He writes:

> It has become more and more rare in Europe for a man to accept being killed for the ideas he defends. Black people in America do it every day. For them, "liberty or death" is not a clichéd slogan. When they join the Black Panther Party, Black people know they will be killed or will die in prison. I shall speak of a man who is now famous, George Jackson; but if the quake his death set off in us has not ceased, we ought also to know that every day young anonymous blacks are struck down in the streets by the police or by whites, while others are tortured in American prisons. Dead, they will survive among us— which isn't much—but they will live among the peoples who have been crushed by the white world, thanks to the resounding voice of George Jackson.[93]

Knowing "they will be killed or will die in prison" characterizes fully a reality of Black radical life.[94] In a sweeping rhetorical move, Genet positions the everyday danger of being Black in the United States while also positing the particular risk—and acceptance of that risk—that life poses. Anti-Black violence, being "crushed by the white world," renders Black radical life "dead," even while "they will survive among us."⁹⁵ The conflation here between Black life and Black death parallels Jackson's own writings on his lifelong incarceration. Burdened with "survival" within conditions of absolute confinement and unfreedom, "dead" here accounts for a kind of haunted legacy, where the promise of revolution is in the name of those who died in pursuit of it. The use of death here motivates revolutionary praxis. Within the same publication as Genet, Michel Foucault, Catherine von Bülow, and Daniel Defert published another essay on how Jackson's murder reveals a nuanced understanding of the vexed relationship between incarceration and Blackness.

In their detailed account of the California Department of Corrections (CDC) and its censorship of visual evidence from the murder scene, as well as the factual inconsistencies of information they *did* release, Foucault et al. call attention to the state's desired secrecy around Jackson's murder. The question they ask, and ultimately answer, is, Why would the state go to such lengths to conceal the details of Jackson's murder? Referring to Jackson's known political education and eventual collective organizing of prisoners across racial lines, they state, "For the officials, it is crucial to break this new front at all costs and to reestablish as soon as possible in the prisons the virulent racism against Black inmates. Therefore, they have to show that the events at San Quentin do not belong to a *new* stage in the political struggle but, rather, constitute a return to the *old* practice of savage massacre."⁹⁶ Addressing Jackson's call in *Blood in My Eye* to "prove our predictions about the future with action," the authors address the ways in which state narratives extinguish revolutionary practice through the "*old* practice of savage massacre."⁹⁷ In other words, the authors suggest that rather than Jackson's murder being a result of revolutionary insurrection led by prisoners, his murder was in actuality the state-sponsored execution of revolutionary potential.⁹⁸ This indictment of the CDC as upholding the legacy of "old" practices of "massacre" allows Foucault et al. to make sense of Jackson's murder—and its subsequent logical fallacies and visual censorship—through an ongoing practice of anti-Black violence.

As the authors argue, Jackson's murder served as an institutional—in this case, by the CDC—performance of structural violence. In a site already saturated with intensified and violent unfreedom, the very public murder of Jackson testified to the "daily violence and the permanent threat of death" experienced by prisoners daily.⁹⁹ Within this suspended condition of ongoing violence performed on one's everyday life, Jackson and other prisoners developed "rigorous tools for learning class hatred and the vigilance and astuteness of war"—in other words, prisoners had (and continue to have) an "experience of warfare."[100] Within this experience, Jackson's "war without terms" echoes again for us. Jackson's death validated those last few lines scribed by the GIP: "Jackson's death is at the origin of the revolts that exploded in prisons, from Attica to Ashkelon. Prison struggle has now become a new front of the revolution."[101]

Endings: Jackson's Library

On September 3, 1971, the CDC recorded and classified ninety-nine books in George Jackson's prison cell. Books ranged from Frantz Fanon's *Black Skin, White Masks* to writings by Mao Tse-tung to Albert Camus's *The Myth of Sisyphus*. Keeping in mind that these books were likely only a partial list of what Jackson was able to attain in prison because of highly restricted and censored access to books, this collection offers a glimpse into Jackson's life and an acute awareness demonstrated by the activist of his afterlife. In much the same way as the objects left behind in Fred Hampton's room, these books tell us about the political life of objects as they act upon Jackson's life and death (plate 35).

This library could be seen as a kind of autobiography, one that returns us to an opening scene of this chapter, where his life is forever changed after Jackson meets "Marx, Lenin, Trotsky, Engels, and Mao."[102] These thinkers are immortalized in their writings, and their legacies are incomplete without careful and considered reading and action. The stakes of this kind of study are indeed weighted beyond prison walls, within a space of complete coercion and confinement.

Ethnic studies scholar Dylan Rodriguez extensively accounts for how the radical prisoner represents a striking alterity, even within Black liberation struggles. In his book, Rodriguez charts the violence of the prison industrial complex and various modes of resistance enacted by those incarcerated. Crucial to the premise of his book is how the impact of writing reshapes and reconditions the terms of warfare imagined by the state as practiced through the prison. The scope of his analysis opens up a rich and dynamic engagement with writings by incarcerated peoples, transforming how we imagine the place of the political prisoner in fights against the brutal and ongoing systemic violence embodied by the prison. Because the "radical prisoner's utter lack of mobility and complete subjection to state surveillance imply that the underlying logic of political agency is one of pure opposition to pure force," prisoners activate political resistance by way of protracted antagonism.[103] We can think of Jackson's own praxis—the relationship he activates between the theories alive in his library and his own practice of writing—as one of political antagonism. In his analysis of political prisoner Marilyn Buck's writings, Rodriguez describes this process as "precisely the body's passage into this relation of force—a disciplinarily structure that *only* exists to legitimate punitive violence—that catalyses the epistemological break necessary for the formation of a unique political antagonism."[104] This unique political antagonism is foregrounded by physical capture—where the body is rendered permanently immobile, arrested, incarcerated. As Rodriguez reminds us, within the US prison regime, the prisoner always represents an oppositional positionality to state power precisely because of how the state manufactures the subject's silence and invisibility. This production of the invisible requires force, as the moment a prisoner enunciates presence (through speech, writing, or the like) is the moment political antagonism takes shape.

Jackson's library, alongside his extensive publication record, can be seen as an articulated afterlife. Nestled alongside these iconic political studies, Jackson kept two copies of his own published work, *Soledad Brother*. By placing his book among those from Marx, Aptheker, and Du Bois, Jackson articulated his legacy: that voice, his written prose, and the politics that prose is meant to enact would live far after he himself would. Reframing Fred Hampton's bedroom within which he was slain, Jackson's library marks a similar kind of political life of objects. What is significantly different in Jackson's case are the intensified carceral conditions in which these objects take flight. In other words, Jackson's library must be thought of in relation to its site specificity. Because Jackson's library was housed in prison—a site of total coercion, violence, and censorship—it is crucial to understand the CDC's documentation as a momentary breach, a subversive and excessive glimmer of Jackson's afterlife. These radical books speak to how political antagonism lives long after Jackson's initial articulation. These objects, catalogued and classified pragmatically as "books taken from cell of George Jackson, A-63837," sustain Black radical articulation and antagonism toward the abolition of all prisons and all those numbered as prisoners.

The United States of Attica

On August 22, 1971, just one day after George Jackson's murder in San Quentin State Prison, prisoners at Attica Correctional Facility in New York showed up to the mess hall donning strips of black cloth on their arms.[1] They refused to eat. Some inside called what the prisoners were doing a "'spiritual sit in' to protest the murder the previous day of a fellow prisoner, George Jackson."[2] News of the mess hall sit-in spread, and soon prisoners in A Block began a mass "sick-in" to "call attention to the dire state of the prison's medical facilities."[3] It was clear that Jackson's murder had given rise to a multiracial, organized groundswell at Attica. Historian Heather Ann Thompson, whose epic *Blood in the Water: The Attica Prison Uprising of 1971 and Its Legacy* has provided the clearest and most insightful chronicle of events during the Attica uprising, notes how deeply Jackson's murder had impacted prisoners in Attica, who had organized across racial lines:

George Jackson had become famous in prison systems across the United States for his extensive writings from inside—expositions on just how racist and brutal America's penal institutions were, particularly for prisoners of color. His killing touched a nerve among the incarcerated everywhere. . . . Prisoners everywhere were convinced that whatever had happened at San Quentin must have involved trigger-happy guards, and now George Jackson was dead.

Like those artists who turned to fugitive imaginaries to create artistic renderings aimed to account for the violence of Jackson's murder, the prisoners in San Quentin did not believe the state's narrative about the slain Panther's death. His death exposed and confirmed the state's murderous tenacity: if prisoner's did not live obedient lives as carceral subjects, they would simply be outright killed; the durational violence of the prison would be traded for a guaranteed immediate death. Jackson's murder was purposeful and without cause. Jackson's murder served as a spark that ignited what would be a five-day takeover of Attica, which would eventually result in one of the bloodiest instances of state violence in US history. On September 13, 1971, Governor Rockefeller ordered hundreds of troops to storm the prison and take it back under state control. He also ordered that these troops open fire on prisoners and prison guards. Thirty-nine people were killed. At least one hundred more were severely injured. This number includes both prisoners and guards.

The Attica Rebellion was a testament to the generative capacity of Black radical death. Jackson's death had motivated an already active Attica Liberation Faction (ALF) to ramp up their efforts. The ALF were a tentative group of multiracial prisoners who sought to organize against the brutally violent conditions in the prison. By June 1971, just months before Jackson's murder, the ALF sent demands to commissioner Russell Oswald. These demands were preceded by a manifesto that opened:

> We the inmates of Attica Prison have come to recognize that because of our posture as prisoners and branded characters as alleged criminals, the administration and prison employees no longer consider or respect us as human beings but rather as domesticated animals selected to do their bidding and slave labor and furnished as a personal whipping dog for their sadistic psychopathic hate.[4]

Modeled after a set of demands issued by prisoners at Folsom State Prison in California, ALF's manifesto and demands were a shared collective spirit taking shape and were undoubtedly influenced by Jackson and his writings. The intensely vivid descriptions of vitriolic and degrading violence dovetails with Jackson's own descriptions of life inside. The manifesto clearly paints a picture of life inside prison walls that shapes solidarity between prisoners across the nation. While the Attica manifesto was not specifically abolitionist in nature, this kind of shared narrative approach—the manifesto and set of demands as a collective narrative device—opens onto how the culture of resistance taking shape adapted elements from Black Power in order to activate this new terrain of prison abolition.

Attica in the Cultural Imagination

In September 1971, the world had a chance to see the horrific scenes of violence that had long been transpiring behind prison walls in the Attica prison. This televisual experience had entered the national and international imaginary and had called for a response by politicians, celebrities, and artists. Bob Dylan got in on the cultural momentum, penning and releasing the song "George Jackson" in November 1971, just months after Jackson was slain. John Lennon and Yoko Ono had a track called "Attica State" on their album *Some Time in New York City*, released in December 1971. This *was* the same album whose opening track sparked rightful criticism as it flattened both misogyny and anti-Black racism into a dangerous equivalent, which says nothing of the audacious use of a violent and derogatory anti-Black word by two non-Black artists. "Attica State" is the third track on the album; the ninth was named after Black freedom fighter Angela Y. Davis. The artistic duo saw both tracks as part of a broader movement toward peace and justice. What movement, exactly, these tracks were in collaboration with remains unclear though both represent the impact of Jackson's murder and Davis's incarceration on a global scale. Dylan, Lennon, and Ono were attempting to throw their cultural capital behind the cause, bringing non-Black, celebrity voices to the edges of an already flourishing Black-led freedom struggle. What these tracks share is an explicit, narrative articulation of the state's murder of Jackson and of the impact of white supremacist violence more generally in the case of Attica.

Meanwhile, in New York City, radical saxophonist Archie Shepp was recording *Attica Blues*, a stunningly gripping album that developed forms of sonic storytelling. Shepp, who took issue with the term *jazz* and preferred to be referred to as an artist in the Black arts movement, developed the album as a conceptual response to the political moment.[5] The same year Muhammed Ali recited his poem for Attica in an interview with Cathal O'Shannon for Irish television, Shepp released *Attica Blues*.[6] *Attica Blues* combines elements of pop, spoken word, and free instrumental composition to make an album that bounces between elements of abstraction and narrativization. The entire album bears the weight of existential crisis, as Shepp's ability to combine poetics with composition swells into moments of mantra, chorus, asynchronous instrumental dissonance, funky cooperation, and shaped registers of harmony and scale. Indeed, the entire album successfully does what Shepp once described as central to his music: "This music must at times terrify! It must shake men by the throats. It must bring social as well as esthetic order to our lives."[7] Music is a social force, not just an aesthetic object of pleasure or leisure, and as a social force, music should have an embodied effect as it strikes the listener into terror, often through righteous rage. Terror disassembles like the disassembled, fragmented horn that shrieks across a given track's intermittent groove or like the deep grief embodied in the phrase "I worry about the human soul," repeated in the album's opening track. This might be the power of Shepp's *Attica Blues*: it combines the qualities of abstraction and narrativization so prevalent in Black art after Attica, especially those works that would emerge directly in response to the rebellion. In what follows, I track how a few artists share the road with Shepp in their visual uptake of the Attica Rebellion and its impact on visions of the Black freedom struggle and the transition from Black Power to prison abolition.

Attica Book is a collection of visual art and poetry organized by the Black Emergency Cultural Coalition (BECC) and Artists and Writers Protest against the War in Vietnam (AWPAWV). The book was edited by artists Benny Andrews (founding member of the BECC) and Rudolf Baranik (founding member of AWPAWV), a collaboration that demonstrated interracial and international solidarity with the struggles for Black and third-world liberation at home and abroad. Andrews and Baranik, both lifelong painters and activists who organized together for years, worked together on the organization, commission, and selection of works as well as provided brief opening remarks. In the spirit of collaboration, there are three epigraphs—one by Andrews, one by Baranik, and one they wrote together, dedicated to the BECC and AWPAWV. All proceeds from the book sales went "towards the distribution of free copies within the prison system."[8] This sentiment is emphasized in bold font in the advertisement's closing line, "To be sold outside—to be given away inside." Sales of the book covered the cost of free copies in prisons nationwide.[9] That "Forty-Eight Leading American Artists" donated these works to be reproduced and accessible to people both inside and outside of prison is of particular significance when we think about how many of these artists participated in the art market. Their contributions model a resistance to the allure of capital presented by the art market and instead present a radically "free" circulation of art for incarcerated peoples. This foregrounding of incarcerated peoples is echoed in the formal organization and content of the book as a whole (plate 36).

Attica Book features fifty-two artists, poets, and writers. Contributors range in race, age, gender, generation, incarceration status, and preferred medium. Known artists like Jacob Lawrence, Romare Bearden, Robert Morris, and Nancy Spero appear alongside incarcerated artists like D. Cusic, Ronald King, and Michael McLaughlin. The book is a radical experiment in how to democratize the art book, as there are no hierarchical presentations of works as each object gets its own page. While the page number and artist name is listed in the main content pages of the book, no other information—medium, year, collection, etc.—is provided. In fact, the final page of content provide a list of "Artists and Poets" but only a given poet's poems have titles; the other artworks are merely attributed to a given artist and described simply by media ("Collage," "Etching," "Woodcut," etc.). Visual artists are limited to one work by one artist. Poets are given more real estate, as each poet has more than one poem included. This suggests a reparative approach to the distribution of space—incarcerated artists are given more space in the book as a mode of emphasizing their voices and attempting to allocate more visibility in light of the histories that have historically silenced and rendered invisible incarcerated voices and experiences. These formal choices of organization reflect a deep material recognition of the many ways incarcerated people have been disenfranchised, and through these nuanced formal choices, there are attempts to redistribute spatial and representational power to the incarcerated artists featured in the book.

The artworks included reflect a variety of styles and aesthetic approaches, foregrounding how the Attica Rebellion gave occasion for a range of artistic movements to be housed within the same pages. In their description of the visual artists included in the book, Andrews and Baranik illustrate this range: "It is right that the artists who make their visual statements in this book should constitute a wide stylistic spectrum, from expressionist outcry to laconic conceptual incision. A collage of indignation, witnessing the communality of America's artists speaking for a shared truth. Also right that the poems and letters should come from the 'inside.'" This description of works from the figurative to the abstract inform the reader that the book's contents may not be as decipherable in terms of political content, but the objects share a general critique of societal norms with an approach to the political as already imbedded within formal considerations in any given work. Take, for example, Melvin Edwards's contribution, which looks like an early reproduction of "Night Chain" (1973), an intaglio print. The print in *Attica Book* features abstracted traces of chain links, cross-hatchings, and what resembles a liquid pool of ink that spills and slips across the top of the print. Because of the stark contrast of black and white, combined with the imprecision and blurs made visible via the etching stage of the intaglio process, it is as if the chains are ghosting the surface, presenting moments of dimensionality and movement. I cannot help but think of the print as a precursor to Edwards's famed "Curtains" (1973), a theatrical drape made exclusively of chain links in Edwards's signature welded sculptural style. The print, however, reads like an early study that uses an alternative medium to explore the artist's concern with steel as a material used both for acts of anti-Black violence and Black labor, thereby signifying dense and complex histories and meanings (plate 37).

The confrontational qualities of the print are especially poignant in *Attica Book*, as these material meanings easily translate in the context of prison labor and violence, thus forming a scathing indictment of anti-Blackness across multiple contexts. Edwards's use of abstraction here gives rise to the social critique imbedded in the formal qualities of materials and processes. While we do not have a direct depiction of violence and labor as centralized in more representational approaches to art-making, we nonetheless are invited to think of how *materials* carry within them histories and meanings that signify their very presence. This Black radical visual language is a prime example of the direct relationship of abstraction to politics, as the critiques of racial capitalism and white supremacy are mobilized through a question about the centrality of the object as a signifier for Blackness, a topic we also considered with the objects that surrogate Hutton's presence in his wake. Edwards's signature approach to abstraction works in tandem with more figurative approaches to Black radicalism after Attica.

Cliff Joseph's "Blackboard" (1972) is an offset lithograph made after the artist's 1969 painting of the same title (plate 38). The lithograph is reproduced in *Attica Book* in photocopied grayscale, while the original lithograph is rich with pinks, browns, reds, yellows, and greens. A Black mother and her son are the main subjects of the work, as both stand in front of a blackboard where the "alphabet of the Black Revolution is scrawled on the black-board."[10] Joseph's lithograph figuratively explores the relationship between Black radical consciousness, education, and futurity—themes that have been explored in relation to Hutton, Hampton, and Jackson's lives. The mother-son pair standing against the backdrop of Black revolutionary cita-tions recall the afterlife of Hampton's legacy vis-à-vis his partner Akua and son Fred Jr. while the citations suggest a deep concern with the new lan-guage of Black radicalism, most poignantly presented with terms like "Black Power" and "Power to the People"—key phrases attached to Hampton's life. The alphabet also resonates with Jackson's studies, as the alphabet similarly reflects historical and contemporary examples of Black freedom fighters and vernacular phrases combined to demonstrate the intimate connections between Black American and Black diasporic peoples. The young son wears a pin with red, black, and green stripes that resemble the Black national flag, his style and demeanor harken Hutton's youthful cool, speaking to the cen-tral role of youth for the movement's future. Like the political posters after Jackson's murder, Joseph's mode of visual communication prioritizes figu-ration as a vehicle for Black Power aesthetics and, as such, blurs fine and political poster art. This approach is shared by Faith Ringgold, whose work *The United States of Attica* is featured on page one in *Attica Book* (plate 39).

Faith Ringgold's 1972 poster *The United States of Attica* offers a visual ac-count of historical and structural violence. The artist notes of the work:

> The United States of Attica (1972), was the most widely distributed Ringgold political poster of the 1970s. This poster was dedicated to the men who died in 1971 at Attica prison for demonstrating against the deplorable conditions. This red, black and green poster depicts a map of the United States. The dates and other details of infamous acts of violence that occurred are posted within each state—such as race riots, witch-hunts, presidential assassinations, lynching's and Indian wars. Around the periphery of the map is a statistical history of the dead, wounded and missing in American wars starting with the 1776 Revolutionary War and ending at the Vietnam War. An appeal for people to add their own updated information was put on the poster.

Organized into four quadrants, each section alternates between red fore-ground and green background and green foreground and red background.

A black line drawing of the continental United States accompanies hand-written text that clutters and crowds the drawing, concentrated in areas where particular violent historical events took place. The surrounding space around the United States features the numbers of the dead from every war since the 1776 Revolutionary War. Two key areas are typeset. The first is at the top-center of the poster, which reads in black type:

THE UNITED STATES OF ATTICA
  FOUNDED BY THE AMERICAN PEOPLE ON SEPT. 13. 1971 AT
ATTICA PRISON, N.Y. WHERE 42 MEN GAVE THEIR LIVES IN A
HEROIC STRUGGLE FOR FREEDOM ...
  THE JUDSON THREE

The second typeset area is in the bottom-center of the poster:

THIS MAP OF AMERICAN VIOLENCE IS INCOMPLETE
  PLEASE WRITE IN WHATEVER YOU FIND LACKING.

I highlight the aesthetic structure of the poster, and emphasize the moments of captioned typeset, in order to give a sense of the artist's radical vision in the founding of a new United States: a post-Black Power, post-Attica nation held together by the chromatic schema of a new nation's flag and colors of red, black, and green, clearly a nod to the Black freedom struggle.[11] By stripping away the nation from its previous name and patriotic colors, and by naming the date of its founding the very same day of the Attica massacre, Ringgold opens up a vision of a nation structured by and free within its founding violence. Each location on the map is tattooed with a list of violent events foundational to its making and, as such, the viewer is called upon to think violence and freedom together as twinned projects of US nation-making.

The September 18, 1971, edition of the *Black Panther* newspaper featured a signature political poster style. While not signed and directly attributed to Emory Douglas, the cover's signature style matches the Minister of Culture's previous aesthetic works, including the poster for George Jackson covered in the previous chapter. If Douglas did not make the cover, he had an influence in its making. In bold, capitalized typeface, just under the newspaper's weekly issue graphic, reads, "MASSACRE AT ATTICA." Yellow and black operate as contrasting colors throughout the collage. The top half of the image is an illustrated prison cell, signaled by the use of vertical bars that track the page, and a drawn lock crested in the upper-right quadrant. Poking through the illustration is a spire that encourages the viewer to cast their gaze down the page to encounter a photographic image of the front gates into Attica Correctional Facility. The viewer's vantage point is frontal, from somewhere in the parking lot or front road, and seems to be flooded with cars and people crowding the entrance to the prison. It's likely this newspaper image was sourced cotemporaneously, as the print's making and its rush and crowd are likely present because of the uprising taking place behind those doors. The typeface, color choice, and use of journalistic media signal the violence that squashed a rebellion, a violence that remained out of sight for the public (plate 40).

The back cover of the issue featured a reprint of a Douglas poster from the August 14, 1971, issue. This too emphasized thick black vertical bars that frame the work's composition. At the left corner of the page sits another lock with an exposed keyhole, leaving the viewer to once again see the composition of a prison cell. This time, though, the keyhole and lock are foiled by the appearance of a symmetrical rectangular box shape in the upper-right quadrant of the poster. This space features cutouts of the stars on the US flag, such that if one turns the poster forty-five degrees to the left, we will see the shape of the familiar national symbol. The stripes are composed of bars from a prison cell, the colors of which are instead substituted for multiple Black people who share the picture's back and foreground. Sourced from photographs and journalistic media, a figure looks out onto a plurality of Black figures from a range of ages, genders, body types, and generations. Scaled at various dimensions with no correlation to the normative protocols of a realism, these cutout, photomontaged figures are everyday Black people whose figurative presence in the poster gives pause to the viewer. This detail makes a case for the foundational entanglement among anti-Black violence, the prison system, and US nation-making projects. Meanwhile, an illustrated wounded Black figure grips the cell bars, leaving the viewer and the drawn figure with the same perspective and gazing from the inside out. The caption above the image reads, "WHY MUST BLACK PEOPLE LOOK AT EACH OTHER THROUGH PRISON BARS? WHERE IS OUR FREEDOM? (plate 41)"

There is much to be said about this front and back cover decision. Taking the prison cell as a central aesthetic device, both works bring together elements of illustration with source materials from various photographic media. As is popular within the illustrated form, caption is concise and clear, both in message and graphic design. Both images use drawing to bring in the viewer through the use of bold black lines and identifiable political tropes. Both deploy photographs as a way to reassemble a sense of the masses, Black collectivity, isolation, and freedom. The prison cell is the ultimate signifier of invisibility, censorship, and isolation—the state's ultimate victory over one's body and personhood. Both take on the question of surveillance and impeded sight, themes that were extensively considered in the murders of Hutton, Hampton, and Jackson. The cover's use of black ink combined with the reproduction of the Attica stone wall that surrounds the prison centralizes how prison is a system that relies on containment, invisibility, separation, and censorship. While the back cover emphasizes how the figure's line of sight is impeded upon by the cell's bars, making it hard to see those just outside the cell door's reach. These aesthetic concerns—with isolation and visibility, censorship and the masses—make the question of Black freedom inextricably bound to questions of sight.

The uprising, and subsequent massacre, was an overwhelming source of political inspiration for artists and activists on the outside. Like Jackson's murder and the kinds of political will and fugitive imaginaries generated despite state censorship of the conditions of his murder, Attica represented both a momentary victory and warning call for activists: the prisoners, for a brief moment, practiced self-determination as takeover, and with reactionary force, the state once again massacred its own people—this time prisoners and guards alike. Attica as a name carried with it a set of politics, a vision of liberation, and the ubiquity of its placeness as one of many sites of ongoing state-sponsored terror. Just as Jackson's name came to carry with it an understanding of a Black collective experience, so too had Attica transformed into a signifier for the state's violence and a collective vision for liberation.

Thought together, the *Black Panther* cover and *United States of Attica* are visions of the structures that govern Black life: state-sanctioned violence, war, militarism, carcerality. Both also identify radical visions of place: prison cells, Attica, the United States. These objects together deploy formal elements that call upon the Black freedom struggle's future terrain: the prison industrial complex and the various localities of judicial policies and vigilante practices that give rise to sustained and durational violence against Black people within and outside of prison walls. Douglas asks where freedom might be located, and Rinngold suggests that perhaps freedom lives in this new image, this imagined place called the United States of Attica. What if we met there, within and beyond the state's grip, to form a new approach to the United States in the hollowed shell of its former self?

Notes

INTRODUCTION. THE VISUAL LIFE OF BLACK POWER

1. Jane Rhodes, "Power to the People: *The Black Panther* and the Pre-Digital Age of Radical Media," in *The Funambulist: Politics of Space and Bodies: Publishing the Struggle*, no. 22 (March–April 2019): 26.

2. Amy Abugo Ongiri, *Spectacular Blackness: The Cultural Politics of the Black Power Movement and the Search for an Aesthetic* (Charlottesville: University of Virginia Press, 2010); Jane Rhodes, *Framing the Black Panthers: The Spectacular Rise of the Black Power Icon* (New York: New Press, 2007).

3. Erika Doss, "'Revolutionary Art Is a Tool for Liberation': Emory Douglas and Protest Aesthetics at *The Black Panther*," *New Political Science* 21, no. 2 (1999): 249; Marc Léger, "By Any Means Necessary: From the Revolutionary Art of Emory Douglas to the Art Activism of Jackie Sumell," *Afterimage* 38, no. 5 (March/April 2011).

4. Geoff Kaplan, "Introduction," in *Power to the People: The Graphic Design of the Radical Press and the Rise of the Counterculture, 1964-1974* (Chicago: University of Chicago Press, 2013).

5. Emory Douglas, "Revolutionary Art/Black Liberation," in *The Black Panthers Speak*, ed. Philip Foner (New York: De Capo Press, 1995), 16.

6. Doss, "Revolutionary Art," 253.

7. Douglas, "Revolutionary Art/Black Liberation," 16.

8. For more on the BPP's uptake of Fanon's notion that violence is a cleansing force for the colonized subject, see chapters 1 and 2.

9. Key texts that have significantly influenced my understanding of the libidinal, social, and political pleasures of anti-Black violence include Huey Copeland, *Bound to Appear: Art, Slavery, and the Site of Blackness in Multicultural America* (Chicago: University of Chicago Press, 2013); Frantz Fanon, *Black Skin, White Masks*, trans. Richard Philcox (New York: Grove Press, 2004); Saidiya Hartman, *Scenes of Subjection: Terror, Slavery, and Self-Making in Nineteenth-Century America* (London: Oxford University Press, 1997); David Marriott, *On Black Men* (New York: Columbia University Press, 2000); David Marriott, *Haunted Life: Visual Culture and Black Modernity* (New Brunswick, NJ: Rutgers University Press, 2007); Steve Martinot and Jared Sexton, "The Avant-Garde of White Supremacy," *Social Identities* 9, no. 2 (2003):169–81; Robyn Wiegman, *American Anatomies: Theorizing Race and Gender* (Durham, NC: Duke University Press, 2002); Frank B. Wilderson III, *Red, White, and Black: Cinema and the Structure of U.S. Antagonisms* (Durham, NC: Duke University Press, 2010).

10. Fred Moten, *In the Break: The Aesthetics of the Black Radical Tradition* (Minneapolis: University of Minnesota Press, 2003); Hartman, *Scenes of Subjection*.

11. Fred Moten, "Review of *Soul: Black Power, Politics, and Pleasure* and *Scenes of Subjection: Terror, Slavery, and Self-Making in Nineteenth-Century America*," *TDR: The Drama Review* 43, no. 4 (1999): 171.

12. Moten, *In the Break*, 170.

13. Hilton Als, "GWTW," in *Without Sanctuary: Lynching Photography in America*, ed. James Allen (Santa Fe, NM: Twin Palms, 2000), 38.

14. Joseph Roach, *Cities of the Dead: Circum-Atlantic Performance* (New York: Columbia University Press, 1996), 28.

15. Roach, *Cities of the Dead*, 2.

16. Harvey Young, *Embodying Black Experience: Stillness, Critical Memory, and the Black Body* (Ann Arbor: University of Michigan Press, 2010), 186.

17. Young, *Embodying Black Experience*, 188.

18. Marta Braun, *Picturing Time: The Work of Étienne Jules-Marey* (Chicago: University of Chicago Press, 1992).

19. Susan Sontag, *On Photography* (New York: Delta, 1977), 14.

20. Friedrich A. Kittler, *Gramophone, Film Typewriter*, trans. Geoffrey Winthrop-Young and Michael Wutz (Stanford, CA: Stanford University Press, 1999), 124.

21. Jason Puskar, "Pistolgraphs: Liberal Technoagency and the Nineteenth-Century Camera Gun," *Nineteenth-Century Contexts* 36, no. 5 (December 2014): 523.

22. Hartman, *Scenes of Subjection*; Eric Lott, *Love and Theft: Blackface Minstrelsy and the American Working Class* (Oxford: Oxford University Press, 1993); Janet Neary, *Fugitive Testimony: On the Visual Logics of Slave Narratives* (New York: Fordham University Press, 2017).

23. Matthew Fox-Amato, *Exposing Slavery: Photography, Human Bondage, and the Birth of Modern Visual Politics in America* (Oxford: Oxford University Press, 2019), 37; Harvey Young, "Still Standing: Daguerreotypes, Photography, and the Black Body," in *Embodying Black Experience: Stillness, Critical Memory and the Black Body* (Ann Arbor: University of Michigan Press, 2010), 26–76.

24. Allen, ed., *Without Sanctuary*; Jaqueline Goldsby, *A Spectacular Secret: Lynching in American Life and Literature* (Berkeley: University of California Press, 2006); David Marriott, *On Black Men* (New York: Columbia University Press, 2000); Dora Apel and Shawn Michelle Smith, *Lynching Photographs* (Berkeley: University of California Press, 2008); Shawn Michelle Smith, "Spectacles of Whiteness: The Photography of Lynching," *Photography on the Color Line: W. E. B. Du Bois, Race, and Visual Culture* (Durham, NC: Duke University Press, 2004); Amy Louise Wood, *Lynching and Spectacle: Witnessing Racial Violence in America, 1880–1940* (Chapel Hill: University of North Carolina Press, 2009).

25. Goldsby, *A Spectacular Secret*, 224, 238.

26. Goldsby, *A Spectacular Secret*, 248.

27. Goldsby, *A Spectacular Secret*, 252.

28. Julianne Burton, "The Camera as 'Gun': Two Decades of Culture and Resistance in Latin America," *Latin American Perspectives: Culture in the Age of Mass Media* 5, no. 1 (Winter 1978): 49, emphasis in original, translation added.

29. Gordon Parks, *A Choice of Weapons* (Minneapolis: Minnesota Historical Society Press, 2010); Greg Thomas, "On *Teza*, Cinema, and American Empire: An Interview with Haile Gerima," *Black Camera* 4, no. 2 (Spring 2013): 9.

30. Kara Keeling, "'We'll Just Have to Get Guns and Be Men': The Cinematic Appearance of Black Revolutionary Women," *Witch's Flight: The Cinematic, the Black Femme, and the Image of Common Sense* (Durham, NC: Duke University Press, 2007), 74–75.

31. Angela Y. Davis, "Afro Images: Politics, Fashion, and Nostalgia," *Critical Inquiry* 21, no. 1 (Autumn 1994): 38.

32. Davis, "Afro Images," 42.

33. Steve Everitt, "A Huey P. Newton Story—People—Bobby Hutton," Public Broadcasting Service, 2002, https://www.pbs.org/hueypnewton/people/people_hutton.html.

34. Jeffrey Haas, *The Assassination of Fred Hampton: How the FBI and the Chicago Police Murdered a Black Panther* (Chicago: Lawrence Hill Books, 2010); Hans Bennet, "The Black Panthers and the Assassination of Fred Hampton," *Journal of Pan African Studies* 3, no. 6 (2010): 215.

35. Wallace Turner, "Two Desperate Hours: How George Jackson Died," *New York Times*, September 3, 1971, https://www.nytimes.com/1971/09/03/archives/two-desperate-hours-how-george-jackson-died-two-desperate-hours-how.html.

36. Webster Melcher, "Photography and Evidence," *Central Law Journal* (April 1922): 242.

37. Deborah Thomas, "Humanness in the Wake of the Plantation," in *Political Life in the Wake of the Plantation: Sovereignty, Witnessing, Repair* (Durham, NC: Duke University Press, 2019), 2.

38. Thomas, "Humanness in the Wake of the Plantation."

39. Michael X. Delli Carpini, "The Black Panther Party: 1966–1982," in *The Encyclopedia of Third Parties in America*, ed. Immanuel Ness and James Ciment (New York: Routledge, 2006), 194.

40. Joshua Bloom and Waldo E. Martin, *Black Against Empire: The History and Politics of the Black Panther Party* (Berkeley: University of California Press, 2013), 2.

41. Bloom and Martin, *Black Against Empire*, 3.

42. Students for a Democratic Society, "Huey Newton Talks to the Movement," Kent State University Libraries, Special Collections and Archives, accessed October 13, 2021, https://omeka.library.kent.edu/special-collections/items /show/3176.

43. Kara Keeling, *Queer Times, Black Futures* (New York: New York University Press, 2019), 36.

44. Keeling, *Queer Times, Black Futures*, 32.

45. Keeling, *Queer Times, Black Futures*, 33.

46. Keeling, *Queer Times, Black Futures*, 36.

47. For more on wake work, see Christina Sharpe, *In the Wake: On Blackness and Being* (Durham, NC: Duke University Press, 2016). For more on waywardness, see Saidiya Hartman, *Wayward Lives, Beautiful Experiments: Intimate Histories of Riotous Black Girls, Troublesome Women and Queer Radicals* (New York: Penguin Random House, 2019).

48. Laura Helton, Justin Leroy, Max A. Mishler, Samantha Seeley, and Shauna Sweeney, "The Question of Recovery: An Introduction," *Social Text* 33, no. 4 (December 2015): 7.

CHAPTER 1. "1,000 BOBBY HUTTONS"

1. Stephen Shames, email correspondence with the author, February 27, 2019. Emory Douglas thought the original photograph was taken by Shames. Shames insists he did not take the photograph. Adrienne Fields, director of legal affairs, Artists Rights Society, email correspondence with the author, February 18, 2020.

2. Gar Smith, email correspondence with the author, February 25, 2019.

3. I have considered the role of "cool" and "shade" in the BPP's embodied visual practices elsewhere. To do so, I combined Robert Farris Thompson's invocation of an "aesthetics of cool" with Krista Thompson's "sidelong glance." For more, see Sampada Aranke, "Shades of Cool," *AQ/SFAQ/NYAQ*, June 21, 2016; Krista Thompson, "A Sidelong Glance: The Practice of African Diaspora Art History in the United States," *Art Journal* 70 (2011): 7–31; Robert Farris Thompson, "An Aesthetic of Cool," *African Arts* 7, no. 1 (1973): 41.

4. I am developing the term *photographic fugitivity* from Krista Thompson's insightful essay on Ivanhoe Martin's appearance and disappearance through

the photographic form. Krista Thompson, "'I WAS HERE BUT I DISAPEAR': Ivanhoe 'Rhygin' Martin and Photographic Disappearance in Jamaica," *Art Journal* 77, no. 2 (Summer 2018), https://artjournal.collegeart.org/?p=10123.

5. Leah Dickerman, David Joselit, and Mignon Nixon, "Afrotropes: A Conversation with Huey Copeland and Krista Thompson," *October* 162 (Fall 2017): 3–18.

6. Dickerman, "Afrotropes," 12, 17.

7. Huey Copeland and Krista Thompson, "Afrotropes: A User's Guide," *Art Journal* 76 (2017): 7–9.

8. Dickerman, "Afrotropes," 4.

9. Dickerman, "Afrotropes," 4.

10. Huey Copeland, *Bound to Appear: Art, Slavery, and the Site of Blackness in Multicultural America* (Chicago: University of Chicago Press, 2013); Dickerman, Joselit, and Nixon, "Afrotropes," 4.

11. Ariella Azoulay, *The Civil Contract of Photography* (London: Zone Books, 2008), 129.

12. Azoulay, *The Civil Contract*, 137.

13. Leigh Raiford, *Imprisoned in a Luminous Glare: Photography and the African American Freedom Struggle* (Chapel Hill: University of North Carolina Press, 2011), 143.

14. Raiford, *Imprisoned*, 143.

15. Raiford, *Imprisoned*, 173.

16. Raiford, *Imprisoned*, 173.

17. Hito Steyerl, "In Defense of the Poor Image," *e-flux*, no. 10 (November 2009): 1.

18. Steyerl, "In Defense," 5–6.

19. Steyerl, "In Defense," 8.

20. Steyerl's engagement with Dziga Vertov's theory of "visual bonds" is particularly illustrative. I paraphrase here to call attention to how her engagement might extend the scope of the "workers of the world" and account for a Black revolutionary force. See Steyerl, 8.

21. Abe Peck, *Uncovering the Sixties: The Life and Times of the Underground Press* (New York: Pantheon, 1985), 183.

22. Peck, *Uncovering*, 183.

23. Environmental and antiwar activist Gar Smith suspects that "the image appears to be a photo of a poster that was created to commemorate Bobby Hutton and the poster incorporated a photo by Alan Copeland. It could be that Alan captured the image of Bobby Hutton reflected on bullet-shattered glass." Gar, email correspondence.

24. Eldridge Cleaver, *Target Zero: A Life in Writing* (Hampshire: Palgrave Macmillan, 2006).

25. Bobby Seale as referenced in Joseph Peniel, *Waiting 'til the Midnight Hour: A Narrative History of Black Power in America* (New York: Holt Paperbacks, 2007), 228.

26. Curtis J. Austin, *Up Against the Wall: Violence in the Making and Unmaking of the Black Panther Party* (Fayetteville: University of Arkansas Press, 2006); Joshua

Bloom and Waldo E. Martin Jr., *Black against Empire: The History and Politics of the Black Panther Party* (Berkeley: University of California Press, 2013); Karen Grigsby Bates, "Bobby Hutton: The Killing That Catapulted the Black Panthers to Fame," NPR, April 6, 2018, https://www.npr.org/2018/04/06 /600055767/bobby-hutton-the-killing-that-catapulted-the-black-panthers -to-fame; Bill Van Niekerken, "The Death of a Black Panther: 50 Years after Bobby Hutton's Killing," *San Francisco Chronicle*, April 24, 2018, https://www .sfchronicle.com/thetake/article/The-death-of-a-Black-Panther-50-years -after-12855923.php.

27. "Two Nations of Black America," *Frontline*, PBS, February 10, 1998.

28. Cleaver, *Two Nations*.

29. Cleaver, *Two Nations*; emphasis added.

30. For more on the relationship between white supremacy and the police as both specifically manifest via sustained and structural anti-Black violence, see Steve Martinot and Jared Sexton, "The Avant-Garde of White Supremacy," *Social Identities: Journal for the Study of Race, Nation, and Culture* 9, no. 2 (June 2003): 169–81.

31. For more on the relationship among anti-Black violence, social death, and carceral subjectivity, please refer to the final chapter of this project, which discusses the murder of George Jackson at San Quentin State Prison.

32. Bloom and Martin Jr, *Black Against Empire*, 425, footnote 18.

33. Ariella Azoulay, *The Civil Contract of Photography* (New York: Zone Books, 2008); Katherine Biber, *Captive Images: Race, Crime, Photography* (Abingdon: Routledge, 2007); Avery Gordon, *Ghostly Matters: Haunting and the Sociological Imagination* (Minneapolis: University of Minnesota Press, 1997); Susie Linfield, *The Cruel Radiance: Photography and Political Violence* (Chicago: University of Chicago Press, 2010); Allan, Sekula, "The Body and the Archive," *October* 39 (1986): 3–64.; Susan Sontag, *On Photography* (New York: Picadour Press, 1977); David Levi Strauss, *Between the Eyes: Essays on Photography and Politics* (New York: Aperture, 2003); Blake Stimson, *The Pivot of the World: Photography and Its Nation* (Cambridge, MA: MIT Press, 2006); Harvey Young, "Still Standing: Daguerreotypes, Photography, and the Black Body," in *Embodying Black Experience: Stillness, Critical Memory, and the Black Body* (Ann Arbor: University of Michigan Press, 2010); "The Law and Science of Evidence," in *Hearsay of the Sun: Photography, Identity, and the Law of Evidence* (January 2009), http://chnm.gmu.edu/aq/photos/frames/essay01.htm.

34. Biber, *Captive Images*, 5.

35. John Berger, "Understanding a Photograph," in *Classic Essays on Photography*, ed. Alan Trachtenberg (New Haven, CT: Leete's Island Books, 1980), 293.

36. Bay Area Television Archive, "Police Chief Charles Gain on Bobby Hutton's Shooting," Diva, accessed March 12, 2022, https://diva.sfsu.edu/bundles/223881.

37. Ward Churchill and Jim VanderWall, *Agents of Repression: The FBI's Secret Wars against the Black Panther Party and the American Indian Movement* (Cambridge, MA: South End Press, 2008), 8.

38. Elizabeth Alexander, "'Can you be BLACK and Look at This?': Reading the Rodney King Video(s)," *Public Culture* 7, no. 1 (1994): 77–94; Azoulay, *The Civil Contract of Photography*; Tina Campt, *Listening to Images* (Durham, NC: Duke University Press, 2018); Gordan, *Ghostly Matters*; Linfield, *The Cruel Radiance*; David Marriott, *On Black Men* (New York: Columbia University Press, 2000); Sekula, "The Body and the Archive," 3–64; Maurice O. Wallace and Shawn Michelle Smith, eds., *Pictures and Progress: Early Photography and the Making of African American Identity* (Durham, NC: Duke University Press, 2012); Michele Wallace, *Dark Designs and Visual Culture* (Durham, NC: Duke University Press, 2004); Deborah Willis, *Picturing Us: African American Identity in Photography* (New York: New Press, 1996).

39. Bates, "Bobby Hutton."

40. Take, for example, Hutton's family's conviction that "Bobby was deliberately shot down by the Oakland police." Keith Power and Bill Van Niekerken, "A Ghetto Tragedy: The Death of a Panther," *San Francisco Chronicle*, April 24, 2018, https://www.sfchronicle.com/thetake/article/The-death-of-a-Black-Panther-50-years-after-12855923.php.

41. Bobby Seale, *Seize the Time: The Story of the Black Panther Party and Huey P. Newton* (Baltimore, MD: Black Classics Press, 1991), 42.

42. "Bobby James Hutton (1950–1968)," Cals: Encyclopedia of Arkansas, accessed March 3, 2020, http://www.encyclopediaofarkansas.net/encyclopedia/entry-detail.aspx?entryID=6040.

43. Seale, *Seize the Time*, 35.

44. Seale, *Seize the Time*, 35.

45. Seale, *Seize the Time*, 35.

46. In *Workers' Control in America: Studies in the History of Work, Technology, and Labor Struggles*, David Montgomery details approaches to workplace needs as the central organizing structure of labor struggles. In it, Montgomery suggests that the workplace was a primary location of politicization and organization. We can see this continued practice in Seale's 1966 decision to work as a foreman for youth. For more information, please refer to Montgomery, *Workers' Control in America: Studies in the History of Work, Technology, and Labor Struggles* (Cambridge: Cambridge University Press, 1979).

47. Seale, *Seize the Time*, 65.

48. Seale, *Seize the Time*, 65.

49. Power and Van Niekerken, "A Ghetto Tragedy."

50. *Berkeley Barb*, 4

51. Glen Coulthard, *Red Skin, White Masks: Rejecting the Colonial Politics of Recognition* (Minneapolis: University of Minnesota Press, 2014); Tiffany Lethabo-King, *The Black Shoals: Offshore Formations of Black and Native Studies* (Durham, NC: Duke University Press, 2019); Aileen Moreton-Robinson, *The White Possessive: Property, Power, and Indigenous Sovereignty* (Minneapolis: University of Minnesota Press, 2015); Andrea Smith, "Heteropatriarchy and the Three Pillars of White Supremacy," in *Color of Violence: The INCITE! Anthology*,

ed. INCITE! Women of Color against Violence (Durham, NC: Duke University Press, 2016), 66–73.

52. Bay Area Television Archive, "Brando & Panthers at Bobby Hutton's Funeral," Diva, accessed March 12, 2022, https://diva.sfsu.edu/bundles/188783.

53. Power and Van Niekerken, "A Ghetto Tragedy."

54. Alexander, "'Can you be BLACK and Look at This?,'" 77–94.

55. Fred Moten, *In the Break: The Aesthetics of the Black Radical Tradition* (Minneapolis: University of Minnesota Press, 2003), 199–200.

56. Stokely Carmichael, "Letter for Lil' Bobby," *Black Panther*, May 4, 1968, 21.

57. Carmichael, "Letter for Lil' Bobby," 21.

58. In regards to the age fourteen reference, I assume that Howe mistakenly refers to Hutton as fourteen at the time of his recruitment into the party. There are no records of a recruit before Bobby Hutton, who was recruited in 1967 at the age of sixteen. Charles Howe, "Black Panthers—What They Want," *San Francisco Chronicle*, May 15, 1968, 18.

59. Cleaver, "Brando & Panthers at Bobby Hutton's Funeral."

60. There is a robust history of armed self-defense within the Black radical tradition, from Nat Turner to the Deacons for Defense to Robert Williams. For more information on the role of armed self-defense within revolutionary Black history, please refer to Lance E. Hill, *The Deacons for Defense: Armed Resistance and the Civil Rights Movement* (Chapel Hill: University of North Carolina Press, 2004); Mabel R. Williams and Sele Nadel-Hayes, *Robert F. Williams: Self-defense, Self-Respect, & Self-Determination* (San Francisco: Freedom Archives, 2005), sound recording.

61. Mumia Abu-Jamal, *We Want Freedom: A Life in the Black Panther Party* (Cambridge, MA: South End Press, 2004), 105.

62. Philip Foner, ed., *The Black Panthers Speak* (New York: Da Capo Press, 1995), 8–9.

63. LeRoi Jones, Warren Rinckle, Curtis Harnack, Charles V. Hamilton, and John Gunther, "Violence in Oakland," *New York Review of Books*, May 9, 1968, https://www.nybooks.com/articles/1968/05/09/violence-in-oakland/.

64. Jones, "Violence in Oakland."

65. Jones, "Violence in Oakland."

66. Churchill and VanderWall, *Agents of Repression*, 8.

67. Huey Newton, "Tribute to Bobby Hutton," *Black Panther*, May 4, 1968, cover.

68. Seale, *Seize the Time*, 235–36.

69. Seale, *Seize the Time*, 236.

70. There is much to be said about masculinist approaches to revolutionary organizing practiced by Newton, Cleaver, and Seale. On one level, the binary between emotional versus pragmatic responses to Hutton's murder can be understood as particularly antifeminist strategies. However, many Black radical women who organized alongside Newton, Cleaver, and Seale offer alternative understandings of women's roles in the BPP and the lifelong struggle against sexism. For more, please refer to Elaine Brown, *A Taste of*

Power: A Black Woman's Story (New York: Pantheon, 1992); Angela Y. Davis, *Angela Davis: An Autobiography* (New York: Random House, 1974).

71. Foner, *The Black Panthers Speak*, xxviii.
72. Fanon, *Wretched*, 44.
73. See Emory Douglas, "On Revolutionary Art," *Black Panther*, 1968.
74. I am indebted to Krista Thompson's insight here on the shift from the evidentiary to the forensic.
75. Leigh Raiford, *Imprisoned in a Luminous Glare: Photography and the African American Freedom Struggle* (Chapel Hill: University of North Carolina Press, 2011), 198.
76. Raiford, *Imprisoned*, 198.

CHAPTER 2. FRED HAMPTON AND THE POLITICAL LIFE OF OBJECTS

Epigraph: As I will discuss in this chapter, the translation of Frantz Fanon is significant to various uptakes of the thinker in Black studies in the United States, which is why I choose to linger on it here. I chose to use the Richard Philcox translation for the opening epigraph of this chapter and my repeated use of the phrase "object among other objects" throughout the chapter. In the Charles Markmann translation, the passage is translated as, "I came into the world imbued with the will to find a meaning in things, my spirit filled with the desire to attain to the source of the world, and then I found that I was an object in the midst of other objects." As I will discuss later, each translation carries with it a different set of emphases in relation to theorizations on Black life. See Frantz Fanon, *Black Skin, White Masks*, trans. Richard Philcox (New York: Grove Press, 2008), 89; Frantz Fanon, *Black Skin, White Masks*, trans. Charles Markmann (New York: Grove Press, 1967), 109.

1. Mark Clark, a twenty-two-year-old Chicago Black Panther, was also killed the night of Fred Hampton's murder. Clark was asleep on a chair in the living room and shot in the chest. As he fell to the ground, Clark's gun (which was rested on his lap) shot into the air, striking no one. The Chicago Police Department claimed they shot into the house only after the BPP shot at them. However, later courtroom evidence showed there were somewhere between eighty-two and ninety-nine shots fired into the house and only one shot was proven to come from a Panther gun. This one shot was, indeed, from Mark Clark's gun. For more detailed information on Clark, please refer to Jeffery Haas's work *The Assassination of Fred Hampton: How the FBI and the Chicago Police Murdered a Black Panther* (Chicago: Chicago Review Press, 2009).

2. Louis J. Massiah, Thomas Ott, and Terry Kay Rockefeller, dir., "A Nation of Law? 1968–1971," *Eyes on the Prize* (Boston: Blackside, 1990), DVD.

3. In 1971, files were discovered after a break-in at the FBI office in Media, Pennsylvania. The release of these documents revealed a massive government counterinsurgent program called the Counter Intelligence Program (COINTELPRO).

The portfolio documents included a floor plan of Hampton's apartment and an outline of the deal to conceal the FBI's role in the assassination of Hampton. In 1970, the survivors and relatives of Hampton sued the federal and local governments for $47.7 million, stating that their civil rights were violated. The case was dismissed after it was determined that the government withheld relevant documents and obstructed the judicial process. A new trial was held in 1979. In 1982, Cook County and the federal government agreed to a settlement of $1.85 million. See the National Archives, "Fred Hampton (August 30, 1948–December 4, 1969)," US National Archives and Records Administration, accessed March 12, 2022, https://www.archives.gov/research/african-americans/individuals/fred-hampton.

4. As described in Joshua Bloom and Waldo E. Martin Jr., *Black against Empire: The History and Politics of the Black Panther Party* (Berkeley: University of California Press, 2013), 241; John Kifner, "Panthers Say an Autopsy Shows Party Official was 'Murdered,'" *New York Times*, December 7, 1969, 68; John Kifner, "Inquiry Is Urged in Slaying of Black Panther," *New York Times*, December 9, 1969, 40.

5. Kifner, "Inquiry Is Urged," 40.

6. John Kifner, "Coroner Seals Panther Slaying Site," *New York Times*, December 18, 1969, 66.

7. Kifner, "Coroner Seals Panther," 66.

8. A. H. Weiler, "The Murder of Fred Hampton," *New York Times*, October 5, 1971.

9. Roger Ebert, "Interview with Mike Gray," Ebert Co., October 11, 1971, https://www.rogerebert.com/interviews/interview-with-mike-gray.

10. Ebert, "Interview with Mike Gray."

11. Museum of Modern Art, 1971, "Controversial Film to Premiere at Museum: *The Murder of Fred Hampton*—Black Panther," press release, 1971.

12. Museum of Modern Art, "Controversial Film."

13. Weiler, "The Murder of Fred Hampton."

14. Ebert, "Interview with Mike Gray."

15. Ebert, "Interview with Mike Gray."

16. Ebert, "Interview with Mike Gray."

17. Ebert, "Interview with Mike Gray."

18. Museum of Modern Art, "Controversial Film."

19. Museum of Modern Art, "Controversial Film."

20. Peter Matthews, "*The Battle of Algiers*: Bombs and Boomerangs," film rerelease booklet (New York: Criterion, 2004), 9.

21. Matthews, "*The Battle of Algiers*," 9.

22. Bloom and Martin, *Black against Empire*, 232.

23. Bloom and Martin, *Black against Empire*, 232.

24. Martin Luther King Jr.'s assassination was one of many deaths that shadowed Hampton's in 1969. King's presence in Chicago just a year prior made the local impact of his death for Black Chicagoans particularly powerful and

undoubtedly shaped how Hampton's death would impact Black radicals locally and nationally. Relatedly, the site of King's death on the balcony of room 306 at the Lorraine Motel in Memphis Tennessee would become the National Civil Rights Museum in 1991. The transformation of the location of King's assassination shares some similarity with that of Hampton's home, but while King's legacy would be institutionalized as a Smithsonian affiliate, Hampton's 2337 West Monroe home would not be transformed into a permanent memorial and exhibition space for the slain leader.

25. Martin Luther King Jr., *Where Do We Go from Here: Chaos or Community?* (Boston: Beacon Press, 1968), 56.

26. Hader Eid and Khaled Gazel, "Footprints of Fanon in Gillo Pontecorvo's 'The Battle of Algiers' and Sembene Ousamne's 'Xala,'" *English in Africa* 35, no. 2 (October 2008): 154.

27. As noted across several sources, Frantz Fanon was required reading for members of the BPP. See Bloom and Martin, *Black against Empire*, 232.

28. Haas, *The Assassination*, 15.

29. Haas, *The Assassination*, 17.

30. Haas, 18; Joseph Boyce, "Friends, Relatives Tell Story of Fred Hampton," *Chicago Tribune*, December 28, 1969, http://gatekeeper.chipublib.org/login?url =https://search-proquest-com.gatekeeper.chipublib.org/docview/169815441 ?accountid=303.

31. Boyce, "Friends, Relatives."

32. Boyce, "Friends, Relatives"; and Haas, *The Assassination*, 18.

33. Boyce, "Friends, Relatives."

34. Boyce, "Friends, Relatives."

35. Huey P. Newton, *War against the Panthers: A Study of Repression in America* (London: Writers and Readers, 2001), 48.

36. Natalie Moore and Lance Williams, *The Almighty Black P. Stone Nation: The Rise, Fall, and Resurgence of an American Gang* (Chicago: Chicago Review Press, 2011).

37. "African Independence," Esri, accessed October 16, 2019, http://education .maps.arcgis.com/home/webmap/viewer.html?webmap=87d01590d1b1445f8e ed3ee22895d3b3.

38. "Decolonization of Asia and Africa, 1945–1960." US Department of State, accessed October 16, 2019, https://history.state.gov/milestones/1945–1952/asia -and-africa.

39. Vijay Prashad, *The Darker Nations: A People's History of the Third World* (New York: New Press, 2007).

40. George Katsiaficas, *The Imagination of the New Left: A Global Analysis of 1968* (Boston: South End Press, 1987).

41. Ward Churchill and Jim Vander Wall brilliantly document state repression of radical social movements in their 2002 book *Agents of Repression: The FBI's Secret Wars against the Black Panther Party and the American Indian Movement*

(Cambridge, MA: South End Press, 2008). In their account of Hampton's death, the authors affirm then-suspected accusations that the state was out to kill, imprison, or, at the very least, repress radical social movements and their leaders. The most infamous government program that spearheaded this repression was the FBI's COINTELPRO, which effectively destroyed radical social movements by engaging a series of tactics, including infiltration, sabotage, arrest, false imprisonment, and, in some cases, murder. This study catalogs each of these tactics as they played out in the Black Panther Party and the American Indian Movement. See Churchill and Vander Wall, *Agents of Repression*.

42. The most notorious call for "law and order" took place during Richard Nixon's 1968 presidential campaign, during which he promised restored civility and a "tough on crime" platform that specifically targeted leadership within radical social movements. For more on the implications of Nixon's 1968 campaign in relation to the then-burgeoning prison industrial complex, refer to Ruth Wilson Gilmore, "Globalisation and US Prison Growth: From Military Keynesianism to Post-Keynesian Militarism," *Race & Class* 40, no. 2–3 (March 1999): 171–88, https://doi.org/10.1177/030639689904000212.

43. As Churchill and Vander Wall have documented extensively in *Agents of Repression*, the state murder and prolonged incarceration of Black Panther Party members and Black liberation freedom fighters in general were unprecedented in relation to other radical organizations. Black radicals still alive that once were affiliated with the BPP continue to be incarcerated today. For more information, see Churchill and Vander Wall, *Agents of Repression*.

44. Government documents and testimonies later revealed that this allegation, along with many other attempts to jail Hampton, was orchestrated by the FBI under COINTELPRO.

45. Gray, *The Murder of Fred Hampton*.

46. Abdul R. JanMohamed, *The Death-Bound-Subject: Richard Wright's Archaeology of Death* (Durham, NC: Duke University Press, 2005), 2.

47. JanMohamed, *The Death-Bound-Subject*, 15.

48. JanMohamed, *The Death-Bound-Subject*, 15.

49. Philip Rosen, "Document and Documentary: On the Persistence of Historical Concepts," in *Theorizing Documentary*, ed. Michael Renov (New York: Routledge, 1993), 58–89.

50. Michael Renov, "Introduction: The Truth About Non-Fiction," in *Theorizing Documentary*, 3.

51. Rosen, "Document and Documentary," 71 (italics in original).

52. Rosen, "Document and Documentary," 70.

53. Trinh T. Minh-ha, "The Totalizing Quest of Meaning," in *Theorizing Documentary*, 100.

54. Minh-ha, "The Totalizing," 21.

55. Renov, "Introduction,"31.

56. Kara Keeling, *The Witch's Flight: The Cinematic, the Black Femme, and the Image of Common Sense* (Durham, NC: Duke University Press, 2007): 74.

57. Keeling, *The Witch's Flight*, 74.

58. Keeling, *The Witch's Flight*, 85.

59. Parry D. Teasdale, *Videofreex: America's First Pirate TV Station & the Catskills Collective That Turned It On* (Hensonville: Black Dome Press, 1999).

60. Steve Dollar, "Before the Internet, There Was a Video Revolution," *Wall Street Journal*, March 7, 2016, https://www.wsj.com/articles/before-the-internet-there-was-a-video-revolution-1457316748.

61. Videofreex, "Fred Hampton: Black Panthers in Chicago," Video Data Bank, accessed March 12, 2022, https://www.vdb.org/titles/fred-hampton-black-panthers-chicago.

62. Many journalistic and first-person accounts corroborate that the attendees into Hampton's home were mostly Black neighbors and Chicago residents. For more, see Joseph Boyce, "Writer Joins Curiosity Seekers in Tour of Black Panther Lair," *Chicago Tribune*, December 13, 1969; Haas, *The Assassination of Fred Hampton*, 18.

63. "Daily Defender Cameraman at Death Scene," *Chicago Daily Defender*, December 6, 1969, 40.

64. Strikingly, on April 9, 1969—the same day that Hampton was convicted of the ice cream truck robbery—Seale and the rest of the Chicago Eight were arraigned on conspiracy charges for their political organizing during the 1968 Democratic National Convention and the uprising that took place by thousands during the convention. For more, see Bloom and Martin Jr., *Black against Empire*, 231.

65. Boyce, "Writer Joins Curiosity Seekers."

66. Boyce, "Friends, Relatives."

67. Bloom and Martin, *Black against Empire*; Salim Muwakkil, "Black Panthers Reconsidered," *Chicago Tribune*, February 28, 2000, https://www.chicagotribune.com/news/ct-xpm-2000-02-28-0002280029-story.html.

68. Frantz Fanon, *Black Skin, White Masks*, trans. Richard Philcox (New York: Grove Press, 2008), 89.

69. Fred Moten, "A Case of Blackness," *Criticism* 50, no. 2 (Spring 2008): 179.

70. Moten, "A Case of Blackness," 179.

71. This original excerpt was taken from a 2013 seminar run by Fred Moten at the University of California, Irvine (UCI), entitled "Just Friends." Moten's seminar directly took on intellectual debates and conversations between himself and Frank B. Wilderson III and Jared Sexton, both of whom reside as faculty at UCI. Versions of the talks given during this seminar appeared across articles, mostly appearing in Fred Moten, "Blackness and Nothingness (Mysticism in the Flesh)," *South Atlantic Quarterly* 112, no.4 (2013): 737–80. For this section, I quote extensively from the early draft of this talk given at UCI. A crude citation appears as Fred Moten, "Just Friends (Black OP_2)" seminar given at University of California, Irvine, 2013, 40.

72. Fanon, *Black Skin*, xvii.

73. Moten, "The Case of Blackness," 177–218; Moten, "Blackness and Nothingness."

74. Moten, "Just Friends," 44.

75. Moten, "Just Friends," 42.

76. Frank Wilderson, *Red, White, and Black: Cinema and the Structure of U.S. Antagonisms* (Durham, NC: Duke University Press, 2010).

77. Fred Moten, *In the Break: The Aesthetics of the Black Radical Tradition* (Minneapolis: University of Minnesota Press, 2003), 1; Huey Copeland and Jared Sexton, "Raw Life: An Introduction," *Qui Parle* 13, no. 2 (2003): 53–62; Saidiya Hartman, *Scenes of Subjection: Terror, Slavery, and Self-Making in Nineteenth Century America* (London: Oxford University Press, 1997), 21; Frank B. Wilderson III, "Of Grammar and Ghosts: The Performative Limits of African Freedom," *Theatre Survey* 50, no. 1 (2009): 119–25.

78. For more on Black studies approaches to this shared history, see Hortense Spillers, "Mama's Baby, Papa's Maybe: An American Grammar Book," *Diacritics* (1986): 65–81; Ronald T. Judy, *(Dis)forming the American Canon: African-Arabic Slave Narratives and the Vernacular* (Minneapolis: University of Minnesota Press, 1993); Hartman, *Scenes of Subjection*; Cedric Robinson, *Black Marxism: The Making of the Black Radical Tradition* (Chapel Hill: University of North Carolina Press, 2000); Frank B. Wilderson III, "Gramsci's Black Marx: Whither the Slave in Civil Society?" *Social Identities* 9, no. 2 (2003): 225–40; Moten, *In the Break*; Christina Sharpe, *Monstrous Intimacies: Making Post-Slavery Subjects* (Durham, NC: Duke University Press, 2010); Zakkiyah Iman Jackson, "Losing Manhood: Animality and Plasticity in the (Neo) Slave Narrative," *Qui Parle* 25, nos. 1–2 (2016): 95–136.

79. Spillers, "Mama's Baby," 72.

80. Spillers, "Mama's Baby," 67.

81. Huey Copeland, *Bound to Appear: Art, Slavery, and the Site of Blackness in Multicultural America* (Chicago: University of Chicago Press, 2013), 10.

82. Copeland, *Bound to Appear*, 50.

83. Sampada Aranke, "Objects Made Black," *Art Journal* 73, no. 3 (2014): 86–88.

84. Copeland, *Bound to Appear*, 10.

85. Joseph Roach, *Cities of the Dead: Circum-Atlantic Performance* (New York: Columbia University Press, 1996).

86. Roach, *Cities of the Dead*, 2.

87. Roach, *Cities of the Dead*, 2.

88. Roach, *Cities of the Dead*, 2.

89. Manning Marable's *Malcolm X: A Life of Reinvention* most clearly discusses how *The Autobiography of Malcolm X*, a collaboration between Malcolm X and Alex Haley, was overstated and oversimplified. Marble contends that the book aimed to articulate a particular image of Malcolm X that would fuel a clearly developed political analysis among its readership. For more, see Manning Marable, *Malcolm X: A Life of Reinvention* (New York: Penguin, 2011).

90. Roach, *Cities of the Dead*, 2.
91. Keeling, *Witch's Flight*, 39.
92. Keeling, *Witch's Flight*, 40.
93. Fanon, *Black Skin*, 109.
94. Philip Foner, *The Black Panthers Speak* (New York: Da Capo Press, 1995), 259.
95. Foner, *The Black Panthers Speak*, 259.

CHAPTER 3. GEORGE JACKSON'S MURDER AND FUGITIVE IMAGINARIES

1. Dan Berger, *Captive Nation: Black Prison Organizing in the Civil Rights Era* (Chapel Hill: University of North Carolina Press, 2014), 133.
2. For an incredibly detailed account, please see Berger, *Captive Nation*, 133–38.
3. George Jackson, *Soledad Brother: The Prison Letters of George Jackson* (Chicago: HarperCollins, 1970); Zach Schrempp, "George Jackson (1941–1971)," Black Past, October 4, 2010, https://www.blackpast.org/african-american-history/jackson-george-1941-1971/.
4. Jackson, *Soledad Brother*, 16.
5. Dylan Rodriguez, *Forced Passages: Imprisoned Radical Intellectuals and the U.S. Prison Regime* (Minneapolis: University of Minnesota Press, 2006).
6. Rodriguez, *Forced Passages*.
7. Rodriguez, *Forced Passages*.
8. George Jackson, *Blood in My Eye* (Baltimore: Black Classic Press, 1972), 182.
9. There is a long history of Black radical uses of so-called criminal acts as methods of resistance. The overturning of lawlessness into a political strategy is an attempt to reconceptualize the state and capitalism as the ultimate criminal institutions, whose ongoing actions and ethos structure life along uneven proportions of death. In other words, to borrow from Achille Mbembe, anti-Black violence is a way of managing Black death under capitalism—thus making the system itself the generative force of criminality. To borrow from Angela Y. Davis's influential study, the very notion of "doing time"—a phrase adopted in prison vernacular to indicate time served inside prison—is wedded to the force of laboring within capitalist structures of temporality. See Angela Y. Davis, *Are Prisons Obsolete?* (New York: Seven Stories Press), 44. To build off this notion, the very computability of time is a result of computing values of capitalist commodities. (With the inception of the 1970s neoliberal prison, these commodities themselves turn perversely into prisoners themselves.) Within this understanding, divorcing Blackness from criminality is an outcome of a kind of anticapitalist and anti-state political consciousness that George Jackson illustratively demonstrates in his writings.
10. Peniel Joseph, *Waiting 'Til the Midnight Hour: A Narrative History of Black Power in America* (New York: Holt, 2006), 142; emphasis added.
11. Joseph, *Waiting 'Til the Midnight Hour*, 142.
12. Joseph, *Waiting 'Til the Midnight Hour*, 272

13. *Black Panther*, November 23, 1967, 11.
14. Gregory Armstrong, preface to *Blood in My Eye*, ix.
15. Jean Genet, preface to *Soledad Brother*; cited in Jean Genet, *The Declared Enemy: Texts and Interviews* (Stanford, CA: Stanford University Press, 2004), 55; emphasis in original.
16. In *Black Skin, White Masks*, Frantz Fanon details the psychic and material affects of Blackness. Within this study, he introduces a way of thinking through the intensified overlapping psychic traumas of Black life called the racial epidermal schema. The epidermal racial schema refers to how Blackness means "existing triply" for Black bodies. Existing triply indicates (1) a dialectic or relationship between one's body and the world or a notion of embodiment of self; (2) existing for the other, the white man; and (3) existing out of historical precedents (racist stereotypes, etc.). The epidermal racial schema is the burden placed on Black bodies to exist in multiple ways. This way of being confines Black bodies to a realm of limited possibilities. See Fanon, *Black Skin, White Masks*, trans. Charles Markmann (New York: Grove Press, 1967), 112.
17. For more information on how the prison industrial complex intensifies the already confirmed relationship between the state and corporate capitalism, please refer to Angela Yvonne Davis and David Barsamian. *The Prison Industrial Complex* (Chico, CA: AK Press, 1999); Ruth Wilson Gilmore, *Golden Gulag: Prisons, Surplus, Crisis, and Opposition in Globalizing California*. Vol. 21 (Berkeley: University of California Press, 2007); Julia Sudbury, *Global Lockdown: Race, Gender, and the Prison-Industrial Complex* (New York: Routledge, 2005).
18. Black radicals and intellectuals often refer to Jackson's murder as an assassination—the political nature of his death. See Larry Ryckman, "TODAY'S FOCUS: Violent Deaths of Jonathan, George Jackson Remembered," Associated Press, 1985. http://www.apnewsarchive.com/1985/TODAY-S-FOCUS-Violent-Deaths-of-Jonathan-George-Jackson-Remembered/id-b2714e0fbf61972b20f3447d6da1e1cc?SearchText=george%20jackson%20murder%201971.
19. Patrick Anderson, *So Much Wasted: Hunger, Performance, and the Morbidity of Resistance* (Durham, NC: Duke University Press, 2010), 11.
20. Ruth Wilson Gilmore, "Globalisation and US Prison Growth: From Military Keynesianism to Post-Keynesian Militarism," *Race & Class* 40, nos. 2–3 (March 1999): 175.
21. Gilmore, "Globalisation," 178.
22. Gilmore, "Globalisation," 176.
23. Gilmore, "Globalisation," 180–82.
24. Angela Y. Davis, *Are Prisons Obsolete?* (New York: Seven Stories Press, 2003), 106
25. Shania Agid, Brooks Berndt, Rachel Herzig, and Ari Wohlfeiler, "The Abolitionist Toolkit," Critical Resistance, October 2004, http://criticalresistance.org/resources/the-abolitionist-toolkit/.

26. Frank B. Wilderson III, "The Prison Slave as Hegemony's (Silent) Scandal," in *Warefare in the American Homeland: Policing and Prison in a Penal Colony*, edited by Joy James (Durham, NC: Duke University Press, 2007), 23; emphasis mine.

27. Wilderson, "The Prison Slave," 32.

28. Wilderson, "The Prison Slave," 33.

29. Jackson, *Soledad Brother*, 16.

30. Stefano Harney and Fred Moten, *The Undercommons: Fugitive Planning and Black Study* (Brooklyn: Minor Compositions, 2013), 56.

31. In many ways, my argument in this section about the prison as a particular kind of state performance of justice can be seen as paradoxical. Let me clarify this argument as a twofold process. On the one hand, as indicated by Davis and Foucault, born out of liberal reforms oriented toward social rehabilitation, prisons aimed to make "good" subjects out of those whose criminal actions have made them "deviant." Out of this notion of rehabilitating the deviant subject and eventually reeducating them through legal torture, prison formation in the 1970s was invested in extended incarceration and ongoing state performances of violence, which is a radical departure from the eighteenth-century imaginary promise of justice seemingly guaranteed by prisons. I do not want to exonerate eighteenth-century disciplinary mechanisms as free of racist practices. Indeed, the history of colonialism, imperialism, and slavery should all be understood as varying degrees of disciplinary measures that both representationally and materially incarcerated racialized subjects into captivity and forced servitude. Rather, I suggest that we think of eighteenth-century models of prisons as operating under a particular ideal that falls apart with the inception of advanced capitalism.

    This early genealogy of incarceration as born out of reform might destabilize more liberal tendencies to think of the current state of prisons as merely needing reforms. In fact, when we think of the prison as birthed from liberal reformist policies, we can see how the current prison phenomenon is a logical conglomerate of state, industry, and liberal desires for rehabilitation. Within the logic of liberal capitalism, the prison as it stands is fulfilling the project it was meant to fulfill.

32. Dylan Rodriguez, "State Terror and the Reproduction of Imprisoned Dissent," *Social Identities* 9, no. 2 (2003): 193.

33. Rodriguez, "State Terror," 194.

34. Rodriguez, "State Terror," 195.

35. Rodriguez, "State Terror," 198.

36. Nicole Fleetwood, *Marking Time: Art in the Age of Mass Incarceration* (Cambridge, MA: Harvard University Press, 2020), 3, 2.

37. Fleetwood, *Marking Time*, 26.

38. Fleetwood, *Marking Time*, 41.

39. In most radical organizing collectives or social movements working toward a more egalitarian political system, praxis refers to the interplay

between theory and practice. Praxis requires constant cyclical movement within taking action, reflecting on the action taken, and then incorporating that theoretical reflection into more directed and effective action. Praxis, in its best form, refuses the anti-intellectualism that inflects most radical organizing spaces toward a more engaged and engaging dialogue between both scholarship and action. For more on praxis, refer to the works of Paulo Freire's *Pedagogy of the Oppressed*; Antonio Gramsci's *Prison Notebooks*; or Assata Shakur's autobiography.

40. Fleetwood, *Marking Time*, 7.
41. In Kojève's reading of Hegel's master-slave dialectic, he offers an analysis that is now central to most understandings of Hegel. Kojeve makes an important intervention on the question of identity and recognition. *He notes that in order for the master to be so, he depends on the existence of the slave.* This is a radical reunderstanding of who actually holds the power in this kind of hierarchy. Therefore, both necessitate the other's recognition. This battle for recognition is where the tension culminates to a "fight to the death." The slave's only road to freedom relies upon a fight to the death between himself and the master. In this formulation, the essential quality of revolutionary praxis negotiates thesis, antithesis, and synthesis in which the slave's struggle for freedom relies on the radical fight-to-death in which the master loses. For more on Kojève's lectures, please refer to Alexandre Kojève, *Introduction to the Reading of Hegel* (Ithaca, NY: Cornell University Press, 1980).
42. What is particularly compelling in Jackson's account is the way that his terminology anticipates and influences Black studies. The language of "premature death," for example, would be crucial in some of the most central writings in the field while Jackson rarely appears in these citations.
43. Paul Gilroy, *The Black Atlantic: Modernity and Double Consciousness* (Cambridge, MA: Harvard University Press, 1993): 68.
44. Gilroy, *The Black Atlantic*, 69.
45. Gilroy, *The Black Atlantic*, 69.
46. Michel Foucault, *Discipline and Punish: The Birth of the Prison*, trans. Alan Sheridan (New York: Vintage Books, 1977).
47. Part of the original pamphlet published by the organization is translated in Joy James, ed., *Warfare in the American Homeland: Policing and Prison in a Penal Democracy* (Durham, NC: Duke University Press Books, 2007).
48. James, *Warfare*, 140.
49. Saidiya Hartman, "Venus in Two Acts," *Small Axe* 12, no. 2 (2008): 1–14.
50. Berger, *Captive Nation*, 94.
51. Fred Moten, *In the Break: The Aesthetics of the Black Radical Tradition* (Minneapolis: University of Minnesota Press, 2003), 210.
52. Lincoln Cushing, *All of Us or None: Social Justice Posters of the San Francisco Bay Area* (Berkeley: Heyday, 2012), ix.
53. Cushing, *All of Us*, viii.
54. Cushing, *All of Us*, ix.

55. Harney and Moten, *Undercommons*, 50.
56. Harney and Moten, *Undercommons*, 50.
57. Harney and Moten, *Undercommons*, 50.
58. Harney and Moten, *Undercommons*, 50.
59. Jackson, *Soledad Brother*, 16.
60. Translated by Hand Aldmairi, correspondence with author, May 19, 2020.
61. Josh MacPhee, "Constructing Third World Struggle: The Design of the OSPAAAL & Tricontinental," *Funambulist* 22 (March 2019): 50.
62. MacPhee, "Constructing," 50.
63. At least one source suggests that this poster was Morante's first for OSPAAAL's *Tricontinental* publication. See "Morante and OSPAAAL," D-aqui, accessed January 7, 2020, https://d-aqui.com/stories/morante-and -the-ospaaal.
64. "Instituto Cubano del Arte y Industria Cinematográficos," EcuRed, ac-cessed May 19, 2020, https://www.ecured.cu/Instituto_Cubano_del_Arte_e _Industria_Cinematogr%C3%A1ficos.
65. Melanie Herzog, *Elizabeth Catlett: An American Artist in Mexico* (Seattle: Univer-sity of Washington Press, 2005); Sarah Kelly Oehler and Esther Adler, eds., *Charles White: A Retrospective*, (New Haven, CT: Yale University Press, 2018).
66. Josh McPhee, interview with author, January 8, 2020; "The Art of the Revolution Will be Internationalist," Internationalist 360, April 11, 2019, https://libya360.wordpress.com/2019/04/11/the-art-of-the-revolution-will-be -internationalist/.
67. Carol Mavor, *Black and Blue: The Bruised Passion of "Camera Lucida," "la Jetée," "Sans Soleil," and "Hiroshima Mon Amour"* (Durham, NC: Duke University Press, 2012), 32–33; emphasis in original.
68. Mavor, *Black and Blue*, 33.
69. There is a dense and complex visual history of (anti)lynching accounted for in the mid-twentieth-century by a spectrum of political leftists and artists, most notably marked by the 1935 exhibition *Struggle for Negro Rights*, orga-nized by the Artists' Union—a collective that had organizational overlap with several Communist-affiliated groups. This exhibition featured works by a cohort of well-known artists from the American Left, including Charles Alston, José Clemente Orozco, and Harry Sternberg. This exhibition embod-ied a commitment to connecting the racial terror embodied in lynching acts to other forms of anti-Black racism under white supremacy and capitalism. I mention it in brief here because in early 1943, Elizabeth Catlett would go on to move to New York City to study lithography with Sternberg at the Art Students League and would befriend Charles Alston soon after. During this time, Catlett's political work with the George Washington Carver school, a "Marxist school for working-class adults in Harlem," combined with her astute aesthetic abilities, would develop her conceptual commitment to images of and for the Black freedom struggle. With her lithographic experience in tow, Catlett would go on to receive a Rosenwald Fellowship in 1946 that would

take her to Mexico City, where she would work with Taller de Gráfica Popular, developing a new skill in linocut prints that would shape her famous *The Negro Woman* series. For more, see Eric Cohn, "Art Fronts: Visual Culture and Race Politics in Mid-Twentieth Century United States," (unpublished PhD diss., University of Pennsylvania, 2010), 135–41; Melanie Herzog, *Elizabeth Catlett*; Helen Langa, *Radical Art: Printmaking and the Left in 1930s New York* (Berkeley: University of California Press, 2004), 283; "Two Antilynching Art Exhibitions: Politicized Viewpoints, Racial Perspectives, Gendered Constraints." *American Art* 13, no. 1 (1999): 26.

70. I am eternally grateful for Krista Thompson's suggestion that I turn to this Catlett print in this section. This chapter would indeed have suffered without such an energizing comparative.

71. Herzog, *Elizabeth Catlett*.

72. Jaqueline Goldsby, *A Spectacular Secret: Lynching in American Life and Literature* (Berkeley: University of California Press, 2006), 252.

73. Goldsby, *A Spectacular Secret*, 253.

74. For more information on this exhibition, see Sampada Aranke, "Studio/ Streets: Faith Ringgold's Sense of Practice," in *The Everywhere Studio,* ed. Alex Gartenfield, Gean Moreno, and Stephanie Seidel (New York: Prestel Publishing, 2018); Julia Bryan-Wilson, *Art Workers: Radical Practice in the Vietnam War Era* (Berkeley: University of California Press, 2009); Faith Ringgold, *We Flew Over the Bridge: The Memoirs of Faith Ringgold* (Durham, NC: Duke University Press, 2005); Michele Wallace and Mary Lodu, "Michele Wallace interviewed by Mary Lodu," *Third Rail*, no. 9, November 2016.

75. Wallace and Lodu, "Michele Wallace interviewed," 32.

76. Sampada Aranke, "Material Matters," *e-flux* 79 (February 2017); Kellie Jones, *Eyeminded: Living and Writing Contemporary Art* (Durham, NC: Duke University Press, 2011); Kellie Jones, *South of Pico: African American Artists in Los Angeles in the 1960s and 1970s* (Durham, NC: Duke University Press, 2017); David Joselit, "Notes on Surface: Toward a Genealogy of Flatness," *Art History* 23 (2000): 19–34; Tobias Wofford, "Can You Dig It? Signifying Race in David Hammons' Spade Series," in *L.A. Object & David Hammons Body Prints*, ed. Lindsay Charwood (New York: Tilton Gallery, 2011), 86–135.

77. Houston A. Baker, *Modernism and the Harlem Renaissance* (Chicago: University of Chicago Press, 1987), 50.

78. Jackson, *Soledad Brother*, 296; emphasis added.

79. While the exact date is unknown, the artist notes starting the collective after the Berkeley Free Speech Movement, sometime after 1964. Interview with Doug Lawler, July 2015, Oakland, California.

80. Lawler, interview, 2015.

81. Lawler, interview, 2015.

82. Lawler, interview, 2015.

83. Lawler, interview, 2015.

84. On August 7, 1970, during the trial of James McClain and with the help of two imprisoned men, Ruchell McGee and William Christmas, an armed Jonathan Jackson held hostage Judge Haley, deputy district attorney Gary Thomas, and three female jurors. Jackson, working under the assumption that his brother George would be present at the trial, promised to free all hostages in exchange for the immediate release of his brother and the two other Soledad Brothers (Fleeta Drumgo and John Cluchette) from prison on that day. As they led all hostages to their getaway van in the parking lot, the Marin Police Department engaged a shoot-out that immediately killed Jonathan, James McClain, William Christmas, and Judge Haley. Ruchelle McGee and Gary Thomas were seriously injured (Freedom Archives, "George Jackson- 41 year commemoration"). Several witnesses overheard what are considered to be Jonathan Jackson's last public words as he intervened in the trial's proceedings by declaring, "All right gentlemen, I'm taking over now." Several of the guns used in the shoot-out were linked to Angela Y. Davis, a prominent theorist and activist who worked in the Soledad Brothers Defense Committee. Davis was charged in August 1970 with aggravated kidnapping and first-degree murder, which forced the activist to go underground until her capture in January 1971. The timeline of her case and incarceration overlapped with Jackson's murder. She was found not guilty in June 1972. Jonathan's murder and Davis's trial deeply and irrevocably impacted Jackson, who in the opening dedication of *Soledad Brother* pens that he dedicates "this collection of letters; to the destruction of their enemies I dedicate my life."

85. For more on this, please refer to André Bazin, "The Life and Death of Superimposition (1946)," *Film-Philosophy* 6, no. 1 (2002); Simone Natale, "A Short History of Superimposition: From Spirit Photography to Early Cinema," *Early Popular Visual Culture* 10, no. 2 (2012): 125–45.

86. Jackson, *Soledad*, 222.

87. Jennifer Devere Brody, *Punctuation: Art, Politics, Play* (Durham, NC: Duke University Press, 2008).

88. Brody, *Punctuation*, 13.

89. Angela Y. Davis, "A Statement on Our Fallen Comrade, George Jackson," *Black Panther*, vol. 3, no. 1, August 28, 1971.

90. For more on Douglas's use of collage, especially in his poster "Our Fight Is Not in Vietnam," see Leigh Raiford, *Imprisoned in a Luminous Glare: Photography and the African American Freedom Struggle* (Chapel Hill: University of North Carolina Press, 2011), 25.

91. Michel Foucault, Catherine Von Bülow, and Daniel Defert, "The Masked Assassination," in *Warfare in the American Homeland: Policing and Prison in a Penal Democracy*, trans. Sirène Harb (Durham, NC: Duke University Press, 2007), 138.

92. Foucault et al., "The Masked Assassination," 138.

93. Jean Genet, "Preface to *L'assassinat de Georges Jackson*," in *The Declared Enemy: Texts and Interviews*, ed. Albert Dichy and trans. Jeff Fort (Stanford, CA: Stanford University Press, 2004), 91.

94. Genet, "Preface," 91.

95. Genet, "Preface," 91.

96. Foucault et al., "The Masked," 147.

97. Jackson, *Blood in My Eye*, 7; Foucault et al., "The Masked Assassination," 147.

98. One could say that Jackson's prisoner-led insurrection and subsequent murder directly influenced the Attica Uprising in September 1971. Attica was the first explicitly prison-abolitionist uprising that was sparked by news of Jackson's murder in San Quentin. For more information on the Attica Rebellion, refer to Tom Wicker, *A Time to Die: The Attica Prison Revolt* (Lincoln: University of Nebraska Press, 1994); Liz Samuel, "Improvising on Reality: The Roots of Prison Abolition," *The Hidden 1970s: Histories of Radicalism*, ed. Dan Berger (New Brunswick, NJ: Rutgers University Press, 2010), 21–38.

99. Foucault et al., "The Masked Assassination," 156.

100. Foucault et al., "The Masked Assassination," 156.

101. Foucault et al., "The Masked Assassination," 156–57.

102. Jackson, *Soledad Brother*,16. For more on Mao's influence on Black radicals in the United States, especially Jackson, see Robin D. G. Kelley, *Freedom Dreams: The Black Radical Imagination* (Boston: Beacon Press, 2002).

103. Dylan Rodriguez, "State Terror and the Reproduction of Imprisoned Dissent," *Social Identities* 9, no. 2 (2003): 196.

104. Rodriguez, "State Terror," 195.

EPILOGUE. THE UNITED STATES OF ATTICA

1. Heather Ann Thompson, *Blood in the Water: The Attica Prison Uprising of 1971 and Its Legacy* (New York: Vintage, 2017), 35.

2. Thompson, *Blood in the Water*, 36.

3. Thompson, Blood, 36.

4. Thompson, Blood, 32.

5. Dan Bolles, "An Interview with Jazz Icon Archie Shepp," *Seven Days: Vermont's Independent Voice*, January 16, 2013, https://www.sevendaysvt.com/vermont/an-interview-with-jazz-icon-archie-shepp/Content?oid=2242673; Nate Chinen, "Archie Shepp: Attica Blues," Pitchfork, May 10, 2020, https://pitchfork.com/reviews/albums/archie-shepp-attica-blues/.

6. For more, see Muhammad Ali, conversation with Cathal O'Shannon, RTÉ Television, July 17, 1972, https://www.youtube.com/watch?v=J8ZWZztobkQ.

7. Martin Williams, "The Jazz Avant Garde, Who's In Charge?" *Evergreen Review* 10 (June 1966): 67; as quoted in John D. Baskerville, "Free Jazz: A Reflection of Black Power Ideology," *Journal of Black Studies* 24, no. 4 (1994): 484–97, http://www.jstor.org/stable/2784566.

8. "A Collection of Powerful Works by Forty-Eight Leading American Artists," advertisement for *Attica Book*, 1972, paper.

9. Lee Bernstein, *America Is the Prison: Arts and Politics in Prison in the 1970s* (Chapel Hill: University of North Carolina Press, 2010): 86.

10. Elsa Honig Fine, *The Afro-American Artist: A Search for Identity* (New York: Rinehart and Winston, 1973); Cliff Joseph, *Artist and Activist*, exhibition, Tyler Fine Art/Aaron Galleries, St. Louis, 2018, https://issuu.com/msmodular72/docs/cliff_joseph_artist_activist.

11. Red, black, and green were first used in the development of the Pan-African flag as commissioned by Marcus Garvey and the United Negro Improvement Association (UNIA). See Barbara Bair and Robert Hill, *Marcus Garvey, Life and Lessons: A Centennial Companion to the Marcus Garvey and Universal Negro Improvement Association Papers* (Berkeley: University of California Press, 1987).

Bibliography

African American Heritage. "Fred Hampton." National Archives. Accessed March 5, 2020. https://www.archives.gov/research/african-americans /individuals/fred-hampton.

"African Independence." Esri. Accessed October 16, 2019. http://education.maps.arcgis .com/home/webmap/viewer.html?webmap=87d01590d1b1445f8eed3ee22895d3b3.

Agid, Shania, Brooks Berndt, Rachel Herzig, and Ari Wohlfeiler. "The Abolition-ist Toolkit." Critical Resistance, October 2004. http://criticalresistance.org /resources/the-abolitionist-toolkit/.

Alexander, Elizabeth. "'Can you be BLACK and Look at This?': Reading the Rod-ney King Video(s)." *Public Culture* 7, no. 1 (1994): 77–94.

Ali, Muhammad. Conversation with Cathal O'Shannon. RTÉ Television, July 17, 1972. https://www.youtube.com/watch?v=J8ZWZztobkQ.

Allen, James. *Without Sanctuary: Lynching Photography in America*. Santa Fe, NM: Twin Palms, 2000.

Aranke, Sampada. "Objects Made Black." *Art Journal* 73, no. 1 (2014): 86–88.

Aranke, Sampada. "Studio/Streets: Faith Ringgold's Sense of Practice." In *The Everywhere Studio*, edited by Alex Gartenfield, Gean Moreno, and Stephanie Seidel. New York: Prestel Publishing, 2018.

Aranke, Sampada. "Style Wars: Shades of Cool." *AQ/SFAG/NYAQ*, June 21, 2016.

Armstrong, Gregory. "Preface." In *Blood in My Eye*, by George Jackson. Baltimore, MD: Black Classics Press, 1972.

"The Art of the Revolution Will be Internationalist." Internationalist 360, April 11, 2019. https://libya360.wordpress.com/2019/04/11/the-art-of-the-revolution-will -be-internationalist/.

Austin, Curtis J. *Up Against the Wall: Violence in the Making and Unmaking of the Black Panther Party*. Fayetteville: University of Arkansas Press, 2006.

Azoulay, Ariella. *The Civil Contract of Photography*. London: Zone Books, 2008.

Bair, Barbara, and Robert Hill. *Marcus Garvey, Life and Lessons: A Centennial Companion to the Marcus Garvey and Universal Negro Improvement Association Papers*. Berkeley: University of California Press, 1987.

Baker, Houston A. *Modernism and the Harlem Renaissance*. Chicago: University of Chicago Press, 1987.

Baskerville, John D. "Free Jazz: A Reflection of Black Power Ideology." *Journal of Black Studies* 24, no. 4 (1994): 484–97. http://www.jstor.org/stable/2784566.

Bates, Karen Grigsby. "Bobby Hutton: The Killing That Catapulted the Black Panthers to Fame." NPR, April 6, 2018.

Bay Area Television Archive. "Brando & Panthers at Bobby Hutton's Funeral." Diva, accessed March 12, 2022. https://diva.sfsu.edu/collections/sfbatv/bundles /188783.

Bay Area Television Archive. "Police Chief Charles Gain on Bobby Hutton's Shooting." Diva. Accessed March 12, 2022. https://diva.sfsu.edu/bundles/223881.

Bazin, André. "The Life and Death of Superimposition (1946)." *Film-Philosophy* 6, no. 1 (2002). https://doi.org/10.3366/film.2002.0001.

Berger, Dan. *Captive Nation: Black Prison Organizing in the Civil Rights Era*. Chapel Hill: University of North Carolina Press, 2014.

Berger, John. "Understanding a Photograph." In *Classic Essays on Photography*, edited by Alan Trachtenberg, 291–95. New Haven, CT: Lette's Island Books, 1980.

Berkeley Barb. March 12, 1968.

Bernstein, Lee. *America Is the Prison: Arts and Politics in Prison in the 1970s*. Chapel Hill: University of North Carolina Press, 2010.

Biber, Katherine. *Captive Images: Race, Crime, Photography*. Abingdon, VA: Routledge, 2007.

Black Panther. November 23, 1967.

Bloom, Joshua, and Waldo E. Martin Jr. *Black against Empire: The History of Black Panther Party*. Berkeley: University of California Press, 2013.

Bolles, Dan. "An Interview with Jazz Icon Archie Shepp." *Seven Days: Vermont's Independent Voice*, January 16, 2013. https://www.sevendaysvt.com/vermont/an -interview-with-jazz-icon-archie-shepp/Content?oid=2242673.

Boyce, Joseph. "Friends, Relatives Tell Story of Fred Hampton." *Chicago Tribune*, December 28, 1969.

Boyce, Joseph. "Writer Joins Curiosity Seekers in Tour of Black Panther Liar." *Chicago Tribune*, December 13, 1969.

Braun, Marta. *Picturing Time: The Work of Étienne Jules-Marey*. Chicago: University of Chicago Press, 1992.

Brody, Jennifer Devere. *Punctuation: Art, Politics, Play*. Durham, NC: Duke University Press, 2008.

Brown, Elaine. *A Taste of Power: A Black Woman's Story*. New York: Pantheon Books, 1992.

Campt, Tina. *Listening to Images*. Durham, NC: Duke University Press, 2018.

Carmichael, Stokely. "Letter for Lil' Bobby." *Black Panther* (May 4, 1968).

Chinen, Nate. "Archie Shepp: Attica Blues." Pitchfork, May 10, 2020. https://pitchfork.com/reviews/albums/archie-shepp-attica-blues/.

Churchill, Ward, and Jim Vander Wall. *Agents of Repression: The FBI's Secret Wars against the Black Panther Party and the American Indian Movement*. Cambridge, MA: South End Press, 2008.

Cleaver, Eldridge. *Target Zero: A Life in Writing*. Hampshire: Palgrave Macmillan, 2006.

Cohn, Eric. "Art Fronts: Visual Culture and Race Politics in Mid-Twentieth Century United States." Unpublished PhD diss., University of Pennsylvania, 2010.

Copeland, Huey. *Bound to Appear: Art, Slavery and the Site of Blackness in Multicultural America*. Chicago: University of Chicago Press, 2013.

Copeland, Huey, and Jared Sexton. "Raw Life: An Introduction." *Qui Parle* 13, no. 2 (2003): 53–62.

Copeland, Huey, and Krista Thompson. "Afrotropes: A User's Guide." *Art Journal* 76, nos. 3–4 (2017): 7–9.

Coulthard, Glen. *Red Skin, White Masks: Rejecting the Colonial Politics of Recognition*. Minneapolis: University of Minnesota Press, 2014.

Cushing, Lincoln. *All of Us or None: Social Justice Posters of the San Francisco Bay Area*. Berkeley, CA: Heyday, 2012.

"Daily Defender Cameraman at Death Scene." *Chicago Daily Defender*, December 6, 1969, 40.

Davis, Angela Y. *Angela Davis: An Autobiography*. New York: Random House, 1974.

Davis, Angela Y. *Are Prisons Obsolete?* New York: Seven Stories Press, 2003.

Davis, Angela Y. "A Statement on Our Fallen Comrade, George Jackson." *Black Panther*, August 28, 1971.

Davis, Angela Yvonne, and David Barsamian. *The Prison Industrial Complex*. Chico, CA: AK Press, 1999.

"Decolonization of Asia and Africa, 1945–1960." US Department of State. Accessed October 16, 2019. https://history.state.gov/milestones/1945–1952/asia-and-africa.

Delli Carpini, Michael X. "The Black Panther Party: 1966–1982." In *The Encyclopedia of Third Parties in America*, edited by Immanuel Ness and James Ciment. New York: Routledge, 2006.

Dickerman, Leah, David Joselit, and Mignon Nixon. "Afrotropes: A Conversation with Huey Copeland and Krista Thompson." *October*, no. 162 (2017): 3–18.

Dollar, Steve. "Before the Internet, There was a Video Revolution." *The Wall Street Journal*, March 7, 2016.

Douglas, Emory. "On Revolutionary Art." *Black Panther*, 1968.

Ebert, Roger. "Interview with Mike Gray." Ebert Co., October 11, 1971. https://www.rogerebert.com/interviews/interview-with-mike-gray.

Eid, Haidar, and Khaled Gazel. "Footprints of Fanon in Gillo Pontecorvo's 'The Battle of Algiers' and Semebene Ousamne's 'Xala.'" *English in Africa* 35, no. 2 (2008): 151–61.

Fanon, Frantz. *Black Skin, White Masks*. Translated by Charles Markmann. New York: Grove Press, 1967.

Fanon, Frantz. *Black Skin, White Masks*. Translated by Richard Philcox. New York: Grove Press, 2004.

Fine, Elsa Honig. *The Afro-American Artist: A Search for Identity*. New York: Rinehart and Winston, 1973.

Foner, Philip. Editor. *The Black Panthers Speak*. New York: Da Capo Press, 1995.

Foucault, Michel, Catherine Von Bülow, and Daniel Defert. "The Masked Assassination." Translated by Sirène Harb. In *Warfare in the American Homeland: Policing and Prison in a Penal Democracy*. Durham, NC: Duke University Press, 2007.

Foucault, Michel. *Discipline and Punish: The Birth of the Prison*. Translated by Alan Sheridan. New York: Vintage Books, 1977.

Fox-Amato, Matthew. *Exposing Slavery: Photography, Human Bondage, and the Birth of Modern Visual Politics in America*. Oxford: Oxford University Press, 2019.

Gates, Henry Louis, Jr. *Two Nations of Black America*. Alexandria, VA: Frontline, PBS Home Video, 2008.

Genet, Jean. "Preface." In *Soledad Brother: The Prison Letters of George Jackson*, by George Jackson. Chicago: HarperCollins, 1970.

Genet, Jean. "Preface to *L'assassinat de Georges Jackson*." In *The Declared Enemy: Texts and Interviews*, edited by Albert Dichy, translated by Jeff Fort. Stanford, CA: Stanford University Press, 2004.

Gilmore, Ruth Wilson. "Globalisation and US Prison Growth: From Military Keynesianism to Post-Keynesian Militarism." *Race & Class* 40, nos. 2–3 (1999): 171–88.

Gilroy, Paul. *The Black Atlantic: Modernity and Double Consciousness*. Cambridge, MA: Harvard University Press, 1993.

Goldsby, Jacqueline. *A Spectacular Secret: Lynching in American Life and Literature*. Chicago: University of Chicago Press, 2006.

Gordon, Avery. *Ghostly Matters: Haunting and the Sociological Imagination*. Minneapolis: University of Minnesota Press, 1997.

Haas, Jeffrey. *The Assassination of Fred Hampton: How the FBI and the Chicago Police Murdered a Black Panther*. Chicago: Chicago Review Press, 2009.

Harney, Stefan, and Fred Moten. *The Undercommons: Fugitive Planning and Black Study*. New York: Minor Compositions, 2013.

Hartman, Saidiya. *Scenes of Subjection: Terror, Slavery, and Self-Making in Nineteenth Century America*. London: Oxford University Press, 1997.

Hartman, Saidiya. "Venus in Two Acts." *Small Axe* 12, no. 2 (2008): 1–14.

Hartman, Saidiya. *Wayward Lives, Beautiful Experiments: Intimate Histories of Riotous Black Girls, Troublesome Women and Queer Radicals*. New York: Penguin Random House, 2019.

Herzog, Melanie. *Elizabeth Catlett: An American Artist in Mexico*. Seattle: University of Washington Press, 2005.

Herzog, Melanie. *Elizabeth Catlett: In the Image of the People*. Chicago: Art Institute of Chicago, 2005.

Hill, Lance E. *The Deacons for Defense: Armed Resistance and the Civil Rights Movement*. Chapel Hill: University of North Carolina Press, 2004.

Howe, Charles. "Black Panthers—What They Want: Interview with Doug Lawler." *San Francisco Chronicle*, May 15, 1968. Oakland, California: July 2015.

"Hutton, Bobby James (1950–1968)." Cals: Encyclopedia of Arkansas. Accessed March 3, 2020. http://www.encyclopediaofarkansas.net/encyclopedia/entry -detail.aspx?entryID=6040.

"Instituto Cubano del Arte y Industria Cinematográficos." EcuRed. Accessed May 19, 2020. https://www.ecured.cu/Instituto_Cubano_del_Arte_e_Industria _Cinematogr%C3%A1ficos.

Jackson, George. *Blood in My Eye*. Baltimore, MD: Black Classic Press, 1972.

Jackson, George. *Soledad Brother: The Prison Letters of George Jackson*. Chicago: HarperCollins, 1970.

Jackson, Iman Zakkiyah. "Losing Manhood: Animality and Plasticity in the (Neo) Slave Narrative." *Qui Parle* 25, nos. 1–2 (2016): 95–136.

Jamal-Abu, Mumia. *We Want Freedom: A Life in the Black Panther Party*. Cambridge, MA: South End Press, 2004.

JanMohamed, Abdul R. *The Death-Bound-Subject: Richard Wright's Archaeology of Death*. Durham, NC: Duke University Press, 2005.

James, Joy, ed. *Warfare in the American Homeland: Policing and Prison in a Penal Democracy*. Durham, NC: Duke University Press Books, 2007.

Jones, Kellie. *Eyeminded: Living and Writing Contemporary Art*. Durham, NC: Duke University Press, 2011.

Jones, Kellie. *South of Pico: African American Artists in Los Angeles in the 1960s and 1970s*. Durham, NC: Duke University Press, 2017.

Joselit, David. "Notes on Surface: Toward a Genealogy of Flatness." *Art History* 23 (2000): 19–34.

Joseph, Cliff. *Artist and Activist*. Exhibition. Tyler Fine Art/Aaron Galleries, St. Louis, 2018. https://issuu.com/msmodular72/docs/cliff_joseph_artist _activist.

Jones, LeRoi, Warren Rinckle, Curtis Harnack, Charles V. Hamilton, and John Gunther. "Violence in Oakland." *New York Review of Books*, May 9, 1968.

Judy, Ronald T. *(Dis)forming the American Canon: African-Arabic Slave Narratives and the Vernacular*. Minneapolis: University of Minnesota Press, 1993.

Katsiaficas, George. *The Imagination of the New Left: A Global Analysis of 1968*. Boston: South End Press, 1987.

Keeling, Kara. *The Witch's Flight: The Cinematic, the Black Femme, and the Image of Common Sense*. Durham, NC: Duke University Press, 2007.

Kelley, Robin D. G. *Freedom Dreams: The Black Radical Imagination*. Boston: Beacon Press, 2002.

King, Martin Luther, Jr. *Where Do We Go From Here: Chaos or Community?* Boston: Beacon Press, 1968.

Kittler, Friedrich A. *Gramophone, Film, Typewriter*. Translated by Geoffrey Winthrop-Young and Michael Wutz. Stanford, CA: Stanford University Press, 1999.

Knifer, John. "Coroner Seals Panther Slaying Site." *New York Times*, December 18, 1969.

Knifer, John. "Inquiry Is Urged in Slaying of Black Panther." *New York Times*, December 9, 1969.

Knifer, John. "Panthers Say an Autopsy Shows Party Official was 'Murdered.'" *New York Times*, December 18, 1969.

Kojève, Alexandre. *Introduction to the Reading of Hegel*. Ithaca, NY: Cornell University Press, 1980.

Langa, Helen. *Radical Art: Printmaking and the Left in 1930s New York*. Berkeley: University of California Press, 2004.

Langa, Helen. "Two Antilynching Art Exhibitions: Politicized Viewpoints, Racial Perspectives, Gendered Constraints." *American Art* 13, no. 1 (1999): 10–39.

Lethabo-King, Tiffany. *The Black Shoals: Offshore Formations of Black and Native Studies*. Durham, NC: Duke University Press, 2019.

Linfield, Susie. *The Cruel Radiance: Photography and Political Violence*. Chicago: University of Chicago Press, 2010.

Lott, Eric. *Love and Theft: Blackface Minstrelsy and the American Working Class*. Oxford: Oxford University Press, 1993.

MacPhee, Josh. "Constructing Third World Struggle: The Design of the OSPAAAL & Tricontinental." *Funambulist* 22 (March 2019). https://thefunambulist.net /magazine/22-publishing-struggle/constructing-third-world-struggle-design -ospaaal-tricontinental-josh-macphee.

Marable, Manning. *Malcolm X: A Life of Reinvention*. New York: Penguin, 2011.

Marriott, David. *On Black Men*. New York: Columbia University Press, 2000.

Martinot, Steve, and Jared Sexton. "The Avant-Garde of White Supremacy." *Social Identities: Journal for the Study of Race, Nation, and Culture* 9, no. 2 (June 2003): 169–81.

Massiah, Louis J., Thomas Ott, and Terry Kay Rockefeller. *Eyes on the Prize: A Nation of Law? (1968–1971)*. Public Broadcasting Service, 1990. DVD.

Matthews, Peter. "*The Battle of Algiers*: Bombs and Boomerangs." Film re-release booklet. New York: Criterion, 2004.

Mavor, Carol. *Black and Blue: The Bruised Passion of "Camera Lucida," "La Jetée," "Sans Soleil," and "Hiroshima Mon Amour."* Durham, NC: Duke University Press, 2012.

Melcher, Webster. "Photography and Evidence." *Central Law Journal* (April 1922): 242–46.

Minh-ha, Trinh T. "The Totalizing Quest of Meaning." In *Theorizing Documentary*, edited by Michael Renov, 90–107. New York and London: Routledge, 1993.

Montgomery, David. *Workers' Control in America: Studies in the History of Work, Technology, and Labor Struggles*. Cambridge: Cambridge University Press, 1979.

Moore, Natalie, and Lance Williams. *The Almighty Black P. Stone Nation: The Rise, Fall, and Resurgence of an American Gang*. Chicago: Chicago Review Press, 2011.

"Morante and OSPAAAL." D-aqui. Accessed January 7, 2020. https://d-aqui.com /stories/morante-and-the-ospaaal.

Moreton-Robinson, Aileen. *The White Possessive: Property, Power, and Indigenous Sovereignty*. Minneapolis: University of Minnesota Press, 2015.

Moten, Fred. "Blackness and Nothingness (Mysticism in the Flesh)." *South Atlantic Quarterly* 112, no. 4 (2013): 737–80.

Moten, Fred. "A Case of Blackness." *Criticism* 50, no. 2 (2008): 177–215.

Moten, Fred. *In the Break: The Aesthetics of Black Radical Tradition*. Minneapolis: University of Minnesota Press, 2003.

Moten, Fred. "Just Friends." Mini seminar, University of California, Irvine, November 7, 2012.

Moten, Fred. "Soul: Black Power, Politics, and Pleasure and Scenes of Subjection: Terror, Slavery, and Self-Making in Nineteenth-Century America (review)." *TDR: The Drama Review* 43, no. 4 (1999): 169–75.

Museum of Modern Art. "Controversial Film to Premiere at Museum: *The Murder of Fred Hampton*—Black Panther." Press release, 1971.

Muwakkil, Salim. "Black Panthers Reconsidered." *Chicago Tribune*, February 28, 2000.

Natale, Simone. "A Short History of Superimposition: From Spirit Photography to Early Cinema." *Early Popular Visual Culture* 10, no. 2 (2012): 125–45.

Neary, Janet. *Fugitive Testimony: On the Visual Logics of Slave Narratives*. New York: Fordham University Press, 2017.

Newton, Huey P. "Tribute to Bobby Hutton." *Black Panther*, May 4, 1968.

Newton, Huey P. *War against the Panthers: A Study of Repression in America*. London: Writers and Readers, 2001.

Niekereken, Bill Van. "The Death of a Black Panther: 50 Years After Bobby Hutton's Killing." *San Francisco Chronicle*, April 25, 2018.

Oehler, Sarah Kelly, and Esther Adler. *Charles White: A Retrospective*. New Haven, CT: Yale University Press, 2018.

Parks, Gordon. *A Choice of Weapons*. Minneapolis: Minnesota Historical Society Press, 2010.

Peck, Abe. *Uncovering the Sixties: The Life and Times of the Underground Press*. New York: Pantheon Books, 1985.

Peniel, Joseph. *Waiting 'Til the Midnight Hour: A Narrative of Black Power in America*. New York: Henry Holt, 2007.

Puskar, Jason. "Pistolgraphs: Liberal Technoagency and the Nineteenth-Century Camera Gun." *Nineteenth-Century Contexts* 36, no. 5 (December 2014): 517–34.

Raiford, Leigh. *Imprisoned in a Luminous Glare: Photography and the African American Freedom Struggle*. Chapel Hill: University of North Carolina Press, 2011.

Renov, Michael. "Introduction: The Truth About Non-Fiction." In *Theorizing Documentary*, edited By Michael Renov, 1–12. New York and London: Routledge, 1993.

Ringgold, Faith. *We Flew over the Bridge: The Memoirs of Faith Ringgold*. Durham, NC: Duke University Press, 2005.

Roach, Joseph. *Cities of the Dead: Circum-Atlantic Performance*. New York: Columbia University Press, 1996.

Robinson, Cedric. *Black Marxism: The Making of the Black Radical Tradition*. Chapel Hill: University of North Carolina Press, 2000.

Rodriguez, Dylan. "State Terror and the Reproduction of Imprisoned Dissent." *Social Identities* 9, no. 2 (2003): 183–203.

Rosen, Phillip. "Document and Documentary: On Persistence of Historical Concepts." In *Theorizing Documentary*, edited By Michael Renov, 58–89. New York and London: Routledge, 1993.

Ryckman, Larry. "Today's Focus: Violent Deaths of Jonathan, George Jackson Remembered." *Associated Press*, San Francisco, 1985.

Samuel, Liz. "Improvising on Reality: The Roots of Prison Abolition." In *The Hidden 1970s: Histories of Radicalism*, edited by Dan Berger. New Brunswick, NJ: Rutgers University Press, 2010.

Sharpe, Christina. *Monstrous Intimacies: Making Post-Slavery Subjects*. Durham, NC: Duke University Press, 2010.

Seale, Bobby. *Seize the Time: A Story of the Black Panther Party and Huey P. Newton*. New York: Random House, 1970.

Sekula, Allan. "The Body and the Archive." *October*, no. 39 (1986): 3–64.

Sontag, Susan. *On Photography*. New York: Picador Press, 1997.

Smith, Andrea. "Heteropatriarchy and the Three Pillars of White Supremacy." In *Color of Violence: The INCITE! Anthology*, edited by INCITE! Women of Color against Violence, 66–73. Durham, NC: Duke University Press, 2016.

Spillers, Hortense. "Mama's Baby, Papa's Maybe: An American Grammar Book." *Diacritics* 17, no. 2 (1987): 65–81.

Stanutz, Katherine. "'Dying, but Fighting Back': George Jackson's Modes of Mourning." *MELUS: Multi-Ethnic Literature of the U.S.* 42, no. 1 (Spring 2017): 32–52.

Steyerl, Hito. "In Defense of the Poor Image." *e-flux*, no. 10 (November 2009).

Stimson, Blake. *The Pivot of the World: Photography and Its Nation*. Cambridge, MA: MIT Press, 2006.

Strauss, David Levi. *Between the Eyes: Essays on Photography and Politics*. New York: Aperture, 2003.

Students for a Democratic Society. "Huey Newton Talks to the Movement." Kent State University Libraries, Special Collections and Archives. Accessed October 13, 2021. https://omeka.library.kent.edu/special-collections/items/show/3176.

Sudbury, Julia. *Global Lockdown: Race, Gender and the Prison-Industrial Complex*. New York: Routledge, 2005.

Teasdale, Parry D. *Videofreex: America's First Pirate TV Station & the Catskills Collective That Turned It On*. Hensonville, NY: Black Dome Press, 1999.

Thomas, Deborah. *Political Life in the Wake of the Plantation: Sovereignty, Witnessing, Repair*. Durham, NC: Duke University Press, 2019.

Thomas, Greg. "On *Teza*, Cinema, and American Empire: An Interview with Haile Gerima." *Black Camera* 4, no. 2 (Spring 2013): 84–104.

Thompson, Heather Ann. *Blood in the Water: The Attica Prison Uprising of 1971 and Its Legacy*. New York: Vintage, 2017.

Thompson, Krista. "'I WAS HERE BUT I DISAPEAR': Ivanhoe 'Rhygin' Martin and Photographic Disappearance in Jamaica." *Art Journal* 77, no. 2 (Summer 2018): 80–99.

Thompson, Krista. "A Sidelong Glance: The Practice of African Diaspora Art History in the United States." *Art Journal* 70, no. 3 (2011): 7–31.

Thompson, Robert Farris. "An Aesthetic of the Cool." *African Arts* 7, no. 1 (1973): 41–91.

Thurston, Thomas. "Hearsay of the Sun: Photography, Identity and the Law of Evidence in Nineteenth Century American Courts." *Hypertext Scholarship in American Studies, American Quarterly* (1996).

"Two Antilynching Art Exhibitions: Politicized Viewpoints, Racial Perspectives, Gendered Constraints." *American Art* 13, no. 1 (1999): 26.

Videofreex. "Fred Hampton: Black Panthers in Chicago." Video Data Bank. Accessed March 12, 2022. http://www.vdb.org/titles/fred-hampton-black-panthers -chicago.

Wallace, Maurice O., and Shawn Michelle Smith, eds. *Pictures and Progress: Early Photography and the Making of African American Identity*. Durham, NC, and London: Duke University Press, 2012.

Wallace, Michele. *Dark Designs and Visual Culture*. Durham, NC: Duke University Press, 2004.

Wallace, Michele, and Mary Lodu. "Michele Wallace Interviewed by Mary Lodu." *Third Rail* 9 (November 2016): 26–36.

Weiler, A. H. "The Murder of Fred Hampton." *New York Times*, October 5, 1971.

Wicker, Tom. *A Time to Die: The Attica Prison Revolt*. Lincoln: University of Nebraska Press, 1994.

Wiegman, Robyn. *American Anatomies: Theorizing Race and Gender*. Durham, NC: Duke University Press. 2002.

Wilderson, Frank B, III. "Gramsci's Black Marx: Whither the Slave in Civil Society?" *Social Identities* 9, no. 2 (2003): 225–40.

Wilderson, Frank B, III. "Of Grammar and Ghosts: The Performative Limits of African Freedom." *Theatre Survey* 50, no. 1 (2009): 119–25.

Wilderson, Frank B, III. "The Prison Slave as Hegemony's (Silent) Scandal." In *Warfare in the American Homeland: Policing and Prison in a Penal Colony*, edited by Joy James. Durham, NC: Duke University Press, 2007.

Williams, Mabel R., and Sele Nadel-Hayes. *Robert F. Williams: Self-Defense, Self-Respect and Self-Determination*. San Francisco: Freedom Archives, 2005. Sound recording.

Williams, Martin. "The Jazz Avant Garde, Who's In Charge?" *Evergreen Review* 10 (June 1966): 67.

Willis, Deborah. *Picturing Us: African American Identity in Photography*. New York: New Press, 1996.

Wilson-Bryan, Julia. *Art Workers: Radical Practice in the Vietnam War Era*. Berkeley: University of California Press, 2009.

Wofford, Tobias. "Can You Dig It? Signifying Race in David Hammons' Spade Series." In *L.A. Object & David Hammons Body Prints*, edited by Lindsay Charwood, 86–135. New York: Tilton Gallery, 2011.

Young, Harvey. "Still Standing: Daguerreotypes, Photography, and the Black Body." In *Embodying Black Experience: Stillness, Critical Memory and the Black Body*, 26–76. Ann Arbor: University of Michigan Press, 2010.

Index

Mancia, Adrienne, 57
Mao Tse-tung, 133. *See also* Jackson, George
Marin County Courthouse, 125
Martin, Jean, 59
Marx, Karl: George Jackson and, 92, 104, 133–34
Mavor, Carol, 115
McLaughlin, Michael, 139
Melcher, Webster, 15
Menard Correctional Facility, 67, 79
Middle Passage, 81–82. *See also* afterlives: of
  slavery
Morante, Rafael, 112–20, 124, 129–30; *Power
  to the People George* (1971), plate 26. *See also*
  OSPAAAL
Morris, Robert, 139
Moten, Fred, 5, 41–42, 78–80, 84, 110–12, 159n71;
  on Mamie Till, 40. *See also* anti-Black vio-
  lence; Black radical; objects
Murder of Fred Hampton, The (film), 19, 55,
  60–61, 69–70, 73, 110, plates, 17–25
Museum of Modern Art (MoMA), 56–57;
  Cineprobe Series, 57
Myth of Sisyphus, The (Camus), 133
mythologies of sight, 107, 109, 114. *See also*
  archive

National Black Political Convention, 95
Newton, Huey, 17, 22–23, 39, 41, 46–50, 89, 90,
  95, 129, 154n70
New York City, New York: American Con-
  temporary Art Gallery, 114; Judson Memorial
  Church, 119; School of the Visual Arts, 114
New York Review of Books, 45
New York Times: Fred Hampton and, 55; *The
  Murder of Fred Hampton* and, 56
Nolen, W. L., 92
North Oakland Neighborhood Anti-Poverty
  Center, 38

Oakland, California, 39, 77; Bobby Hutton's
  murder, 32, 55; Lake Merritt, 44; North
  Oakland Anti-Poverty Center, 38; Oakland
  Museum of California (OMCA), 125; Oakland
  Police Department, 21, 32–34, 36–38, 45, 48,
  51, 153n40; St. Augustine's Episcopal Church,
  129
objecthood, 7, 65, 79–82, 84, 87
objectification, 7
objects, 23–24; aesthetic, 6, 15, 18, 22–25, 27–29,
  81, 111, 114, 125, 138–40; body and, 7–8, 61,

78–80, 83–84, 87; Fanon and, 78–80, 155n;
  methodologies and, 9, 14, 15, 18–19, 25–26,
  110–11; political life of, 31, 35, 37, 39–40, 54–56,
  75–77, 84–87, 92, 114, 133–34, 139–40, 144;
  resistance of, 7, 84–85; and subject, 4, 9–10,
  27–29, 65, 70, 77–84
O'Neal, William, 54
Organization of Solidarity of the People of
  Asia, Africa, and Latin America (OSPAAAL),
  43, 112–16, 124; *Power to the People George*
  (1971), plate 26. *See also* Morante, Rafael
O'Shannon, Cathal, 138

Parks, Gordon: *A Choice of Weapons*, 12
Peltier, Leonard, 95. *See also* American Indian
  Movement (AIM)
People's Flag Show, The, 119
People's Law Office (PLO), 33, 66, 74
performance studies, 97, 128; performance
  theories of embodiment, 4
photographic fugitivity, 24, 26, 150n4. *See also*
  Afrotrope; law: photography and
police: Chicago Police Department, 54–55,
  65–66, 74, 155n1; Oakland Police Department, 21, 32–34, 36–38, 45, 48, 51, 153n40;
  Gain, Charles, 36–37; Richmond Police
  Department, 1. *See also* anti-Black violence;
  COINTELPRO; FBI; violence
political life of objects, 53, 76, 92, 133–34.
  See also objects
political poster, 2, 18, 20, 23, 25, 50, 111, 113, 119,
  124, 141, 142. *See also* revolution and art
political prisoner, 14, 20, 95–96, 102, 111, 127,
  133, 134. *See also* abolition; prison industrial
  complex
Pontecorvo, Gillo, 58–59
Pratt, Geronimo, 95
praxis: aesthetic, 19; definition of, 163n39; fight
  to the death as, 164n41; Fred Hampton and,
  63, 85; George Jackson and, 92, 103–4, 106,
  114, 125, 128; political, 2, 89, 114; revolutionary, 18, 63, 85, 92, 106, 128, 131–32, 164n41.
  See also revolution
prison industrial complex, 89, 97–98, 100, 102,
  133, 144, 158n42, 162n17
Prison Information Group (Groupe
  d'information sur les prisons [GIP]), 107, 131.
  See also Foucault, Michel
propaganda, 3. *See also* revolution: art and
Puskar, Jason, 9–10